REGULATING HATE SPEECH CREATED BY GENERATIVE AI

REGULATING HATE SPEECH CREATED BY GENERATIVE AI

Edited by Jay Liebowitz

CRC Press
Taylor & Francis Group
AN AUERBACH BOOK

First edition published 2025
by CRC Press
6000 Broken Sound Parkway NW, Suite 300, Boca Raton, FL 33487-2742
and by CRC Press
2 Park Square, Milton Park, Abingdon, Oxon, OX14 4RN

CRC Press is an imprint of Taylor & Francis Group, LLC

Library of Congress Cataloging-in-Publication Data
A catalog record for this title has been requested.

ISBN: 9781032648170 (hbk)
ISBN: 9781032644349 (pbk)
ISBN: 9781032654829 (ebk)

DOI: 10.1201/9781032654829

Typeset in Adobe Garamond Pro, Avenir LT Pro
by DerryField Publishing Services

Trademarks Used in This Book

Apple and Siri are registered trademarks by Apple, Inc.
Amazon and Alexa are registered trademarks by Amazon Technologies, Inc.
Anthropic and Claude are registered trademarks by Anthropic, PBC.
AOL is a registered trademark by AOL LLC.
ATT is a registered trademark by AT&T Intellectual Property II, L.P.
BAIDU is a registered trademark by Baidu, Inc.
BigBear.ai is a registered trademark by BigBear.ai, LLC.
BuzzFeed is a registered trademark by BuzzFeed, Inc.
C3.AI is a registered trademark by C3.AI, Inc.
Comcast is a registered trademark by Comcast Corporation.
EY is a registered trademark by EYGN Limited.
Facebook is a registered trademark by Meta Platforms.
Gab Online is a registered trademark by Gab Online, LLC.
GitHub is a registered trademark by GitHub, Inc.
Google, AdSence, Bard, Deepmind, Gemini, and YouTube are registered trademarks by Google LLC.
Grammarly is a registered trademark by Grammarly, Inc.
HBO is a registered trademark by Home Box Office, Inc.
Instagram is a registered trademark by Instagram, LLC.
LinkedIn is a registered trademark by LinkedIn Corporation.
Microsoft, Azure, and Bing are registered trademarks by Microsoft Corporation.
MidJourney is a registered trademark by MidJourney, Inc.
NBCUniversal is a registered trademark by NBCUniversal Media, LLC.
NVIDIA is a registered trademark by NVIDIA Corporation.
OpenAI, ChatGPT, DALL-E, and GPT are registered trademarks by OpenAI, Inc.
Reddit is a registered trademark by Reddit, Inc.
SSPS is a registered trademark by International Business Machines, Inc.
Stable Diffusion is a registered trademark by Stability AI Ltd.
Tesla is a registered trademark by Tesla, Inc.
TikTok is a registered trademark by Bytedance Ltd.
Time is a registered trademark by Time, Inc.
Tumblr is a registered trademark by Tumblr, Inc.
Twitch is a registered trademark by Twitch Interactive, Inc.
Twitter is a registered trademark by Twitter, Inc.
Unix is a registered trademark by X/Open Company Limited.
Verizon is a registered trademark by Verizon Trademark Services LLC.
Wikipedia is a registered trademark by Wikimedia Foundation, Inc.
YAHOO is a registered trademark by YAHOO Inc.

Contents

List of Figures and Tables

Foreword

A Holistic Framework for Hate Speech Modelling

Pompeu Casanovas[1]* and Andre Oboler[2]

[1]IIIA-CSIC, Barcelona, Spain, IDT-UAB, Barcelona, Spain; La Trobe LawTech Research Group, Melbourne, Australia

[2]Online Hate Prevention Institute (OHPI) and La Trobe LawTech Research Group, Melbourne, Australia

*Corresponding author

At the beginning of her autobiographic book, *The Hate Race* (2016), writer Maxine Beneba Clarke shares her own experience with racism. We place it at the beginning of our Foreword lest we lose sight of the problem we are dealing with when applying artificial intelligence (AI) techniques to hate speech. This episode occurred in North Road, not far from where we live in Melbourne, but in some ways, it is timeless and placeless. It could have occurred near the reader's home.

> *I don't want sympathy. I want to un-hear what I just heard, un-experience what just happened. If racism is a shortcoming of the heart, then experiencing it is an assault on the mind. You should go drown your f---en' kid! Go the f--k back you where you come from, n----r. The cumulative effect of these incidents is like a poison: it eats away the very essence of your being. Left unchecked, it can drive you to the unthinkable.*

A few months ago, again not far from North Road, a young man posted a video of himself making hateful comments related to local and world events. He was doxed and harassed intensely online. He committed suicide within a few days. The problem of hate speech involves words that hurt, words that harm, and words that that can kill. Beyond the impact on individuals, they create hostile environments at the societal level, undermining not only community harmony but democracy itself. Is there any antidote for this poison?

Obtaining consensus on definitions for hate speech and AI systems is a complicated task. However, to legislate, regulate, or mitigate the problem, governments, rulers, and technology platforms themselves usually need to start by defining the thing they seek to control or regulate. Clear rules, scalability, and interoperability across national, international, and global jurisdictions beyond the narrow limits of the nation state depend in part on this common endeavour.

There is an ongoing effort in this direction both in the AI community and in international organisations. For instance, in recent months Organisation for Economic Co-operation and Development (OECD) members approved a revised version of the organisation's definition of an AI system, which has in turn received many comments, leading to a second revision that is still being considered. The current definition says:

> *An AI system is a machine-based system that, for a given set of human-defined explicit or implicit objectives, infers, from the input it receives, how to generate outputs such as predictions, content, recommendations, or decisions that can influence physical or virtual environments. Different AI systems vary in their levels of autonomy and adaptiveness after deployment.*

This endeavour is about gathering and synthesizing different types of information processing from generative, symbolic, and swarm AI, including neural networks, machine and deep learning, knowledge representation, natural language processing, large language models, multi-agent systems, algorithmic governance, machine perception, and computer vision.

However, AI opportunities come at the same time as threats grow in an increasingly conflictive world. As noticed by a recent UN Report of December 2023, the so-called 'AI divide' lurks within a larger and developmental divide. More than 2.6 billon people still lack access to the Internet. Broadband access, affordable devices and data, digital literacy, are simply not there for many human beings. At the same time, interstate and intrastate violence is clearly gaining traction, mainly for political or geopolitical reasons, in several countries that are outside this division. In contrast to the expectations at the beginning of the century, it seems that violence—all types of violence, including race, gender, and culture—is a rising trend in developed countries.

The expansion of the Internet and the widespread use of smart phones play a role, but AI is increasingly a significant contributing factor. Recommender algorithms on video platforms lead users to extremism, then accelerating their radicalisation. Democratic processes such as elections are becoming more polarising, with generative

AI being used to micro target demographics and seed divisions. AI is furthering divisions in times of war as well: in the Russia-Ukraine conflict, a deep fake sought to convince people President Volodymyr Zelenskyy had surrendered. In the Israel-Hamas war, AI created lifelike images of carnage to intensify emotional responses.

Hate speech is generally characterized as the verbal component of violence, a first level susceptible to escalation into physical harm, or which may remain at the level of hostility in social interactions. However, there is an element of ambiguity in this conceptualization that should be highlighted. In the definitions and indicators related to violence and Internet technologies, it is usually assumed that it is possible to construct relatively reliable metrics to indicate the evolution or social progression of the phenomenon. It is a discourse stemming from social and political sciences.

This is not the case with hate speech. Social psychologists have long noted that the Internet does not create or encourage new emotions, but rather intensifies and modulates existing ones. Discourse and speech, whether about love or hatred, find a new channel for the expression of feelings that are experienced in its various phases (creation, transmission, and reception) with a speed, intentionality, and intensity unknown until that moment. It is the ability to impact and cause harm that has changed. Hateful content from one person can go viral, reaching millions; one victim can be impacted by a flood of abusive messages from different people through an orchestrated campaign; or a hostile environment can be created that seeks to exclude people from an online community or an entire platform.

Perhaps this is why law and jurisprudence have taken action on the matter. The notion of *hate speech* does not come from linguistic pragmatics, discourse analysis, conversation analysis, or the qualitative social and political sciences of the nineties. It comes from the regulatory field of jurisprudence, with its background of constitutional and political law. From this point of view, it constitutes the reverse and limit of expressions with a long doctrinal history, such as *free speech* in the Common Law tradition and *liberté d'expression, Redefreiheit,* or *libertad de expresión* in the tradition of Civil Law. Both are related to the idea of the rule of law and the restrictions and liberties it entails to preserve the right of citizens to a dignified life free of illegitimate coercion. In its origins, it is also related to the fight against racism and for civil rights in the US and to the reaction against totalitarian forms of government that took place in Europe and in the countries of the Commonwealth after the Second World War.

While the US is exceptional, with its First Amendment protecting hate speech from government regulation unless it falls into a categorical exception such as speech inciting imminent lawless action or fighting words, other countries have generally held that equality and non-discrimination should also be considered in the enactment of free speech rights and a balance found. This is an issue that has been discussed by relevant legal and sociolegal scholars, such as Ronald Dworkin,

Jürgen Habermas, and Jeremy Waldron, among many others. In recent times, it has been linked to the fourth generation of human rights, focusing on the use of appropriate technologies to ensure human dignity.

There are two types of legal definitions. The first consists of the legislative version of notions of a more general scope. This would be the case with "artificial intelligence" or "technology." It becomes necessary to indicate which meaning has been chosen to be consistent in the Act, Directive, or Regulation that is being drafted. The second has another character, since it constitutes a strictly legal definition—that is, a constitutive semantic field delimiting the conditions and effects of a specific regulation. Hate speech falls into this second category, and this is the reason it is so difficult to reach a general definition.

In 2019, the United Nations Strategy and Plan of Action on Hate Speech specified that there is no international legal definition. Hate speech should be understood as:

> *. . . any kind of communication in speech, writing or behaviour, that attacks or uses pejorative or discriminatory language with reference to a person or a group on the basis of who they are, in other words, based on their religion, ethnicity, nationality, race, colour, descent, gender or other identity factor.*

The UN document specified that, rather than prohibiting hate speech as such, International Law prohibits the incitement to discrimination, hostility, and violence.

In 2023, a most recent summary—*Understanding Hate Speech**—identifies three important attributes: (1) hate speech can be conveyed through *any form of expression* (including images, cartoons, memes, objects, gestures, and symbols, offline or online); (2) it is *discriminatory* or *pejorative* of an individual or group; and (3) it expands the original definition to all types of *identity factors*—that is, "religion, ethnicity, nationality, race, colour, descent, gender", but also "language, economic or social origin, disability, health status, or sexual orientation, among many others".

This certainly draws a broad reference framework. It is further complicated by the fact that some hate narratives are used interchangeably against many groups, while other narratives are specific to attacking a particular group. Antisemitism, for example, manifests as both generic racism against Jews, and with specific narratives such as claims of blood libel, deicide, or Holocaust denial. However, if an AI system "is a machine-based system that infers from the input it receives how to generate outputs such as predictions, content, recommendations, or decisions that can influence physical or virtual environments", how could AI systems proceed to generate a set of appropriate requirements within this framework? What level of design autonomy would be needed to prevent the development and effects of hate

* https://www.un.org/en/hate-speech/understanding-hate-speech/what-is-hate-speech

speech online and offline? How could threats be detected? To what extent? And how could these AI systems be validated against real human behaviour? Moreover, do they raise any type of regulatory issues from an ethical and governance perspective?

The book that the reader is holding, edited by Jay Liebowitz, explores this new hybrid space of human-machine interaction (HMI), in which hate speech is represented and computed through algorithms and AI generative systems. It is exploratory because there are still many problem-solving challenges to be faced, and it is innovative because it is not assuming that solutions lie only in technological advancements but also on a broader scale. In this sense, large language models can and are being considered from a holistic view—that is, from the different dimensions and layers of regulatory and legal governance.

For instance, academia and industry have developed some deep learning (DL) and natural language processing (NLP) models to detect online hate speech automatically. But most existing methods adopt a supervised approach depending on already labelled datasets. Hence, they may experience biases coming from this training. They will also struggle with the use of rapidly changing coded language and messages that require a leap of inference.

One example seen recently was a cartoon image of a crying Hitler with a speech bubble saying, "I want to turn back time and try again". The post had over 3,600 positive reactions and over 1,100 shares. The text might be extracted from the image, but lacking context is not in itself hate speech. An image of Hitler might be identified by facial recognition software, but a stylised cartoon, while readily identifiable to humans, poses a problem for AI, unless a specific model is developed.

There is no single way to overcome these challenges. Many strategies are possible and can be implemented. Some focus on the prompting phase; others operate on the fine-tuning stage based on transfer learning; while others target automatically generated responses to create conversational contexts. Counter narratives—informed textual responses automatically generated—are another recent strategy to prevent hate content from spreading further. The model finally adopted in the design will depend on the vision of the type of actions that are worth taking, including perspectives on privacy, security, and end users' participation. Any model will need a fallback to a human system to handle those cases the AI is unable to address.

The creation of the counterfactual wall claimed by Maxine Beneba Clarke to un-hear and un-experience hate speech is only possible by leaning in to her suggestion of unlearning what we should never have learned—that is, in our own version, acknowledging the fact that human beings and machines are capable of creating new learning contexts that must be configured and understood as a symbiotic, hybrid reality that is both equal to and different from the one we have known until now. Not realizing this fact would imply returning to a cyclical repetition of errors that would do nothing to help us get out of the dead end that hatred represents.

Preface

Unfortunately, we live in dangerous and volatile times. We see what has happened with unrest around the world. The use of social media has added fuel to this fire, and now we are seeing hatred being created partly, whether intentionally or not, through Generative AI (GenAI).

According to the U.S. Government Accountability Office, GenAI is a technology that can create content, including text, images, audio, or video, when prompted by a user (GAO, 2023). GAI generates its content using large language models (LLMs), and there are many advantages of using GenAI, including summarizing information, enabling automation, and improving productivity.

However, with this new technology, there are numerous challenges that have been created, including trust and oversight concerns, false information, economic issues, privacy risks, and even national security risks (GAO, 2023). This begs some questions regarding policy context, including: (1) What AI guidelines can best ensure GenAI systems are used responsibly, and are GenAI systems following existing guidance? (2) What standards, regulations, policies, or guardrails need to be put in place to evaluate the methods and materials used to train GenAI models to ensure the fairness and accuracy of their responses for different use cases? (Denning, 2023).

These types of questions are some of the reasons for stimulating the writing of this book. GenAI is a "hot" topic these days. AI prompt engineering is an extremely sought-after field. GenAI can dramatically escalate the ease of use for the average person; however, the potential for abuse of these technologies is a great concern. An Anti-Defamation League (ADL) survey found that 84% of Americans are worried that GenAI will increase the spread of misinformation and hate (Greenblatt, 2023). Jonathan Greenblatt, the CEO of ADL, advocates that, when integrating GenAI tools into their organizations and workplaces, leaders should institute the following: making trust and safety a top priority; establishing high guardrails and insisting on transparency; and safeguarding against weaponization.

The European Union signed the Europe AI Act in December of 2023. In the United States, President Biden signed an executive order in October of 2023 on AI safety and ethics. In addition, the U.S. has created the Blueprint for the AI Bill of Rights and the NIST AI Risk Management Framework. At the very least, guardrails on GenAI should be put in place as frameworks on the source data and rules of ethics. The Center for Countering Digital Hate* found that in their tests of Google®'s Bard®, 78 out of 100 prompts Bard generated were false and harmful narratives (the Pro version of Google Deepmind®'s Gemini® became available to the public in December 2023). The problem with these GenAI systems is that they can easily produce misinformation, as they are being trained on large amounts of often biased and inaccurate data and seems to be a "black box."

I want to thank our thoughtful contributors to this book in addressing GenAI and these related concerns and issues. I am very grateful for the worldwide perspectives from our leading international contributors on this subject. In addition, a debt of gratitude goes to John Wyzalek, Stephanie Kiefer, Theron Shreve, and Susan Culligan for their continued support of my publishing work on emerging topics.

In our VUCA (Volatile, Uncertain, Complex, Ambiguous) environment, we need to develop guidelines for addressing how Generative AI can be regulated to reduce online hate and secure justice in the digital environment. Peter Denning, Distinguished Professor of Computer Science at the Naval Postgraduate School, perhaps said it best:

> *A chatbot prompt is a probe into the conversation of a crowd. Its responses are likely to be abstractions that were not said but are close to what has been said in the training texts. Because the crowd may not be representative of the communities we want to address, we must use these tools very carefully . . . The road to trustworthy uses of this technology will be long* (Denning, 2023, p. 27).

According to EY®, with respect to GenAI, organizations should take into account the following aspects (Garg, 2023):

1. **Privacy and security:** Are adequate measures in place to protect sensitive information and prevent any compromise of security?
2. **Legal compliance:** Have appropriate steps been taken to adhere to all regulatory requirements?
3. **Ethics and data bias:** What measures can be implemented to prevent biased outcomes and mitigate potential negative reputation effects?
4. **Copyright and patents:** Have the necessary licenses been obtained for training data? Can AI potentially generate new inventions?
5. **Mitigating incorrect consumption:** How can the risk of GenAI hallucinations be minimized to ensure safe usage?

* www.counterhate.com

References

Denning, P. (2023, June). The profession of IT: Can generative AI bots be trusted? *Communications of the ACM, 66*(6).

GAO (2023, June). U.S. Government Accountability Office, GAO-23-106782: Science & Tech Spotlight: Generative AI, science, technology assessment, and analytics. https://www.gao.gov/products/gao-23-106782.

Garg, P. (2023). The future of consulting in the age of Generative AI. EY.

Greenblatt, J. A. (2023, June 2). AI-generated hate is rising: 3 things leaders should consider before adopting the new tech. https://techcrunch.com/2023/06/02/ai-generated-hate-is-rising-3-things-leaders-should-consider-before-adopting-intelligent-technologies.

—Jay Liebowitz, D.Sc.
Professor and Director of the AI-EDGE Center
Crummer Graduate School of Business
Rollins College
Winter Park, FL

List of Contributors

Ana Donner Abreu
Federal University of Santa Catarina, Brazil

Amir Adler
Braude College of Engineering, Israel; Massachusetts Institute of Technology, USA

Emanuela Bran
National University for Science and Technology Politehnica Bucharest, Neo Networking SRL & University of Bucharest, Romania

Francisco J. Cantu-Ortiz
Tec de Monterrey, Mexico

Pompeu Casanovas
IIIA-CSIC, Barcelona, Spain, IDT-UAB, Barcelona, Spain; La Trobe LawTech Research Group, Melbourne, Australia

Michael Cowling
Central Queensland University, Australia

Joseph Crawford
University of Tasmania, Australia

Patricia de Sa Freire
Federal University of Santa Catarina, Brazil

Mirko Farina
Institute for Digital Economy and Artificial Systems: Xiamen University, China, and Lomonosov Moscow State University, Russia

Andrea Lavazza
Centro Universitario Internazionale, Arezzo and University of Pavia, Italy

Jay Liebowitz
Crummer Graduate School of Business, Rollins College, USA

Florinda Matos
ISCTE-University Institute of Lisbon, Portugal

Einat Minkov
University of Haifa, Israel

Andre Oboler
Online Hate Prevention Institute, La Trobe University, Australia

Andreas Oranje
National Conference of Bar Examiners, USA

Roberto Carlos dos Santos Pacheco
UFSC-Federal University of Santa Catarina, Brazil

Joanna Paliszkiewicz
Warsaw University of Life Sciences-Szkoła Główna Gospodarstwa Wiejskiego, Poland

Sagi Pendzel
University of Haifa, Israel

Ricardo Pereira
UFSC—Federal University of Santa Catarina, Brazil

Cosima Rughiniş
University of Bucharest, Romania

Răzvan Rughiniş
National University for Science and Technology; Politehnica Bucharest & Romanian Academy of Scientists, Romania

Neri dos Santos
UFSC-Federal University of Santa Catarina, Brazil

Edyta Skarzynska
Warsaw University of Life Sciences-Szkoła Główna Gospodarstwa Wiejskiego, Poland

Idit Yutav Sohlberg
Department of Economics and Business Administration, Ariel University, Israel

Tomer Wullach
OriginAI, Israel

Xiao Yu
Sichuan Center for Digital Development, China

Avi Zigdon
Department of Health Systems Management, School of Health Sciences, Ariel University, Israel

Moti Zwilling
Department of Economics and Business Administration, Ariel University, Israel

About the Editor

Dr. Jay Liebowitz is Professor of Business Innovation and Industry Transformation and Director of the AI-EDGE Center in the Crummer Graduate School of Business at Rollins College in Winter Park, Florida. He has recently served as the inaugural Executive-in-Residence for Public Service at Columbia University's Data Science Institute. He was previously a Visiting Professor in the Stillman School of Business and the MS-Business Analytics Capstone & Co-Program Director (External Relations) at Seton Hall University.

Dr. Liebowitz previously served as the Distinguished Chair of Applied Business and Finance at Harrisburg University of Science and Technology. Before HU, he was the Orkand Endowed Chair of Management and Technology in the Graduate School at the University of Maryland University College (UMUC). He served as a Full Professor in the Carey Business School at Johns Hopkins University.

Dr. Liebowitz was ranked one of the top 10 knowledge management researchers/practitioners out of 11,000 worldwide, and was ranked #2 in KM Strategy worldwide, according to the January 2010 *Journal of Knowledge Management*. At Johns Hopkins University, he was the founding Program Director for the Graduate Certificate in Competitive Intelligence and the Capstone Director of the MS-Information and Telecommunications Systems for Business Program, where he engaged over 30 organizations in industry, government, and not-for-profits in capstone projects.

Prior to joining Hopkins, Dr. Liebowitz was the first Knowledge Management Officer at NASA Goddard Space Flight Center. Before NASA, Dr. Liebowitz was the Robert W. Deutsch Distinguished Professor of Information Systems at the University of Maryland-Baltimore County, Professor of Management Science at George Washington University, and Chair of Artificial Intelligence at the U.S. Army War College.

Dr. Liebowitz is the Founding Editor-in-Chief of *Expert Systems With Applications: An International Journal* (published by Elsevier, ranked as a top-tier journal; Thomson Impact Factor from June 2021 is 8.665). He is a Fulbright Scholar, IEEE-USA Federal Communications Commission Executive Fellow, and Computer Educator of the Year (International Association for Computer Information Systems).

Dr. Liebowitz has published over 45 books and myriad journal articles on knowledge management, analytics, financial literacy, intelligent systems, and IT management and served as the Editor-in-Chief of *Procedia-CS* (Elsevier). He is also the Series Book Editor of the *Data Analytics Applications* book series (Taylor & Francis) as well as the Series Book Editor of the new *Digital Transformation: Accelerating Organizational Intelligence* book series (World Scientific Publishing).

In October 2011, the International Association for Computer Information Systems named the "Jay Liebowitz Outstanding Student Research Award" for the best student research paper at the IACIS Annual Conference. Dr. Liebowitz was the Fulbright Visiting Research Chair in Business at Queen's University for the Summer 2017 and a Fulbright Specialist at Dalarna University in Sweden in May 2019. He is in the Top 2 percent of the top scientists in the world, according to a 2019 Stanford Study.

As of 2021, he is the Visiting Distinguished Professor at the International School for Social and Business Studies in Slovenia. His recent books are: *Data Analytics and AI* (Taylor & Francis, 2021), *The Business of Pandemics: The COVID-19 Story* (Taylor & Francis, 2021), *A Research Agenda for Knowledge Management and Analytics* (Elgar Publishers, 2021), *Online Learning Analytics* (Taylor & Francis, 2022), *Digital Transformation for the University of the Future* (World Scientific, 2022), and *Cryptocurrency Concepts, Technology, and Applications* (Taylor & Francis, April 2023). He has lectured and consulted worldwide.

Chapter 1

Generative AI and Social Engines of Hate

Răzvan Rughiniș,[1] Cosima Rughiniș,*[2] and Emanuela Bran[3]

[1] National University for Science and Technology, Politehnica Bucharest & Academy of Romanian Scientists
[2] University of Bucharest
[3] National University for Science and Technology, Politehnica Bucharest, Neo Networking SRL & University of Bucharest
* Corresponding author

Acknowledgment: This work was funded by the Innovative Solution for Optimizing User Productivity through Multi-Modal Monitoring of Activity and Profiles—OPTIMIZE/*Solutie Inovativa de Optimizare a Productivitatii Utilizatorilor prinMonitorizareaMulti-Modala a Activitatii si a Profilelor*—OPTIMIZE project, Contract number 366/390042/27.09.2021,MySMIS code: 121491

1.1 Introduction

In the fast-changing world of digital communication, artificial intelligence (AI) and generative AI bring new challenges and potential for hate speech regulation. The impact of generative AI on hate speech cannot be fully understood in isolation from other AI technologies and broader social forces. This chapter examines the complex relationship between generative AI and the social and technological processes that generate hate speech in the digital society.

To effectively identify generative AI's contributions to hate speech dynamics, *primary* and *secondary* hate engines must be distinguished. The primary engines are social and psychological systems that perpetuate violence, exploitation, and injustice without mediation or recourse. These engines fuel chronic anger, which can become hate. Secondary engines legitimate, amplify, normalize, nuance, and personalize hate. They create and spread vocabularies and worldviews that motivate hate speech and actions, typically targeting specific social groups. In particular, mass media and social media disseminate and fuel hate speech, thus perpetuating and refining these hateful worldviews and justifications.

The specificity of generative AI in hate speech regulation requires intense attention. Still, we should remain aware that generative AI is only part of a digital communication ecology. Hate speech is also shaped by other AI tools. Thus, while focusing on generative AI, our analysis must also evaluate how diverse AI technologies contribute convergently to hate speech's creation and governance. This holistic approach will help us comprehend the issues and potential solutions for regulating hate speech in the AI era.

1.2 The social generation and amplification of hate

Hatred is entrenched in society's social fabric, in which interactions may cause anger, fear, and victimization. These emotions result from the primary engines of hate—namely, societal processes and systems that create or perpetuate injustice, inequality, and violence.

These engines revolve around victimization. Individuals or groups who perceive themselves as victimized can feel angry and afraid. This is especially true when the perceived harm is persistent and leaves little chance for remedy, justice, or forgiveness. Tajfel et al. (1979) show how in-group and out-group interactions might worsen these feelings in social identity theory. Groups that people feel they belong to (in-groups) typically define themselves in opposition to out-groups they regard as different, inferior, or threatening. Negative stereotyping and dehumanization of the out-group can reinforce victimization and aggressive cycles.

Social mechanisms that enhance political polarization and economic inequality fuel hate. When societies are more divided economically, politically, or culturally, misunderstanding and conflict increase (Rughiniş & Flaherty, 2022). Extremist beliefs and the growing wealth disparity reflect these divisions. Wilkinson and Pickett (2010) explain how social inequality increases violence and mistrust. Civil wars and ethnic conflicts demonstrate these processes. Ethnic tensions and nationalism fueled the 1990s Yugoslav Wars. These confrontations were about geographical disputes, long-standing grudges, historical injustices, and ethnic group oppression. A complex history of ethnic discord and inequity led to the 1994 Rwandan genocide. One of the worst mass murders in modern history occurred when the Hutu majority dehumanized the Tutsi minority through political manipulation and propaganda.

The secondary engines of hate—societal norms, discourses, and media mechanisms—justify, promote, and perpetuate hate. Hate speech is not just a result of direct interactional animosity but also of broader cultural frames and media propagation. These secondary engines are driven by "vocabularies of motive" (Mills, 1940) and "rules of feeling" (Hochschild, 1979). Vocabularies of motive, according to Mills, are the language and narratives societies use to justify and legitimize hateful behavior. These vocabularies may justify and elevate hate in a given situation or, on the contrary, downplay it and pursue empathy, understanding, or forgiveness. Hochschild's rules of feeling examine cultural norms that govern hate expression. These laws determine when, how, and who can be hated.

Mass media, and now social media and its AI infrastructure, amplify and shape hate-filled interactions. Through recommendation algorithms and the ensuing echo chambers, social media platforms segregate toxic discourses from more mediating or empathic ones. This seclusion can normalize and intensify hate speech in bubbles. Alt-tech platforms even use hate stratification (Munn, 2023) for avoiding social pressure against explicit forms of hate, concealing toxic elements from new users and expanding the platform's audience by slowly radicalizing individuals.

For example, Hochschild's *Strangers in Their Own Land* (2016) illustrates at a broad social scale how these primary and secondary hate engines work in concert. Hochschild examines how victimization can explain growing US economic and social polarization, particularly among populations left behind by globalization and demographic changes. This narrative often leads to xenophobia and hate speech toward immigrants and other "outsiders." The book shows how cultural discourses and media portrayals can turn frustrations into focused hate.

1.3 AI contribution to the primary engines of hate

The rise of AI has transformed our digitalized societies, and its use has also exacerbated social inequality, exploitative interactions, and a sense of unfairness, stoking hate (Obreja & Rughiniș, 2023). These unanticipated effects raise concerns about the role of AI in society's widening divisions, especially in work and economic inequity (Budeanu & Rosner, 2021; Budeanu et al., 2023).

The growing divide between digital platform designers and managers and their users is one influence of AI. AI-powered big-tech corporations are becoming quasi-monopolies (Mitchell, 2021; von Thun, 2023). They solidify their influence and capture more wealth from tiny firms and from individuals who are dependent on these platforms using powerful AI algorithms. This technology thus appears unfair to social actors who supply material and labor to these platforms but receive a disproportionately small share of the profits.

Platform work, gig work, and "ghost work" are replacing solid, rewarding occupations. Many jobs, from taxi drivers and warehouse workers to translators, journalists, and writers, have been altered in the digital age. In particular, the human workforce regulating and filtering hate speech online often works under poor conditions (Perrigo, 2023; Newton, 2019) and is not protected from the psychological stress caused by extensive exposure to hate content.

Algorithmic management technologies, a product of AI advancement (Wood, 2021), control workers, reducing autonomy and causing despair and unhappiness. These programs can set work schedules, evaluate performance, and even fire employees without human oversight, creating a stressful, insecure workplace.

AI has thus contributed to the growth of the "precariat," a tech-regulated class of workers. These include "content creators" who earn little from their work across platforms, while tech elites profit greatly from this unstable labor (Daub, 2020). This dramatic gap may promote hate by contributing to a cultural narrative of inequality and injustice.

AI has made many advances, but it has also deepened societal disparities and contributed to exploitative labor. AI indirectly fuels hate by worsening these difficulties, producing a climate of injustice and victimization. To ensure fairness and social justice in AI research and use, these concerns must be addressed.

Generative AI has exacerbated insecure work and economic inequality, including in professional groups formerly considered immune to automation. This technology has raised worries and reactions from creative industries about its effects on employment and creative work (Bran et al., 2023).

One example was the screenwriting (Coyle, 2023) and acting (Dalton, 2023) industry turmoil. Professionals in these fields protested and struck due to generative AI's capacity to write convincing scripts and even digitally reproduce human performances. These people worry that AI-generated material may marginalize or replace their skills. This reflects broader concerns about job security and the value of human innovation in the face of AI.

The music sector also has a strong argument. Generative AI has advanced in classical and contemporary music composition, both instrumental and vocal (Palamara, 2023). This advancement has sparked legal disputes over copyright, creativity, and creator rights. Technology that can quickly produce large and diverse amounts of music challenges musicians' and composers' creative processes and also their livelihoods.

A similar disruption has taken a toll on the community of artists (Xiang, 2023) who create visual content for games, film, media, and entertainment. The fact that these large models feed on the artists' creativity, while earning immense sums of money for other social actors and endangering their jobs, led to outrage across platforms.

In literature and journalism, generative AI's ability to produce logical and entertaining content has led to further litigation and legal problems. Writers and journalists worry that AI can write news stories, novels, and other content which may reduce the need for human-written works (Barbaro & Frenkel, 2023). These advances have raised ethical and economic questions concerning AI's effects on creative industries, and people (Serrano et al., 2023) fight for preserving, only for humans and not for machines, the right to freedom of expression and the right to freedom of the arts and sciences.

In essence, generative AI threatens creative jobs, which were formerly assumed to be immune to automation, while also disrupting established practices in learning and education across disciplines. This technology may replace a large share of human creative work, affecting employment and professionalization in these areas and raising questions about human creativity's value and distinctiveness. Generative AI can fuel hate by escalating perceived injustice and fears of unemployment and economic insecurity in formerly safe industries.

1.4 AI contribution to secondary engines of hate

AI promotes and amplifies hate online through several main processes (see Figure 1.1 on next page). AI's algorithmic *personalization* of social media recommendations, message flows, and wallpapers reinforces users' ideas and *polarizes* them. *Filter bubbles* and *echo chambers* limit diversity and isolate people in ideological silos. *Deepfakes* and other AI-enabled technologies can also create and spread fake information that incites hatred and distrust. AI algorithms also *accelerate* the spread of unconfirmed or fake news by decreasing attention spans and making consumers more sensitive to unverified claims. This, along with increasingly unclear *accountability* in relation to who is the creator or the publisher of a discourse, obscures its source and culpability, making hate prevention harder.

1.4.1 AI role in the spread and amplification of hate

The rise of AI in the digital economy has fueled hate and has amplified, refined, and consolidated hateful discourses. Social media personalization algorithms create echo chambers by filtering content that matches users' pre-existing viewpoints, limiting diversity, and often intensifying hateful convictions. The lack of transparency in AI decision-making, especially in deep learning models, and the black box nature of AI models makes it hard to understand specific content suggestions or labeling, which could lead to unaccountable and unregulated hate speech or,

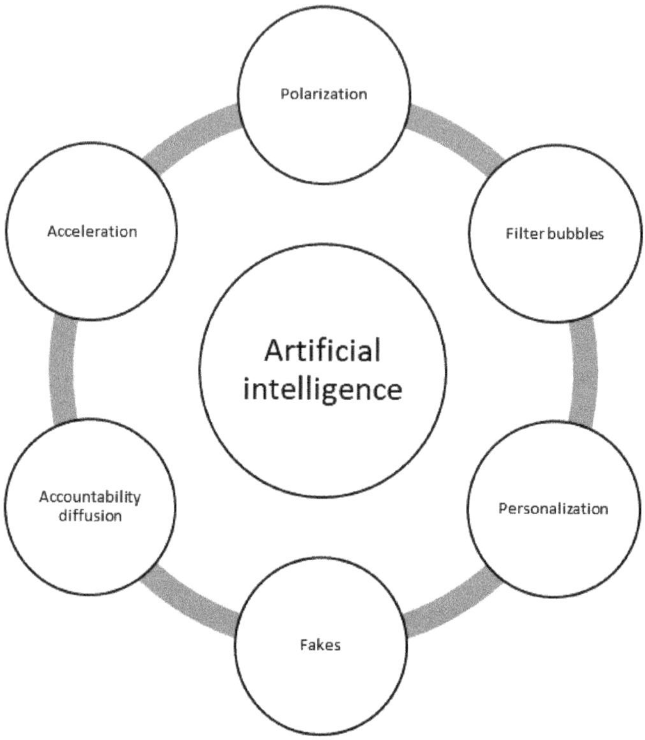

Figure 1.1 Intertwined processes of hate amplification driven by AI

conversely, to censorship. AI-driven bots allow for viral and large-scale propagation of hate speech, propaganda, and misinformation. Digital platforms that prioritize user engagement over ethics risk amplifying controversial and hateful narratives.

Several studies and reports have shown that AI-driven algorithms distribute and amplify hate speech. Violence in Myanmar and Sri Lanka and conversations of hate on YouTube®, Twitter®, and Instagram® show how modern technologies can inadvertently foster hate at scale, including self-hate. Facebook®'s algorithms "proactively amplified" anti-Rohingya propaganda in Myanmar, aggravating atrocities. According to Amnesty International®, Facebook's flawed algorithms and profit-driven approach contributed to crimes, creating an echo chamber that incited hatred (Amnesty International, 2022; De Guzman, 2022 ; Stecklow, 2018).

In a similar vein, the Sri Lankan government blocked Facebook in 2018 due to its inability to control hate speech, which was inciting national mob violence.

AI limits in recognizing context and geographical nuances have made it difficult to moderate content, especially in non-English-speaking countries (Udupa et al., 2023), leading to the uncontrolled rise of hate speech (Wijeratne, 2020).

Opinion polarization has also been linked to social media algorithms. According to Brown et al. (2022), YouTube's recommendation algorithm does not direct most users to extremist content, but it does narrow their ideological views. A modest ideological echo chamber may influence the propagation of specific material by pulling readers to the extremes of the political spectrum.

More recently, Hickey et al. (2023) found that Twitter hate speech increased after Elon Musk bought it and dismantled the platform's moderation teams and infrastructure. The study found bots increasingly spreading hate speech and misinformation. In another area, Instagram's algorithmically driven feeds, which are personalized to each user's engagement patterns, have been shown to affect teen mental health and lead to self-hate, notably as regards body image, creating anxiety, depression, and eating disorders (Austin, 2021). The website hooks vulnerable kids into a harmful cycle of negative social comparison and unattainable body and attractiveness standards. According to whistleblower Frances Haugen, Instagram has acknowledged this issue internally, although the response has been condemned as insufficient (Wetsman, 2021).

Moreover, authoritative governments can use AI to monitor and profile dissenters and excluded groups (Feldstein, 2022; Asher-Schapiro, 2021). Such use can exacerbate state-endorsed discrimination and hatred. This is also a risk for AI tools used by police and law enforcement (such as predictive policing or facial recognition) in democratic countries (Bailey et al., 2020). When AI-driven systems, especially in policing, disproportionately target or misidentify members of certain communities, it deepens social divisions. This disproportionate concentration undermines faith in these technologies and increases mistrust in marginalized communities, isolating them and fostering prejudice and hate.

1.4.2 Generative AI and the creation of novel expressions and legitimations of hate

With the rise of generative AI, hate speech may be even more amplified, personalized, and nuanced (Ocampo et al., 2023). Many AI systems, including generative AI, suffer from algorithmic bias—a major concern. These systems trained on large datasets may absorb historical and contemporary biases. Without adequate calibration and control, generative AI can magnify and reinforce these prejudices, perpetuating stereotypes and discrimination.

Generative AI's ability to create novel material can promote hate by spreading sophisticated vocabularies of motive. First, generative AI can create personalized vocabularies of hate, based on recipient beliefs or specific situations. Similar to

AI-driven phishing, these systems can develop hate arguments that resonate more with an individual depending on their cultural, historical, or personal background. Soon, harassment by automated troll bots might be replaced by harassment by autonomous conversational agents (Hinduja, 2023). The AI models can also better legitimize and intensify hateful attitudes by appealing to relevant historical tales and contemporary music or invoking relevant influencers.

Second, AI can message at scale while keeping personalization, increasing its impact. Generative AI can shape social narratives by personalizing and distributing hate messages to large audiences. Each recipient feels like the message was written for them (Weaver, 2023), boosting its likelihood of resonating and internalizing hate.

Finally, generative AI can create hyper-realistic images of hateful events. By convincingly presenting fake scenarios, AI can affect public opinion, validate prejudices, or inspire enmity toward certain groups or individuals. Deepfakes can rework historical narratives or create fresh lies that justify hate in novel and appealing ways, making them a powerful tool. For example, generative AI has already played a part in the Israel-Hamas war, with deepfake images spreading to promote specific narratives and elicit stronger support (Eisele, 2023).

For example, generative AI has also helped spread pseudoscientific content (BBC World Service, 2023), especially in pseudo-archaeology (Kurnick, 2020). Conspiracy theories, such as those purporting that aliens manufactured ancient relics, have spread thanks to this technology's convincing photographs and videos. This story typically minimizes the achievements of other cultures, especially non-Western or marginalized ones. AI-generated images can encourage xenophobic worldviews, weakening the public recognition of these civilizations' historical and cultural achievements. The ease with which generative AI can create realistic and appealing visual content has helped such theories gain traction and credibility, expanding their effect and reach.

As hate speech, generative AI's growing role in deepfake pornography (Home Security Heroes, 2023) has serious consequences. Deepfake pornography uses AI to produce or edit videos of people having sexual encounters without their consent. Women have been victimized and objectified by this technology. Facing deepfake pornography causes psychological suffering and social stigma. AI businesses and online platforms acknowledge the harm caused by such information but also admit to the difficulties in stopping its creation and transmission.

Noelle Martin's experience (Kudaki, 2023) shows how deepfake pornography traumatizes. Martin struggled to delete deepfake pornographic photographs of herself online and was victim-blamed. This example illustrates how deepfake pornography perpetuates hate by violating individuals' dignity and agency, causing continuing psychological suffering. As their technologies are misused to create explicit content, OpenAI® and Stability AI have taken steps to limit explicit image generation. OpenAI deleted sexual content from their DALL-E data, whereas Stability AI added filters to Stable Diffusion® to prevent explicit imagery. The possibility for manipulation of these technologies remains, making it difficult to prevent their exploitation for deepfake pornography. Twitch®, Apple®, and Google® app stores have amended deepfake pornography policies. Twitch banned graphic deepfakes, including those in streams, and Apple and Google removed a sexually provocative app. These measures highlight the growing awareness of the negative effects of deepfake pornography, which mostly targets women.

1.5 Regulating hate created with AI

1.5.1 Regulating the primary engines of hate

A multifaceted approach that includes technological, legal, and social measures is needed to regulate AI's contribution to the main engines of hate, such as economic or ethnic conflicts, inequities, and ongoing injustices. AI-driven platforms exacerbate social inequality and polarization, hence macro-social solutions are needed (Rughiniș, 2022). Strong antitrust regulations can prevent monopolies, especially by firms using AI. To protect workers from AI-driven precarity and exploitation, labor protection regulations are necessary. In particular, generative AI presents unique content generation and dissemination issues, hence meaningful and enforceable copyright regulations are needed to protect human authors.

Keeping humans in the loop is crucial to this regulatory framework. This ensures that AI decision-making is monitored and guided by human judgment, especially in ethical, cultural, or societal sensitive situations. High-quality and nuanced human judgment is needed at all points in the development and deployment of AI-enhanced hate speech detection and filtering tools.

Policies should also discourage the premature and accelerated deployment of AI technology that could replace human labor without considering social and economic implications. This means making AI-augmented workplace transitions fair, inclusive, and mindful of social impacts. A holistic approach to regulation would address AI's direct outputs and the structural conditions that allow AI to fuel hate.

1.5.2 Regulating the secondary engines of hate

Regulating polarization, personalization, filter bubbles, and echo chambers

Engagement-optimized recommendation algorithms drive digital polarization, personalization, filter bubbles, and echo chambers. Although mainly designed to engage consumers, such algorithms also promote information that evokes strong negative emotions such as indignation, anger, and hate. In this situation, algorithm regulation is important. Governments and regulators should require technology companies to disclose content prioritization algorithms.

In addition to enhanced transparency, personalization should be limited. Personalization can improve user experience, but over-customization can isolate people in ideological bubbles. Regulators should encourage platforms to use serendipity and diversity in their recommendation systems. Generative AI, which can create personalized hateful content, requires distinctive ethical guidelines. Platforms should be held accountable for the harmful content their AI systems generate (O'Carroll, 2023), ensuring that they do not perpetuate or amplify hateful narratives or information.

Regulating deepfakes and fake news

Deepfakes have ushered in a new realm of hate speech, raising complex ethical and legal challenges. Central to any regulatory approach is the issue of consent. Nonconsensual deepfakes, where individuals' likenesses are used without their permission, should be explicitly prohibited by law. This is particularly pertinent in the context of deepfake pornography, a distressingly common misuse of the technology. Governments and regulatory bodies must classify nonconsensual deepfake pornography as a criminal offense, recognizing its profound psychological and reputational impact on victims.

Beyond the issue of consent, there is the broader challenge of fake news propagated through deepfakes. Regulation should require platforms to implement rigorous content verification tools and procedures, ensuring that deepfake content is promptly detected and flagged. Collaboration with independent fact-checking organizations could further enhance the veracity of information circulating online. Moreover, public education campaigns are pivotal. By raising awareness about the capabilities and potential misuse of deepfake technology, individuals can be better equipped to critically assess and discern genuine content from manipulated media.

It is also essential to foster an environment of corporate accountability. Platforms that fail to adequately monitor and mitigate the spread of deepfake content should face substantial penalties. This will incentivize the continuous development and application of detection tools, making it more challenging for malicious actors to exploit the technology for spreading hate or misinformation.

Regulating accountability diffusion

In the AI landscape, accountability often gets obscured, especially when models generate content in tandem with users. A pivotal step in addressing this challenge is to establish clear regulations around the responsibility of AI models and the organizations that produce and train them. These entities should be held accountable for the content co-authored by their models, particularly if it falls under harmful or hateful categories (Henderson et al., 2023). This would necessitate redefining the boundaries of AI's role from a neutral tool to an active participant in content generation, thereby ensuring that companies take proactive measures in curbing the negative potential of their AI systems.

An equally critical aspect is the human involvement in the AI pipeline, especially in areas concerning hate speech detection and moderation (Gillespie, 2020). Individuals—often referred to as *ghost workers*—who label data, train models, and moderate content play a crucial role in shaping the ethical boundaries of AI. Their involvement often goes unnoticed and undervalued, leading to subpar working conditions, low remuneration, and exposure to potentially traumatic content. Regulatory bodies should enforce standards ensuring these workers receive proper compensation, health benefits, and adequate protection against work-related trauma. A concerted effort must be made to halt the race to the bottom in terms of payment and conditions for these crucial roles. Elevating the status, rewards, and protections for these individuals will not only uphold their dignity but also enhance the quality and ethics of AI systems they help build.

Finally, transparency is the bedrock of trustworthiness in AI. Promoting transparent datasets and models is essential to engender public confidence and ensure robustness in AI products that detect hate speech. Clear documentation of data sources, model architectures, and decision-making processes would provide stakeholders with insights into how decisions are made and where potential biases might emerge. A transparent approach would also enable external audits, further ensuring that AI systems align with societal values and ethical considerations.

Regulating acceleration

The hyper-accelerated pace of information dissemination in the digital age, fueled in part by the use of bots and autonomous agents, plays a pivotal role in the erosion of collective attention spans and the rise of impulsive reactions to unverified information. Addressing this requires a multifaceted approach, beginning with the discouragement of bots and autonomous agents in the diffusion of messages on social networks. Regulatory bodies can enforce tighter controls on automated accounts, making it harder for them to operate without clear identification markers. By doing so, users would be more aware when they are interacting with or receiving information from automated entities, thereby placing a higher value on genuine human communication.

Rewarding human communication can also be instrumental. Platforms can be incentivized, through policy or public pressure, to design algorithms that prioritize content generated by human users over automated ones. Such a paradigm shift would amount to algorithmic time work (Flaherty, 2003; Rughiniș & Flaherty, 2019) that elevates authentic, reflective, and nuanced discussions over high-speed, automated content dumps. Furthermore, introducing features that promote "slow information processing" can be invaluable, creating time capital for users (Matei & Preda, 2020). This could manifest as built-in waiting periods before sharing articles, nudges to read full articles instead of just headlines, or prompts that encourage users to reflect before commenting or sharing. Moreover, platforms can be encouraged to introduce "information digestion" features: spaces or modes where users can contemplate and discuss content at a more leisurely pace, decreasing the intensity of negative emotions.

Regulating generative AI models throughout their development pipeline

Generative AI models warrant meticulous oversight throughout their developmental cycle (Hacker et al., 2023). The bedrock of any robust AI system lies in its training data. Ensuring high-quality training data means not just securing vast amounts of information but ensuring that this information is representative, unbiased, and devoid of harmful or hateful content (Hurlburt, 2023). Regulatory bodies should work in tandem with AI developers to set standards for data collection, annotation, and validation. Periodic audits of training datasets, possibly through third-party entities, can ensure adherence to these standards.

Complementing the training data is the process of training, which is equally critical. Regulations can mandate that companies implement best practices that minimize the chances of AI models producing harmful outputs. This could involve techniques such as differential privacy to maintain data anonymity or adversarial training (*red teaming*) to make models robust against generating biased or hateful responses. AI developers should be encouraged, if not required, to maintain logs of training iterations, allowing for traceability in case of undesirable outcomes. Furthermore, specific beneficial scenarios for generating sensible content should be taken into account on the basis of context (Stapleton et al., 2023), such as in the case of *green teaming* for education and training purposes or empowering vulnerable communities to fight back in a peaceful manner.

The ability to distinguish between human-generated and AI-generated content is also gaining importance, especially as generative models become more sophisticated. Developing methods for watermarking AI-generated content can offer a viable solution. For textual content, this might involve subtle markers or metadata tags, while for visual imagery, imperceptible watermarks or digital signatures can be embedded. By doing so, consumers of the content will be aware of its origin, allowing them to exercise discernment. This becomes especially critical in contexts where AI-generated content might be mistaken for genuine human-created media, potentially leading to misinformation.

Beyond these measures, it is essential to foster a culture of open dialogue and collaboration between regulators, AI practitioners, and the broader public. Community-driven oversight, where users and experts alike can provide feedback on AI model behaviors, can supplement regulatory efforts. Moreover, transparency in model architectures, decision-making processes, and potential limitations should be encouraged, fostering an environment in which generative AI is used responsibly and ethically.

For example, The European Union's AI Act, landmark legislation governing artificial intelligence use in Europe, addresses the issue of hate speech in AI through several key mechanisms (European Commission, n.d.; European Parliament, 2023; Reuters, 2023). It proposes a risk-based classification of AI tools, with high-risk categories including law enforcement and migration, where hate speech could be a significant concern. The Act's expansive governance covers AI systems that generate content, predictions, or decisions, ensuring that sectors where hate speech might be generated or propagated are regulated. It imposes strong transparency obligations on AI systems that interact with humans or generate deepfake content, aiding in identifying and mitigating AI-generated hate speech. For high-risk AI tools, such as those used in critical infrastructure or law enforcement, the Act mandates rigorous risk assessments and scrutiny by authorities, which includes evaluating their potential to generate or propagate hate speech.

The Act also discusses the regulation of General Purpose AI Systems (GPAIS) like generative AI models, with lawmakers considering designating all forms of GPAIS as high risk, impacting how technology companies address hate speech generation. Violations of AI Act carry substantial fines, emphasizing the severity of non-compliance. Specifically for generative AI such as ChatGPT®, the Act imposes requirements such as disclosing AI-generated content, preventing the generation of illegal content including hate speech, and publishing training data summaries. This regulatory framework is complemented by existing EU laws against hate speech, with the European Commission working towards criminalizing a broader range of hate speech and hate crimes, enhancing the legal framework against hate speech in conjunction with the AI Act.

1.6 Conclusions

In addressing the challenge of regulating hate speech generated or amplified by AI, including generative AI, a broader approach is essential. This approach must not only focus on the generative AI systems themselves but also on the primary and secondary engines of hate, encompassing the wider communication ecosystem in which these technologies operate. Regulation should redress and prevent AI use for social polarization and labor exploitation.

There is a strong interplay between generative AI and other AI tools, such as recommendation and decision-making algorithms, in data enhancement and bias dynamics. Generative AI, capable of producing diverse content, contributes to the datasets utilized by recommendation algorithms. This synergy brings risks of amplifying hate speech if the content generated by the AI harbors biases or harmful elements that the recommendation systems fail to adequately filter. Simultaneously, generative AI holds potential in mitigating biases within decision-making algorithms. By generating unbiased, varied datasets, it can aid these algorithms in making more equitable and non-discriminatory decisions. Nonetheless, this interaction necessitates oversight to ensure that biases, particularly those leading to the creation or perpetuation of hate speech, are not transferred or exacerbated within these interconnected AI systems.

Keeping humans in the loop is paramount; human oversight and ethical judgment are crucial in monitoring and guiding AI behavior, especially in nuanced areas like hate speech. It is vital to prevent the rapid acceleration and dissemination of harmful content, leaving room for human deliberation and interrupting potential feedback loops that can amplify hate. Transparency and accountability should be key pillars of this regulatory framework, ensuring that AI systems operate within ethical boundaries and societal norms. In addition, focusing on data quality and bias mitigation, especially in generative AI, is essential to prevent the perpetuation of hate speech. Collaborative efforts between AI developers, policymakers, and societal stakeholders are necessary to balance the benefits of AI with the need to protect against its potential harms, creating a responsible and safe digital environment.

References

Amnesty International (September 29, 2022). Myanmar: Facebook's systems promoted violence against Rohingya; Meta owes reparations—New report. https://www.amnesty.org/en/latest/news/2022/09/myanmar-facebooks-systems-promoted-violence-against-rohingya-meta-owes-reparations-new-report/

Asher-Schapiro, A. (January 13, 2021). Chinese tech patents tools that can detect, track Uighurs. Reuters. https://www.reuters.com/article/us-china-tech-uighurs-idUSKBN29I300

Austin, B. (October 8, 2021). How social media's toxic content sends teens into 'a dangerous spiral'. Harvard School of Public Health News. https://www

.hsph.harvard.edu/news/features/how-social-medias-toxic-content-sends-teens-into-a-dangerous-spiral/

Bailey, J., Burkell, J., & Steeves, V. (August 24, 2020). AI technologies—like police facial recognition—discriminate against people of colour. The Conversation. https://theconversation.com/ai-technologies-like-police-facial-recognition-discriminate-against-people-of-colour-143227

Barbaro, M., & Frenkel, S. (2023). The writers' revolt against A.I. companies. NY Times. https://www.nytimes.com/2023/07/18/podcasts/the-daily/ai-scraping.html

BBC World Service (September 14, 2023). Bad science: AI used to target kids with disinformation on YouTube. https://www.youtube.com/watch?v=ojjn9T_fuUw

Bran, E., Rughiniș, C., Nadoleanu, G., & Flaherty, M. G. (2023). The emerging social status of generative AI: Vocabularies of AI competence in public discourse. In *Proceedings of the 24th International Conference on Control Systems and Computer Science* (CSCS) (pp. 391–398). IEEE.

Brown, M. A., Bisbee, J., Lai, A., Bonneau, R., Nagler, J., & Tucker, J. A. (2022). Echo chambers, rabbit holes, and algorithmic bias: How YouTube recommends content to real users. SSRN Electronic Journal. https://doi.org/10.2139/ssrn.4114905

Budeanu, A. M., & Rosner, D. (2021). Big data as capital. A case study on the Innovation Labs Tech Accelerator. In *23rd International Conference on Control Systems and Computer Science* (CSCS) (pp. 469–475). IEEE.

Budeanu, A. M., Țurcanu, D., & Rosner, D. (2023). European perceptions of artificial intelligence and their social variability. An exploratory study. In *24th International Conference on Control Systems and Computer Science* (CSCS) (pp. 436–443). IEEE.

Coyle, J. (September 28, 2023). In Hollywood writers' battle against AI, humans win (for now). AP News. https://apnews.com/article/hollywood-ai-strike-wga-artificial-intelligence-39ab72582c3a15f77510c9c30a45ffc8

Dalton, A. (November 11, 2023). Hollywood actors union board approves strike-ending deal as leaders tout money gains and AI rights. AP News. https://apnews.com/article/actors-strike-deal-d5f9769fd8a263170141a60da64cdc98

Daub, A. (2020). *What tech calls thinking: An inquiry into the intellectual bedrock of Silicon Valley*. FSG Originals. ISBN 978-0374538644.

De Guzman, C. (September 28, 2022). Meta's Facebook algorithms 'proactively' promoted violence against the Rohingya, new Amnesty International report asserts. Time. https://time.com/6217730/myanmar-meta-rohingya-facebook/

Eisele, I. (November 10, 2023). Fact check: AI fakes in Israel's war against Hamas. Deutsche Welle. https://www.dw.com/en/fact-check-ai-fakes-in-israels-war-against-hamas/a-67367744

European Commission (n.d.). Combating hate speech and hate crime: Measures to prevent and combat different forms of hatred and to protect victims. https://commission.europa.eu/strategy-and-policy/policies/justice-and-fundamental-rights/combatting-discrimination/racism-and-xenophobia/combating-hate-speech-and-hate-crime_en

European Parliament (June 14, 2023). EU AI Act: First regulation on artificial intelligence. https://www.europarl.europa.eu/news/en/headlines/society/20230601STO93804/eu-ai-act-first-regulation-on-artificial-intelligence

Feldstein, S. (October 27, 2022). China's high-tech surveillance drives oppression of Uyghurs. Bulletin of the Atomic Scientists. https://thebulletin.org/2022/10/chinas-high-tech-surveillance-drives-oppression-of-uyghurs/

Flaherty, M. G. (2003). Time work: Customizing temporal experience. *Social Psychology Quarterly*, 17–33.

Gillespie, T. (2020). Content moderation, AI, and the question of scale. *Big Data & Society, 7*(2). doi:10.1177/2053951720943234

Hacker, P., Engel, A., & Mauer, M. (June, 2023). Regulating ChatGPT and other large generative AI models. In *Proceedings of the 2023 ACM Conference on Fairness, Accountability, and Transparency* (pp. 1112–1123).

Henderson, P., Hashimoto, T., & Lemley, M. (2023). Where's the liability in harmful AI speech? *Journal of Free Speech Law, 3,* 589.

Hickey, D., Schmitz, M., Fessler, D., Smaldino, P. E., Muric, G., & Burghardt, K. (2023). Auditing Elon Musk's impact on hate speech and bots. In *Proceedings of the International AAAI Conference on Web and Social Media, 17* (pp. 1133–1137).

Hinduja, S. (May 10, 2023). Generative AI as a vector for harassment and harm. Cyberbullying Research Center. https://cyberbullying.org/generative-ai-as-a-vector-for-harassment-and-harm

Hochschild, A. R. (1979). Emotion work, feeling rules, and social structure. *American Journal of Sociology, 85*(3), 551–575.

Hochschild, A. R. (2016). *Strangers in their own land: Anger and mourning on the American right.* New York: The New Press.

Home Security Heroes (2023). State of deepfakes: Realities, threats, and impacts. https://www.homesecurityheroes.com/state-of-deepfakes/#key-findings

Hurlburt, G. (2023). What if ethics got in the way of generative AI? *IT Professional, 25*(2), 4–6.

Kudacki, A. (April 16, 2023 at Associated Press). Deepfake porn could be a growing problem amid AI race. El Pais. https://english.elpais.com/science-tech/2023-04-16/deepfake-porn-could-be-a-growing-problem-amid-ai-race.html

Kurnick, S. (August, 2020). "Aliens built the Pyramids" and other absurdities of pseudo-archaeology. TED Talks. https://www.ted.com/talks/sarah_kurnick_aliens_built_the_pyramids_and_other_absurdities_of_pseudo_archaeology

Matei, Ş., & Preda, M. (2020). Time capital as a social imaginary. *Journal of Comparative Research in Anthropology & Sociology, 11*(1).

Mills, C. W. (1940). Situated actions and vocabularies of motive. *American Sociological Review, 5*(6), 904–913.

Mitchell, S. (December 1, 2021). Report: Amazon's toll road. Institute for Local Self-Reliance. https://ilsr.org/amazons-toll-road/

Munn, L. (2023). Surface and sublevel hate. *Big Data & Society, 10*(1), 20539517221148136.

Newton, C. (February 25, 2019). The trauma floor: The secret lives of Facebook moderators in America. The Verge. https://www.theverge.com/2019/2/25/18229714/cognizant-facebook-content-moderator-interviews-trauma-working-conditions-arizona

Obreja, D. M., & Rughiniş, R. (2023). The moral status of artificial intelligence: Exploring users' anticipatory ethics in the controversy regarding LaMDA's sentience. In *24th International Conference on Control Systems and Computer Science* (CSCS) (pp. 411–417). IEEE.

Ocampo, N. B., Sviridova, E., Cabrio, E., & Villata, S. (2023). An in-depth analysis of implicit and subtle hate speech messages. In *Proceedings of the 17th Conference of the European Chapter of the Association for Computational Linguistics* (pp. 1997–2013). Association for Computational Linguistics.

O'Carroll, L. (October 24, 2023). EU 'in touching distance' of world's first laws regulating artificial intelligence. The Guardian. https://www.theguardian.com/technology/2023/oct/24/eu-touching-distance-world-first-law-regulating-artificial-intelligence-dragos-tudorache

Palamara, J. (August 14, 2023). 3 ways AI is transforming music. The Conversation. https://theconversation.com/3-ways-ai-is-transforming-music-210598

Perrigo, B. (January 18, 2023). Exclusive: OpenAI used Kenyan workers on less than $2 per hour to make ChatGPT less toxic. Time. https://time.com/6247678/openai-chatgpt-kenya-workers/

Reuters Explainer (March 22, 2023). What is the European Union AI Act? https://www.reuters.com/technology/what-is-european-union-ai-act-2023-03-22/

Rughiniş, R. (2022). *Societatea digitală. Stăpâni, cetățeni sau sclavi?* Bucharest: Humanitas Publishing House.

Rughiniş, C., & Flaherty, M. G. (2019). Algorithmic discrimination and its temporal logics. Extended abstract for Digital Humanities in the Nordic Countries Conference. https://cst.dk/DHN2019Pro/abstracts/Rughinis-Flaherty-DHN%20abstract-FINAL.pdf

Rughiniş, C., & Flaherty, M. G. (2022). The social bifurcation of reality: Symmetrical construction of knowledge in science-trusting and science-distrusting discourses. *Frontiers in Sociology, 7*, 782851.

Serrano, M. A., Bensimon, M., Pfister Fetz, N., & George, N. (July 26, 2023). European Writers' Council (EWC) second statement on the AI Act proposal. European Writers' Council. https://europeanwriterscouncil.eu/23ewc_on_aiact/

Stapleton, L., Taylor, J., Fox, S., Wu, T., & Zhu, H. (2023). Seeing seeds beyond weeds: Green teaming generative AI for beneficial uses. arXiv preprint *arXiv: 2306.03097.*

Stecklow, S. (August 15, 2018). Why Facebook is losing the war on hate speech in Myanmar. A Reuters special report. https://www.reuters.com/investigates/special-report/myanmar-facebook-hate

Tajfel, H., Turner, J. C., Austin, W. G., & Worchel, S. (1979). An integrative theory of intergroup conflict. In M. J. Hatch and M. Schultz (Eds.), *Organizational Identity: A Reader* (pp. 56–65). Oxford: Oxford University Press.

Udupa, S., Maronikolakis, A., & Wisiorek, A. (2023). Ethical scaling for content moderation: Extreme speech and the (in)significance of artificial intelligence. *Big Data & Society, 10*(1), 20539517231172424.

von Thun, M. (October 23, 2023). Monopoly power is the elephant in the room in the AI debate. Tech Policy Press Newsletter. https://techpolicy.press/monopoly-power-is-the-elephant-in-the-room-in-the-ai-debate/

Weaver, M. (July 6, 2023). AI chatbot 'encouraged' man who planned to kill queen, court told. The Guardian. https://www.theguardian.com/uk-news/2023/jul/06/ai-chatbot-encouraged-man-who-planned-to-kill-queen-court-told

Wetsman, N. (October 6, 2021). Facebook's whistleblower report confirms what researchers have known for years. The Verge. https://www.theverge.com/2021/10/6/22712927/facebook-instagram-teen-mental-health-research

Wijeratne, Y. (July 23, 2020). Facebook, language and the difficulty of moderating hate speech. LSE Blogs. https://blogs.lse.ac.uk/medialse/2020/07/23/facebook-language-and-the-difficulty-of-moderating-hate-speech/

Wilkinson, R., & Pickett, K. (2009). *The spirit level: Why equality is better for everyone.* London: Penguin.

Wood, A. J. (2021). Algorithmic management consequences for work organisation and working conditions (No. 2021/07). European Council. JRC Working Papers Series on Labour, Education and Technology.

Xiang, C. (December 14, 2022). Artists are revolting against AI art on ArtStation. Vice. https://www.vice.com/en/article/ake9me/artists-are-revolt-against-ai-art-on-artstation

Chapter 2

Generative Artificial Intelligence: Introduction, Application, Trends, and Ethics

Francisco J. Cantu-Ortiz

Tec de Monterrey, Mexico

2.1 Introduction

During the last two decades, we have seen impressive progress in the field of generative artificial intelligence (GAI) that made it possible to build language models that can interact with users and generate content at an expert human-level performance in many areas of application (Campbell, 2023). *Language models* are probabilistic models of a human language associated with words from a corpus of text to make semantic predictions within a user conversation. Language models are commonly used in natural language processing (NLP) and applied in chatbot conversational tasks such as automated customer service, language translation, speech and face recognition, and other interactive tasks.

Chatbots contain various restrictions that lessen their scope of application in conversational activities. Among these shortcomings are the reduced context that chatbots operate on; the limited number of pre-programmed rules in the context; the domain-dependent and relatively small scale of the datasets they make use of; and the inherent limitation in generating text, images, or speech when interacting with users. All these weaknesses frequently result in customer dissatisfaction and frustration, leaving a negative feeling about company service.

Large language models (LLMs) are a type of language model applied for general-purpose language understanding and generation using massive amounts of data to learn billions of parameters during their training phase. They are designed to address the limitations of traditional chatbots. LLMs are generative models built from the probability distribution of a series of words from a natural language to predict the next words in an interactive narrative context.

The most successful LLMs are called *transformers,* a type of artificial neural networks which are trained using machine-learning techniques from text corpora that can generate content such as text, speech, video, music, and other output in multiple problem domains (Min et al., 2024). Transformers incorporate the *Attention* algorithm—a groundbreaking contribution developed by Vaswani et al. (2017) at Google® to address the limitations of deep learning methods. The use of the Attention mechanism invented at Google was a point of inflexion in the resurgence of current LLMs (Vaswani et al., 2017).

The features and capacities of LLMs inherent to generative AI can be seen as a first step forward in the long-term aim of building machine artificial general intelligence (AGI) based on algorithms and manipulation of symbol simulating or even surpassing human capacities (Salmi, 2023). Flying, running, or swimming observed in biological beings like birds, horses, or fish was a human longing that was eventually achieved with the construction of mechanical airplanes, trains, or submarines, respectively. Something similar may happen in the future with the rise of generative AI models.

Regarding current generative AI models, ChatGPT® from OpenAI® is the most well-known and successful LLM, which has attracted wide attention, becoming a "viral Internet sensation" (Jenkins et al., 2013). Other generative AI models chatbots competing with ChatGPT include Bard®* (Aten, 2024) from Google, LLaMA from Meta, Ernie Bot from Baidu®, and Claude® from Anthropic®. Microsoft® launched a version of its search engine Bing® based on ChatGPT.

OpenAI launched ChatGPT on November 30, 2022, and released a free-access test version that immediately became highly popular among Internet users and gained worldwide attention. One month after its launch, ChatGPT reported over 100 million users, becoming the fastest-growing consumer software tool ever. As a comparison, TikTok® took about nine months and Instagram® about two and a half years to reach 100 million users (Hu, 2023).

---

* As of this writing, Google is rebranding its AI products and introducing new ways to interact with its most powerful model, Gemini®.

Due to its great capacity to understand natural language and respond with useful information, ChatGPT has attracted ample interest in industry, academia, media, and the community. Because of its success, companies are integrating ChatGPT in customer support, whereas scholars are investigating its use for various application domains and scientific disciplines. Now, OpenAI offers ChatGPT Plus, a commercial paid version of ChatGPT with more advanced features (Alawida et al., 2023).

On the other hand, Google launched only a restricted version of Bard in the USA on March 2, 2023, as a standalone web application and a text user interface. A disclaimer appears saying that Bard "may display inaccurate or offensive information that doesn't represent Google's views." Bard was announced in the European Union in July of 2023 after solving data protection concerns by EU members. After several updates during the summer of 2023, Bard is being used by Google users with mixed feelings when comparing it with ChatGPT performance owing to the caution and conservative stance in user conversations.

Until October 19, 2023, the web version of Bard was presented as an "experiment" with the disclaimer, "Tell me what's on your mind, or pick a suggestion. I have limitations and won't always get it right, but your feedback will help me improve." Media columnists from *The New York Times, The Washington Post,* CBS, and others have criticized Bard and published pessimistic reports after comparing Bard with ChatGPT performance.

Regarding generative AI chatbot capabilities, they can sustain human-like interaction in a meaningful and useful way from prompts given by users. In addition to producing summaries, essays, images, video, and speech, generative AI chatbots can engender computer code from a user specification and carry out creative work, including writing poetry and songs and playing computer games.

Overall, the use of generative AI systems has proved useful in solving problems from business, economic, culture, and artistic work and are deemed to have the potential to transform most industries, including business, economics, government, entertainment, art, and design (Fui-Hoon Nah et al., 2023).

In the following sections, we elaborate on the various aspects of generative AI models as follows:

- In Foundations, we explain the main AI techniques used in building generative AI models.
- The next section, Leading Generative AI Models, explains the architecture of ChatGPT, Bard, and other models.
- The section on Prompt Engineering gives an overview of this emerging field about the user-machine interaction in generative AI models.
- Application and Trends describes uses of generative AI models in relevant fields.
- Ethical Aspects presents ethical concerns related to the use of generative AI tools and the need for new legislation regulating AI technologies.
- Finally, we end the chapter with the Conclusions section.

2.2 Foundations

In this section, we briefly describe the artificial intelligence and statistics techniques employed to build generative models for human-computer interaction. These include natural language processing, machine learning, and related methods. We present them in a bottom-up fashion, presenting first the most fundamental techniques followed by the ones built upon them in a layered fashion.

2.2.1 Natural language processing

To understand natural language, a machine converts a corpus of text into tokens, vectors, and embeddings, applying algorithms of tokenization, vectorization, and word embedding, respectively (Liu et al., 2023).

Tokenization creates a vocabulary of words from a corpus of text. It divides the text into individual units known as *tokens.* A vocabulary is the set of unique tokens found within the corpus. Tokens can be punctuation marks, words, or sentences and are transformed into vectors by an embedding process.

Vectors are numerical representations of the words along several dimensions, where each dimension represents a meaning of the words in the text. The meaning is obtained by using an *embedding* algorithm that consists in training the vectors with a deep learning model like a generative, deep learning or transformer model in a process called *encoding.* This allows the model to automatically understand the meaning of words and how they relate to each other. Vectors are used to provide answers in a user interaction with a process called a *decoder.* The encoder takes an input sequence of words and creates a context representation, whereas the decoder takes the context as input and creates an output sequence.

As part of the training process, an encoder-decoder network can be built using a recurrent neural network to perform tasks such as question-answers, text summarization, machine translation, dialogue, sentiment analysis, and other tasks.

The number of dimensions in a word vector is its *dimensionality.* A high-dimensional word vector would allow it to capture a wide range of characteristics and nuances of the word, but this also means that it would require more data and computation for training and use (Asudani et al., 2023).

2.2.2 Generative models

A *generative model* is a statistical model of the joint probability distribution $P(X, Y)$ of an observable variable X and a target variable Y, or of an observation x given a target value y. Such models define classifiers which can be used to "generate" random instances or outcomes either of an observation and a target (x, y) or of an observation x given a target value y, represented symbolically by $P(X \mid Y = y)$.

A *discriminative model* is defined symmetrically as a model of the conditional probability of the target Y, given an observation x, $P(Y \mid X = x)$. A discriminative model can be used to isolate the value of the target variable Y, given an observation x. Examples of generative models are naïve Bayes classifiers and linear discriminant analysis, whereas logistic regression is an instance of a discriminative classifier.

The term *generative model* is also used to describe models that generate instances of output variables in a way that have no clear relationship to probability distributions over potential samples of input variables. Generative adversarial networks (GAN) are examples of this class of generative model and are evaluated by the similarity of outputs to potential inputs. Such models are not considered classifiers (Eigenschink et al., 2023).

2.2.3 Supervised learning

A *supervised learning* method acts like a tutoring system in which learning occurs by overseeing a learner giving a sample of cases with pairs of input and the correct answer to that input. Given the right answer for every input value is called a *labeling* process.

From the input-output set of samples, a model is learned by a training task that consists in building a function that discovers a relationship between input and output values from a training subset of the dataset. The function is then examined in a complementary test subset of the data set to determine its accuracy and other statistic parameters. Then, the function learned is used to predict values given new input values. The accuracy of the learning function will depend on its generalization capacity to predict correct answers for unseen input instances (Baladram et al., 2020).

To illustrate supervised learning, consider the case of customer churning in a bank. Churning occurs when profitable clients using credit cards leave the bank and the bank needs to take action to retain such clients. One way to do this is to give a supervised learning algorithm a dataset of clients containing attributes such as client income, amount of credit, monthly purchases, and other financial information, along with a label indicating the status of the clients indicating "active client" or "lost client." Then the algorithm learns a function that predicts the probability of churning for new clients based on the values of the attributes (Jeyaprakaash & Sashirekha, 2022).

In contrast to supervised learning, *unsupervised learning* occurs from entirely non-labeled data, which means that there is no tutoring or supervision in the learning process. The dataset is explored without human intervention to discover patterns via clustering algorithms that identify similarities among instances and assign a label or a class to similar objects. Unsupervised learning is widely used in exploratory data analysis, customer segmentation, and image recognition (Hinton et al., 1999).

A third type of learning method is *semi-supervised learning,* which uses a combination of supervised methods in which a small part of the dataset is manually labeled, followed by an unsupervised method which takes the largest amount of unlabeled data of the same dataset to automatically generate labels. Semi-supervised learning is used by LLMs in which the dataset is extremely large (Zhong, 2018).

Reinforcement learning is a method in which a learner searches for the optimal behavior in an environment to obtain maximum reward. The optimal behavior is learned through interactions with the environment and observations of how it responds. It resembles children exploring the world around them and learning the actions that help them achieve a goal. The learner must independently discover the sequence of actions that maximize the reward with a trial-and-error search. The method can learn successful actions in an unseen environment without the help of a supervisor (Abhishek & Manisha, 2018).

2.2.4 Neural networks

Artificial neural networks of neural networks (NNs) are machine-learning models that are inspired by the structure and operation of biological neural networks of the brains of living organisms. A brain neuron is emulated by a node which is called an *artificial neuron,* and brain synapses correspond to edges connecting the nodes. There may be vertical layers of internal neurons called *hidden layers* connecting input with output nodes.

Artificial neurons receive signals from their inputs, compute a number, and pass the result to neurons in the next layer. The computation is made by a non-linear function of the sum of its inputs. Learning occurs by adjusting weights associated to neurons and edges to augment or decrease the strength of the signal represented by the number computed by the neuron.

In supervised learning, the computed number at the output layer is compared with the desired output, and an error is calculated using a cost function and sent back to previous layers using a learning algorithm called *backpropagation.* The function *mean squared error*—which is the expected value of the squared difference between the predicted and observed results—is a well-known cost function used in neural networks and regression analysis.

Neurons may have a threshold such that a signal is fired only if the computed number crosses a predefined threshold. Network layers may perform different computations on their inputs that travel from the first to the last layer and may traverse the layers several times (Alexander, 2020).

2.2.5 Common types of neural networks

In this section we explain the three more commonly used neural network architectures employed in machine learning.

In a *feed-forward network* (FFN), the signals computed at each node travel forward from input to output layer in one-way direction.

In a *recurrent neural network* (RNN), signals can go back to previous hidden layers iteratively. RNNs are used in text understanding, which is an iterative process. When we read a sentence, we process each word, stacking them up to the end of the sentence. Stacking information of like elements that repeat over time is well performed by RNNs and is commonly used to build encoder-decoder networks.

Long short-term memory (LSTM) is a recurrent neural network that deals with the *vanishing gradient problem* present in traditional recurrent neural network. It is called *long* because it provides a short-term memory to traditional recurrent neural networks that can last thousands of timesteps. It is used in classification, prediction with time series such as in handwriting, speech recognition, machine translation, speech activity detection, robot control, video games, and healthcare.

The *vanishing gradient problem* is encountered when training a neural network with gradient-based learning and backpropagation. In each iteration of training, each of the neural network weights receives an update proportional to the partial derivative (gradient) of the error function with respect to the current weight. The problem is that the gradient will be very small, preventing the weight from changing its value.

In a *convolutional neural network,* computations are made in a neuron applying to inputs a convolution function, which is defined as the integral of the product of two other functions after one of them is shifted and reflected around the *y*-axis of the other function.

2.2.6 Deep learning

Deep learning means having a large enough number of hidden layers to increase the learning capacity of the neural networks in complex domains.

The parameters in a deep learning method include the weights, bias, and learning rate of the network. Parameters are learned by iterative training over a large dataset, followed by a fine-tuning of the parameters for diverse applications.

Deep-learning architectures include deep neural networks, deep belief networks, deep reinforcement learning, recurrent neural networks, convolutional neural networks, and transformers. They have been successfully applied in computer vision, speech recognition, natural language processing, machine translation, and image processing, as well as in domains such as medical diagnosis, material inspection, obstacle avoidance, path planning, other cognitive tasks, and board game programs, where they have produced results comparable to, and in some cases surpassing, human expert performance (Patterson, 2016).

2.2.7 Large language models

As said before, a *language model* is a type of generative model applied to natural language. The model generates probabilities of a series of words taken from a corpus of text on which the model was trained. It is based on an assumption that the probability of the next word in a sequence depends only on a fixed size window of previous words. *N*-grams are an example of language models based on a window of size *N*.

Large language models (LLMs) are a type of language model trained by generating probabilities applying feed-forward neural networks and deep-learning algorithms called *transformers* to an enormous corpus of text, including billions of parameters and training samples (Maddigan & Susnjak, 2023).

One example of an LLM architecture is GPT (generative pre-trained transformer) from OpenAI used in ChatGPT, while PaLM (Pathways Language Model) from Google is other influential LLM that supports Bard.

LLMs are successfully used in speech recognition, language translation, natural language generation, text summarization, handwriting recognition, and information retrieval, among other tasks.

2.2.8 Deep generative models

The combination of deep-learning neural networks with generative models makes it possible to have powerful architectures known as deep generative models (DGMs). When DGMs are applied to a large corpus of data, the learning performance of such models scales up, producing remarkable results in real-world problem domains (Eigenschink et al., 2023).

Popular DGMs include variational autoencoders (VAEs), generative adversarial networks (GANs), and auto-regressive models. For instance, GPT is a DGM based on auto-regressive neural networks that contain billions of parameters trained in massively large datasets. The dataset used to train the model was obtained from various Internet sources, including public webpages, blogs, articles, books, Wikipedia®, and other collections (Song et al., 2023).

DGMs like GPT were developed to predict the next word in a sentence or paragraph written by the user given a context. This next word must be meaningful in the phrase and the whole conversation.

2.2.9 Transformers

A *transformer* is a deep-learning architecture based on DGMs that supersedes recurrent neural networks and long short-term memory in reducing training time by implementing parallelization of text processing with a parallel multi-head attention mechanism (Dufter et al., 2022).

Attention, also called *self-attention,* is a seminal algorithm discovered by Vaswani et al. (2017) at Google that resembles human attention to concentrate thought in a single event. Self-attention is computed with numerical weights for each word in the text. If weights change during each runtime, they are called *soft weights.* If weights are pre-trained, fine-tuned, and remain frozen, they are called *hard weights.*

The self-attention mechanism captures dependencies between the tokens in an input sequence and determines the weight of each token and their relative importance via semantic similarity between vectors using the dot product. The dot product of two vectors determines the cosine distance between the two vectors, considering their amplitude and the angle. The higher the dot product between two embeddings, the more semantically similar they are, indicating their importance in the overall context of the input sequence.

Each word is represented by an embedding, which consists of a vector of real numbers that encodes the meaning of the word in such a way that words that are closer in the vector space are expected to be similar in meaning. Word embeddings are obtained using language-modeling and feature-learning techniques, where words or phrases from the vocabulary are mapped to vectors of real numbers. Self-attention addresses the limitations of recurrent neural networks, where words in a sentence are processed sequentially. Recurrent neural networks favor more recent words at the end of a sentence, while earlier words receive less attention, so it gives all words equal access to any part of a sentence in a faster parallel scheme (Vaswani et al., 2017).

2.3 Leading generative AI models

In this section, we analyze the architecture and internal structure of the leading generative AI and LLMs which have been acclaimed and are the dominant players in the technology contest we are immersed on.

2.3.1 ChatGPT

ChatGPT, which stands for Chat Generative Pre-Trained Transformer, is a foundation model based on an LLM architecture developed by OpenAI. A foundational model is a generative AI model trained on massive dataset and adapted to diverse application tasks. ChatGPT users can dialog and hold a conversation from a user specification of answer length, format, style, level of detail, and language.

GPT is a family of generative transformers based on deep neural networks and the transformer architecture. It is pre-trained on large data sets of unlabelled text and is able to generate useful content for user applications. OpenAI has released the highly influential *GPT foundation models,* which have been sequentially numbered to comprise its GPT-*n* series GPT-1, GPT-2, GPT-3, GPT-3.5, and GPT-4. GPT-3.5 was trained and fine-tuned over 175 billion network parameters and 399 billion tokens, while GPT-4 training is estimated around 1.7 trillion (1.7×10^9) network parameters.

ChatGPT was not trained for a specific task or for a particular domain. It was trained to predict the next word in a text conversation with a user. ChatGPT was trained on a large dataset containing a great number of cases of concrete assignments in many problem domains. Consequently, ChatGPT can perform a wide variety of tasks using adequate prompt engineering practices. The user can assist the pre-trained model by adding more examples relevant to the problem being solved (Johri, 2023).

In addition to holding a human-like conversation, ChatGPT can compose songs, invent fairy tales, and write homework assignment essays. It also can answer test questions at an above-average level, generate business ideas, write poetry, translate, summarize text, write or debug computer programs, emulate a Unix® system, play games, and many other tasks.

2.3.2 ChatGPT limitations

Among ChatGPT limitations is the fact that sometimes it writes answers that are apparently correct, but they turn out to be nonsense or wrong. This problem occurs for most LLMs and is called *hallucination.*

Another limitation is the fact that ChatGPT does not have the latest information. Up to November of 2023, ChatGPT-3.5 shows information until January 2022, whereas the last ChatGPT-4 update is until April of 2023. Their massive datasets were trained up to those dates. Also, ChatGPT cannot access the Internet, so it is not aware of, nor can it discuss, current events worldwide.

On the other hand, the reward model of ChatGPT was designed around human supervision, and as a result, the training can be too specific, preventing generalization to new questions of unseen cases.

One more limitation is about generating long-form structured content and its tendency to give answers in list forms with bullets.

Finally, ChatGPT has trouble understanding context in which there is sarcasm, humor, or irony, which is difficult to understand and respond with out-of-context answers (Koubaa et al., 2023).

2.3.3 Bard (now Gemini)

The term *Bard,* adopted by Google to dub its generative AI solution in response to the challenge risen by ChatGPT, was the title given to poets from an ancient Celtic order of composers and reciters of poetry. These would be persons who composed and recited epic or heroic poems, often while playing the harp, lyre, or the like.

Bard is built upon PaLM, the transformer-based LLM developed by Google mentioned above and announced in April 2022. It remained private until March 2023, when Google launched an interface for PaLM and several other technologies.

PaLM is pre-trained on a corpus of 780 billion tokens that comprise various natural language tasks, use cases, and around 540 billion parameters. This dataset includes filtered webpages, books, Wikipedia articles, news articles, source code obtained from open-source repositories on GitHub®, and social media conversations.

It is used in a range of tasks, including commonsense reasoning, arithmetic reasoning, joke explanation, code generation, and language translation.

In contrast to ChatGPT, Google Bard can provide results by retrieving information from the Internet using Google's search engine. This is an advantage for scholars or anyone gathering fresh information for any purpose. It can provide up-to-date responses to prompts across diverse topics and disciplines.

Bard can translate dozens of languages, helping people communicate with a smooth translation. It can also read content in other languages and process speech commands with a microphone in the screen menu.

2.3.4 Bard limitations

Bard shares many of the same limitations shown by ChatGPT. One of them is its tendency to provide prejudiced, partial, erroneous, or fragmentary information. Bard is trained on big datasets that contain some inaccuracies, as with ChatGPT. Users must check the information obtained, which may demand additional time. Also, Bard may fail to produce long-form content, a feature that ChatGPT is able to deal with more easily.

Sometimes Bard cannot capture the context and responds with non-pertinent answers. Users must provide relevant context and feed-in sharpen prompts to generate improved responses following prompt engineering practices. Another limitation is that Bard does not provide appropriate references or pointers of the answers it provides. This hindrance makes Bard difficult to use for academic or research purposes.

Bard shows impediments regarding abridged creativity and its tendency to give responses that are repetitive or obvious for the user. The same is true when Bard is asked to compose poems or music and produces works that have already been published by someone else (Qin et al., 2023).

ChatGPT and Bard are generative AI models that receive text as input and generate text as output. In contrast, DALL-E® is a generative AI tool from OpenAI that receives a description of a scene in natural language as input and produces digital images as output. It uses a version of the LLM GPT-3 (Gamoura et al., 2023). Codex is another generative AI tool from OpenAI that reads a user specification of a computer programming task in English and generates the computer code that achieves that task (Kurtukova et al., 2022).

Claude from Anthropic is a generative AI model that receives text or an image as input and generates text as output in various forms. GPT-3 is the LLM supporting Claude, and Claude could be a serious competitor to ChatGPT. Anthropic is a startup founded by OpenAI ex-employees in 2021 who were concerned with the safety deficiencies of GPT.

2.3.5 *Hardware*

Generative AI tools use special hardware infrastructure to perform massive computations required in the training and maintenance of large corpus of data. Moore's law, an empirical observation proposed in 1965, states that the number of transistors in an integrated circuit (IC) doubles about every two years. This prediction is expected to reach physical limits inherent to silicon-based circuits before 2030.

In the meantime, advancements in semiconductor technology including HBM, DDR, and DIMM circuits are being used to train and apply generative AI models. HBM stands for high-bandwidth memory, DDR is double data rate synchronous dynamic random-access memory, and DIMM means dual in-line memory module. The Azure® supercomputing infrastructure from Microsoft uses Graphical Processing Units (GPUs) from NVIDIA®. There are estimates that 30,000 NVIDIA GPUs, each costing approximately $30,000, were used to power ChatGPT in 2023. Along with parallel computing, these VLSI (very large scale integration) circuits have contributed to getting efficient implementation of generative AI tools (Steven Woo, 2023).

2.4 Prompt engineering

With the widespread adoption of generative AI models in business, academia, and everyday applications, *prompt engineering* has emerged as a crucial competitive tool. It is the bridge ensuring that these powerful models are used effectively, making generative AI models more accessible and user-friendly.

To make them effective for complex problem solving, generative AI models are trained in massively large datasets. Thus, guiding the user in navigating such a big corpus of data is a relevant task. Prompt engineering is an emerging field in generative AI that looks to assist the human-computer interaction in having users asking the right questions, providing useful hints or giving instructions to get meaningful and contextually relevant answers.

Any cue given by the user to the machine is referred to as a *prompt.* Crafting the right prompt can make the difference between a model's understanding the user request or misinterpreting it and going astray. Nonetheless, prompt engineering is not just about getting the right answer but also about making sure the model understands the context, the intent behind each query, the nuances, and the user motivation in interacting with the model (Korzynski et al., 2023).

As a way of example, when interacting with voice assistants such as Siri® or Alexa®, we are doing a kind of basic prompt engineering. Although voice requests are usually simple, the meaning of words and context are fundamental to get consequential replies.

2.4.1 A prompt engineering guide

Jessica Shieh from OpenAI provides a document with best practices for prompt engineering with ChatGPT and OpenAI API for generative AI models (Shieh, 2023). Matt Crabtree also presents a guide and analyzes aspects the user may consider to craft utility prompts as follows (Crabtree, 2023):

- **Context:** Provide the circumstances and conditions in which the user-computer interaction is happening. For instance: "Give me a listing of the maximum daily interest rate paid on the stock exchange on Nasdaq in New York on October 23–27, 2023." Here the context is given by the ups and downs of the stock exchange market.
- **Instruction:** This refers to the task to be performed: "Calculate the maximum daily interest rate paid in the given context."
- **Input data:** Here we provide specific data that helps to give a specific answer: "Nasdaq in New York on October 31, 2023."
- **Expected output format:** Here we are just requesting a listing of percentage number, but other formats may be specified.

Prompt engineering is a competence for designing and refining prompts to elicit specific responses; the prompt engineer role has swiftly surfaced as a job position in many organizations and is now seen as a digital competence professionals must attain to secure advantageable outcomes in the use of generative AI.

2.4.2 Prompt engineers

Matt Crabtree (2023) explains that the skills a prompt engineer must hold to perform this job are both soft and hard abilities. Soft abilities include communication aptitude to convey ideas, collaborate with teams, and understand user needs; subject matter expertise, proficiency in language, grammar, and semantics to craft effective prompts; critical thinking to evaluate model outputs; identifying biases and ensuring ethical AI practices; and creativity.

Being a scientific discipline that emerged from generative AI methods and techniques, hard or technical abilities of NLP, LLMs, experimentation and iteration, and data analysis methods are also required for a prompt engineer. This is why it is important for prompt engineers to have a certain level of technical knowledge in addition to soft skills. Such technical knowledge of the architecture and internal structure of generative AI tools, or at least an awareness of such methods, is crucial to ask the right questions and achieve purposeful and worthwhile responses. Crabtree (2023) considers methods that include model architectures, tokenization, model parameters, temperature and top-K sampling, and loss function and gradients.

- **Model architectures:** As we have seen, LLMs such as GPT and Bard allow models to handle vast amounts of data and understand context through self-attention mechanisms. As a result, crafting effective prompts often requires an understanding of the model architectures on which they rely.
- **Tokenization:** Tokenizing input data into tokens, which are smaller chunks of text, is one of the first tasks in NLP. The choice of the type of tokenization applied—character, word, sentence, paragraph, or byte-pair—can influence how a model interprets a prompt. A word tokenized differently may yield diverse outputs.
- **Model parameters:** LLMs have billions of parameters. These parameters are fine-tuned during the training process and determine how the model responds to a prompt. Understanding the relationship between these parameters and model outputs can aid in crafting more effective prompts.
- **Temperature setting:** Temperature is a parameter that controls the randomness of LLM output. Temperature setting and top-K sampling are techniques used to determine the randomness and diversity of outputs. A higher temperature will result in text that is more creative and imaginative but potentially less accurate, while a lower temperature will result in more accurate and factual text. Designers often adjust these settings to optimize model outputs.
- **Loss functions and gradients:** The model's behavior is influenced by the loss and gradient functions used for training and learning. While prompt engineers don't typically adjust these directly, understanding their impact can provide insights into model behavior.

Other techniques explained by Crabtree (2023) to interact with a generative AI model are as follows:

- **Zero-shot prompting:** This technique involves providing the model with a task it has not seen during its training. It tests the model's ability to generalize and produce relevant outputs without relying on prior examples.
- **Few-shot prompting:** Here, the model is given a few examples (shots) to guide its response. By providing context or previous instances, the model can better understand and generate the desired output—for example, showing a model several examples of translated sentences before asking it to translate a new one.
- **Chain-of-thought (CoT):** This involves guiding the model through a series of reasoning steps. By breaking down a complex task into intermediate steps or "chains of reasoning," the model can achieve better language understanding and more accurate outputs.

2.4.3 Prompt engineering platforms

Korzynski et al. (2023) describe resources and platforms that facilitate the process of prompt engineering in generative AI models. Some of them are:

1. *Prompting Guide,* which provides foundational knowledge on prompt crafting, methodologies, and models
2. *PromptBase,* a large database of prompts compatible with ChatGPT, Midjourney®, and DALL-E that serves as a marketplace for buying and selling prompts
3. *OpenPrompt,* an open-source framework that allows for the exploration of prompt learning
4. *ShareGPT,* which offers a platform with over 31,000 posts and comment around ChatGPT and its commands and serves as a plugin for learning and sharing new prompts
5. *OpenAI Best Practices,* which provides insights and best practices directly from OpenAI, aids users especially at the onset of their AI journey

Other resources and platforms are displayed in Korzynski et al. (2023).

2.5 Application and trends

There are numerous applications of generative AI chatbots (Fui-Hoon Nah et al., 2023). In education, the emergence of generative AI models has had a disruptive impact in both student learning and teaching, especially in learning assessment and evaluation, with ethical implication in student authorship of exams and homework assignments (Kelly et al., 2023).

In business, companies are transforming the way they interact with their clients, using generative AI chatbots instead of traditional pre-preprogramed bots, providing focused and relevant answers to user queries. Firms are also redesigning their business process models (Kanbach et al., 2023) and supply chain systems (Walter, 2023).

They are also applying generative AI chatbots for energy management and other related fields (C. Zhang et al., 2024). In the medical field, there is active research in applying generative AI models to most areas of health (Zhang & Kamel Boulos, 2023).

An important trend is about prompt engineer jobs. *Time® Magazine* reports that companies ranging from big techs to startups are recognizing the value of specialists in designing prompts in generative AI models. As these models are becoming more integrated into products and services, the expertise of a prompt engineer makes sure that these solutions are effective, user-friendly, and contextually relevant (Popli, 2023).

Smith (2023) reports that Robin Li, the co-founder and CEO of the Chinese AI giant Baidu, predicts that, "In ten years, half of the world's jobs will involve prompt engineering, and those who cannot write prompts will become obsolete." Although this prediction may be overoptimistic, it marks a trend to observe in the following years.

Regarding stock markets, companies such as C3.AI®, Buzzfeed®, BigBear.ai®, and SoundHound AI, as well as cryptocurrency and Wall Street firms, have reported increases in their stock price of between 20% and 120% because of the introduction of ChatGPT to their toolkits.

2.6 Ethical aspects

In addition to the business, economic, and employment issues, there are ethical considerations of generative AI technology that must be addressed to regulate the use of chatbots in society.

One important limitation in the design of generative AI models is that the datasets on which these models are trained may contain inaccuracies and inconsistencies, so ChatGPT, Bard, or other chatbots are prone to capturing biased and sometimes prejudiced data regarding race, social position, demographics, and gender orientation, among others (Gonzales, 2023).

Regarding plagiarism, identfying the real author of an article, essay, or document in an academic or business environment is a current concern. This has to do with the ability of generative AI tools to write coherent, human-like documents that seem to have been written by humans, whether a student, a researcher, or professional. There are cases of scientific articles that included ChatGPT as a co-author. Scientific publishers *Nature* and *Science* prohibited the appearance of text produced by LLMs in their own journals (Zohny et al., 2023).

With respect to privacy and intimacy, a big challenge is making sure that sensitive information from individuals gathered by chatbots is kept private and secure to maintain confidence in the use of AI technologies. Regarding cybersecurity issues, ChatGPT has been used to write phishing emails and malware using the Codex tool (Bale et al., 2024).

Concerned about safety and ethical aspects, Anthropic designed its tool Claude following the principles defined in a "constitutional AI document" that promotes freedom, human respect, and privacy and prevents toxic, sexist, or racist responses (Newstex, 2023).

Nightfall AI (2023) defines "constitutional AI" as "the convergence of legal frameworks, particularly constitutional principles, with AI systems." Its objective is "to embed and ensure AI operations are in alignment with the legal and ethical principles enshrined in national constitutions or other foundational legal documents." In order to achieve this goal, they propose "crafting AI systems that not only recognize but also respect rights, privileges, and values at the heart of our societal contracts."

The Anti-Defamation League (ADL) highlights some key questions that should be asked about generative AI (GAI). One question looks at, "How can we prevent GAI from being weaponized in sowing disinformation and harassment?" The other questions ADL poses are: "How can we safeguard against the possibility of GAI systems producing original, convincing, and potentially radicalizing hateful content?"; "What data accessibility and transparency standards should be established in using GAI?"; "How can we ensure all companies and organizations incorporate trust and safety practices when using GAI?"; "How can we use GAI to improve content moderation and decrease harassment?" ADL presents examples, the need to acquire consciousness about the seriousness with which these questions must be considered, and their potential solutions (ADL, 2023).

We would like to highlight the need for revising current laws and creating regulations, policies, guardrails, or similar courses of action for dealing with generative AI to illuminate potential online hatred, harassment, or bias demeanor against vulnerable or unguarded groups or individuals, or simply among rival ideological collectives (Amlani et al., 2023).

Following this line of thought, on September 7, 2023, UNESCO released the "Guidelines on Generative AI in Education, Urging Global Regulation & Data Privacy Protection," encouraging communities to take appropriate steps to deal with groundbreaking AI technologies and their impact on society (UNESCO, 2023a). On September 28, 2023, the World Economic Forum issued a press release citing that UNESCO "has produced the first-ever global guidance" advising colleges and universities "to rapidly adjust to generative AI." (UNESCO, 2023b). In June 2023, the European Parliament passed Europe's AI Act, and in the Fall of 2023, President Biden signed an executive order in the US on AI safety considerations.

Worldwide interest in generative AI and its consequences cause the need to create legislation or frameworks that address and mitigate hate and unethical behavior. The beneficial use of generative AI technologies is now an important field of research and opportunity for future law making and jurisprudence.

As for future development, OpenAI must design training algorithms that would allow ChatGTP to operate with up-to-date data. In addition to considering their limitations, OpenAI, Google, Meta, X, and other big-tech companies must address the ethical issues just described and contribute to establishing new legislation in accordance with the digital transformation of modern society.

There are several issues that could be addressed in the future such as:

1. Should chatbots be trained within a particular cultural environment?
2. Should chatbots be educated rather than trained?
3. How do we make sure there is not an ideological background in the training process?
4. If the training adopts a constitutional AI approach, which country's constitution must it be trained on, or should it be trained in universal human values instead?
5. Do chatbots know each other, and if so, can they collaborate to solve problems or must they compete among themselves?

These and other questions could be investigated in future research efforts.

2.7 Conclusion

We presented an overview of generative AI technologies, describing the AI and statistics methods on which they are founded. These include natural language processing, machine learning, generative models, deep learning, large language models, and transformers and the novel algorithm called self-attention that was a key discovery in the generalization of chatbots in domain-independent application and common-sense reasoning.

This was an important step forward in the long-term goal of building machine general intelligence. We portrayed general aspects of ChatGPT, Bard, and other salient chatbots and the way they are being applied in several problem domains such as education, medicine, engineering, music, art, and other areas of demand. We addressed the emerging field of prompt engineering and the appearance of jobs called prompt engineers.

Finally, we outlined a few ethical aspects in the use of generative AI technologies that present key challenges to prevent hate, discrimination, and offensive behavior. Doing this demands the formulation of regulatory and legal aspects to trust, make appropriate use of, and facilitate the spread of generative AI technologies.

References

Abhishek, N., & Manisha, B. (2018). *Reinforcement learning: With Open AI, TensorFlow and Keras Using Python*. New York: Apress.

ADL (2023, May 14). Six pressing questions we must ask about generative AI. NewsBank, Inc. https://infoweb.newsbank.com/apps/news/document-view?p=AWNB&docref=news/1918812DF868D778

Alawida, M., Mejri, S., Mehmood, A., Chikhaoui, B., & Abiodun, O. I. (2023). A comprehensive study of ChatGPT: Advancements, limitations, and ethical considerations in natural language processing and cybersecurity. *Information (Switzerland), 14*(8). https://doi.org/10.3390/info14080462

Alexander, D. (2020). *Neural networks: History and applications*. https://search.ebscohost.com/login.aspx?direct=true&db=e000xww&AN=2323785&lang=es&site=eds-live&scope=site

Amlani, N., Samuel, K., & Noah, B. (2023, October). Generative AI: How existing regulation may apply to AI-generated harmful content. NewsBank, Inc.

Asudani, D. S., Nagwani, N. K., & Singh, P. (2023). Impact of word embedding models on text analytics in deep learning environment: A review. *Artificial Intelligence Review, 56*. https://doi.org/10.1007/s10462-023-10419-1

Aten, J. (2024, February 8). Google just killed Bard and replaced it with Gemini. It's more than just a name change. Inc. https://www.inc.com/jason-aten/google-just-killed-bard-replaced-it-with-gemini-its-more-than-just-a-name-change.html

Baladram, M. S., Koike, A., & Yamada, K. D. (2020). Introduction to supervised machine learning for data science. *Interdisciplinary Information Sciences, 26*(1), 87–121. https://doi.org/10.4036/iis.2020.a.03

Bale, A. S., Dhumale, R. B., Beri, N., Lourens, M., Varma, R. A., Kumar, V., Sanamdikar S., & Savadatti, M. B. (2024). The impact of generative content on individuals privacy and ethical concerns. *International Journal of Intelligent Systems and Applications in Engineering, 12*(1), 697–703.

Campbell, C. (2023). Ready or not, generative AI is here to stay. *Journal of Advertising Research, 63*(3), 202–204. https://doi.org/10.2501/jar-2023-019

Crabtree, M. (2023, August). What is prompt engineering? A detailed guide. *Datacamp*, 1–7.

Dufter, P., Schmitt, M., & Schütze, H. (2022). Position information in transformers: An overview. *Computational Linguistics, 48*(3), 733–763. https://doi.org/10.1162/coli_a_00445

Eigenschink, P., Reutterer, T., Vamosi, S., Vamosi, R., Sun, C., & Kalcher, K. (2023). Deep generative models for synthetic data: A survey. *IEEE Access, 11*(March), 47304–47320. https://doi.org/10.1109/ACCESS.2023.3275134

Fui-Hoon Nah, F., Zheng, R., Cai, J., Siau, K., & Chen, L. (2023). Generative AI and ChatGPT: Applications, challenges, and AI-human collaboration. *Journal of Information Technology Case and Application Research, 25*(3), 277–304. https://doi.org/10.1080/15228053.2023.2233814

Gamoura, S., Koruca, H. İ., & Urgancı, K. B. (2023). Exploring the transition from "contextual AI" to "generative AI" in management: Cases of ChatGPT and DALL-E 2. 12th International Symposium on Intelligent Manufacturing and Service Systems, 368–381. https://doi.org/http://10.0.3.239/978-981-99-6062-0_34

Gonzales, B. M. (2023). All things work. *HR Magazine, Society for Human Resource Management.* https://www.shrm.org/topics-tools/news/all-things-work#f-contenttypefiltertag =Feature

Hinton, G. E., & Sejnowski, T. J. (1999). *Unsupervised learning: Foundations of neural computation, vii–xv.* (Series: Co). Cambridge, MA: Bradford.

Hu, K. (2023, February). ChatGPT sets record for fastest-growing user base—Analyst note. Reuters, 3. https://www.reuters.com/technology/chatgpt-sets-record-fastest-growing-user-base-analyst-note-2023-02-01/

Jenkins, H., Ford, S., & Green, J. (2013). *Spreadable media: Creating value and meaning in a networked culture.* (JSTOR, Ed.). https://www.jstor.org/stable/j.ctt9qfk6w

Jeyaprakaash, P., & Sashirekha, K. (2022). Accuracy measure of customer churn prediction in telecom industry using Adaboost over Decision Tree algorithm. *Journal of Pharmaceutical Negative Results, 13*(SO4), 1495–1504. https://doi.org/10.47750/pnr.2022.13.s04.179

Johri, S., & Moncada-Reid, C. (2023, June). The making of ChatGPT: From data to dialogue. *Science in the News.* Cambridge University. https://sitn.hms.harvard.edu/flash/2023/the-making-of-chatgpt-from-data-to-dialogue/

Kanbach, D. K., Heiduk, L., Blueher, G., Schreiter, M., & Lahmann, A. (2023). The GenAI is out of the bottle: Generative artificial intelligence from a business model innovation perspective. *Review of Managerial Science.* https://doi.org/10.1007/s11846-023-00696-z

Kelly, A., Sullivan, M., & Strampel, K. (2023). Generative artificial intelligence: University student awareness, experience, and confidence in use across disciplines. *Journal of University Teaching & Learning Practice, 20*(6).

Korzynski, P., Mazurek, G., Krzypkowska, P., & Kurasinski, A. (2023). Artificial intelligence prompt engineering as a new digital competence: Analysis of generative AI technologies such as ChatGPT. *Entrepreneurial Economic and Business Review, 11*(3). doi: 10.15678/EBER.2023.110302

Koubaa, A., Boulila, W., & Ghouti, L. (2023). Exploring ChatGPT capabilities and limitations: A survey. *IEEE Access, 11*(September), 118698–118721. https://doi.org/10.1109/ACCESS.2023.3326474

Kurtukova, A., Romanov, A., Shelupanov, A., & Fedotova, A. (2022). Complex cases of source code authorship identification using a hybrid deep neural network. *Future Internet, 14*(10). https://doi.org/10.3390/fi14100287

Liu, P., Yuan, W., Fu, J., Jiang, Z., Hayashi, H., & Neubig, G. (2023). Pre-train, prompt, and predict: A systematic survey of prompting methods in natural language processing. *ACM Computing Surveys, 55*(9). https://doi.org/10.1145/3560815

Maddigan, P., & Susnjak, T. (2023). Chat2VIS: Generating data visualizations via natural language using ChatGPT, Codex and GPT-3 large language models. *IEEE Access, 11*(April), 45181–45193. https://doi.org/10.1109/ACCESS.2023.3274199

Min, B., Ross, H., Sulem, E., Veyseh, A. P. B., Nguyen, T. H., Sainz, O., Agirre, E., Heintz, I., & Roth, D. (2023). Recent advances in natural language processing via large pre-trained language models: A survey. *ACM Computing Surveys, 56*(2), 1–40. https://doi.org/10.1145/3605943

Newstex, L. (2023, October 23). A ChatGPT rival just published a new constitution to level up its AI guardrails, and prevent toxic and racist responses. The Business Insider. https://0-search-ebscohost-com.biblioteca-ils.tec.mx/login.aspx?direct=true&db=edsgao&AN=edsgcl.770013893&lang=es&site=eds-live&scope=site. Accessed on 16 November 2023.

Nightfall, A. (2023, November). Constitutional AI: The essential guide. https://www.nightfall.ai/ai-security-101/constitutional-ai#implications-and-future-pathways

Patterson, J., & Gibson, A. (2017). *Deep learning: A practitioner's approach.* O'Reilly Media. ISBN13: 9781491914250.

Popli, N. (2023). The AI job that pays up to $335K—And you don't need a computer engineering background. Time Magazine. https://time.com/6272103/ai-prompt-engineer-job/

Qin, H., Ji, G., Khan, S., Fan, D., Khan, F. S., & Van Gool, L. (2023). How good is Google Bard's visual understanding? An empirical study on open challenges. arXiv (Cornell University). https://doi.org/10.1007/s11633-023-1469-x

Salmi, J. (2023). A democratic way of controlling artificial general intelligence. *AI and Society, 38*(4), 1785–1791. https://doi.org/10.1007/s00146-022-01426-x

Shieh, J. (2023, November). Best practices for prompt engineering with OpenAI API. *OpenAI,* 1–4. https://help.openai.com/en/articles/6654000-best-practices-for-prompt-engineering-with-openai-api

Smith, C. S. (n.d.). Mom, Dad, I want to be a prompt engineer. Forbes. https://www.forbes.com/sites/craigsmith/2023/04/05/mom-dad-i-want-to-be-a-prompt-engineer/?sh=2028990359c8

Song, J., Lee, Y. C., & Lee, J. (2023). Deep generative model with time series-image encoding for manufacturing fault detection in die casting process. *Journal of*

Intelligent Manufacturing, 34(7), 3001–3014. https://doi.org/10.1007/s10845-022-01981-6

Steven Woo, R. (2023, August). Understanding the compute hardware behind generative AI. *All About Circuits,* 1–4. https://www.allaboutcircuits.com/industry-articles/understanding-the-compute-hardware-behind-generative-ai/

UNESCO (2023a, September). UNESCO releases guidelines on generative AI in education, urging global regulation & data privacy protection. *Business World.*

UNESCO, P. O. N. (2023b, September 28). Generative AI has disrupted education. Here's how it can be used for good—UNESCO. *Gale, Cengage Learning.*

Vaswani, A., Shazeer, N., Parmar, N., Uszkoreit, J., Jones, L., Gomez, A. N., Kaiser, L., & Polosukhin, I. (2017). Attention is all you need. *Advances in Neural Information Processing Systems,* 5999–6009. https://search.ebscohost.com/login.aspx?direct=true&db=edsarx&AN=edsarx.1706.03762&lang=es&site=eds-live&scope=site

Walter, S. (2023). AI impacts on supply chain performance: A manufacturing use case study. *Discover Artificial Intelligence, 3*(1). https://doi.org/10.1007/s44163-023-00061-9

Zhang, C., Lu, J., & Zhao, Y. (2024). Generative pre-trained transformers (GPT)-based automated data mining for building energy management: Advantages, limitations and the future. *Energy and Built Environment, 5*(1), 143–169. https://doi.org/10.1016/j.enbenv.2023.06.005

Zhang, P., & Kamel Boulos, M. N. (2023). Generative AI in medicine and healthcare: Promises, opportunities and challenges. *Future Internet, 15*(9), 286. https://doi.org/10.3390/fi15090286

Zhong, G. (2018). *Semi-supervised learning: Background, applications and future directions.* New York: Nova.

Zohny, H., McMillan, J., & King, M. (2023). Ethics of generative AI. *Journal of Medical Ethics, 49*(2), 79–80. https://doi.org/10.1136/jme-2023-108909

Chapter 3

The Mechanics and Validation of Generative AI Outcomes

Andreas Oranje

National Conference of Bar Examiners, USA

3.1 Introduction

The main purpose of this chapter is to unpack the mechanics within generative AI that lead to the introduction of hate and targeting of hate towards specific groups or people. The main thesis is that AI is a protraction and implication of human behavior and human behavior alone. AI, at its best, democratizes access to expertise and removes barriers of inherited affluence. At its worst, however, it reinforces and amplifies extreme positions ("reductive AI") while inhibiting dialogue and, therefore, learning. To mitigate this, we propose three measures: (1) triangulation of generated content via k-class validation, (2) an evaluation process that pursues falsification following Popperian falsification principles, and (3) deep investment in training and education.

Generative AI has become a topic of choice for pessimists and optimists alike. Proclamations that range from complete doom as the end of all human value on the one hand, to infinite opportunity for human prosperity on the other, are part of daily content streams across almost every media platform. Generative AI is deceptively simple yet overtly complex, but it certainly does not lend itself to any sort of generalized statement or prediction. Understanding the mechanics of generative AI, even at a relatively conceptual level, can provide important insight into how adverse outcomes arise. Whether through a lack of accuracy or extreme compartmentalization, the way we arrive at generative AI is at its core a human endeavor that reflects human behavior, norms, and values. This sobering realization is important if we are to understand how generative AI can create hate and what some potential solutions are to reducing and regulating hate.

The basic premise of broad generative AI is that there are extremely large models that contain enough building blocks that can be reconfigured and combined to generate anything anyone would want. In fact, generative AI does not make any claims about the accuracy or usefulness of what it generates. The only value that generative AI creates is responding to general wants or desires. Early on, there was a notion that generative AI would make search engines obsolete, as the entire human universe would already be encapsulated inside the underlying models, and search could simply be skipped. Moreover, there was even the notion that the infinite combinations that would be possible with generative AI would far outpace regular human unpredictable creativity. Or rather, that human creativity was far more limited than one might want to accept. Fortunately, or unfortunately, the value that humans add might not be in generating answers or solutions, but in uniquely generating needs and wants.

AI can largely be divided into *evaluative* and *generative* applications, although combination tools in the form of agents and multimodal AI are becoming more ubiquitous. However, those are beyond the reach of this chapter. Evaluative applications attempt to evaluate a new case based on a model derived from a set of existing cases with respect to some usually singular outcome.

The general goal is a decision. Under this trained model and given this new case, what will be the most likely outcome? The basics of statistical prediction apply (e.g., a linear regression of several buyer characteristics onto the likelihood a particular purchase is made), although the prediction models are far more complex, the amount of data that drives these complex prediction models is far more voluminous, and, therefore, the computation required is far more intense.

In fact, while machine learning models have been around for a long time, breakthroughs in computations have popularized these models and the expansion into sophisticated neural network and deep (multi-layered) learning algorithms to train models. Still, the decision to make is whether to offer a discount or not to lure this person into purchase mode, to incessantly advertise your product on every page the potential buyer subsequently visits, or to push specific content that resonates with this consumer to sell more advertisements to this now captive, capitalized audience.

In generative AI applications, the goal is to create mostly written text or images that are subsequently used for further consumption, rather than to make a single decision. This could be as simple as an email or a news article and as complex as an image. Current applications of generative AI rely on some level of recursion and iteration. More specifically, the next object x_{n+1} (e.g., character, pixel, tone) is roughly found by selecting the object with the highest probability, given everything that came before, including anything just generated by the algorithm, and a model *M* that represents all possible relationships between a universe of objects *X* and, what is more important, billions or more of combinations of those objects:

$$Max(p(x_{n+1}|x_n,M))$$

The algorithms, while increasingly sophisticated, have not necessarily driven the ubiquity of AI. It comes down to four factors:

1. Advances in computing that have made possible what was theoretically always available, particularly in terms of distributed computing across many cloud services and personal devices
2. Access to the algorithm through smart user interfaces, without the need to deeply understand computing or AI
3. Rapid digitization of our society and, therefore, availability of data in a readily usable format
4. Encapsulation of generic AI capabilities into automated processes

The second point is particularly important in light of OpenAI®'s ChatGPT® interface, Microsoft®'s investment in OpenAI® and other generative AI companies, and the integration of various co-pilots and other engines (e.g., DALL-E) into widely available, existing tools either already used by or, if not, certainly accessible to hundreds of millions every day (e.g., Bing®). As such, it's the interface and the ability to translate requests, even if not fully formed, into valuable AI generated objects. This is why Google® has been so successful as a search engine—it seems to know what you are looking for before you do, and it is integrated in just about any computer or smart phone browser.

We see a lot of discussion currently about prompt engineering as a profession and underdeveloped skill, since making the generative AI do what you want still turns out to be less than straightforward. Of course, we expect this to improve over time, but that is still a lot harder to improve than just a search. Yet, the power of AI in the end comes from that easy, in-system access for many people.

In the remainder of this chapter, we will discuss the mechanics of how hate is created and perpetuated on such a wide basis and what can be done to diminish the reductive nature of many AI applications.

3.2 Key factors

There are a number of key factors that determine how generative AI models are developed and how their application can lead to adverse effects. This includes the model *M* itself, the evolution of communication, the evolution of personalization, and the depth of knowledge present. Each of these will be discussed in turn.

3.2.1 M

The model *M,* introduced above, is at the core of laying the foundation for the generation of hate. There are a number of factors that set the model up to include hate, two of which are particularly salient: *data generation* and *data expansion.* Up front, the models discussed in this chapter are large-scale, general-use models that are based on general data. There are lots of special-use applications in generative AI to which little of the following applies and in which the regulation of hatred tends not to be an ongoing concern. These models tend to be highly effective for a narrow application and not very useful outside of that environment. Large models, on the other hand, attempt to be useful across a large number of cases and carry varied degrees of largely unverified bias across all those cases.

The model is created by absorbing, almost indiscriminately, unimaginably large amounts of written, spoken, or visual data and calculating all the relations in that data. The key in, for example, large language models (LLMs) is that the data is taken from mostly publicly available sources, especially the Internet. Therefore, there may be some expert sources (e.g., Wikipedia® is generally extensively vetted and continuously open for correction), but there will be lots of non-expert materials and very likely far more than expert sources because of the extremely low barriers to placing those materials on the Internet. In fact, making it easy to create and share content is the core business model of many large, powerful, and profitable companies in the publishing and social media space. And, therefore, we have an overwhelming generation of content that is entirely unvetted drowning out the far fewer vetted, expert-crafted sources. This is a direct result of the evolution of publishing from "one-to-many" (e.g., newspapers, television, radio, and magazines singularly cater to many consumers) to "many-to-many" (i.e., everyone is a writer, publisher, and media consumer).

In addition to the ease with which unvetted material and content is generated, not only is resharing, cross-posting, and modifying materials made possible but is highly encouraged in the user interfaces of most self-publishing platforms (e.g., Reddit®, LinkedIn®, Facebook®, Instagram®, TikTok®, X, Tumblr®) through prominently displayed and promoted buttons and tools. This is, of course, a logical result of the fact that viral content generates exponentially better advertisement revenue in the world of ad space bidding by AdSense®. This exacerbates the notion that unvetted materials not only are generated, but also are multiplied much faster than expert crafted materials.

The fact that it has become so easy for anyone to publish and distribute content is in principle positive, as it democratizes access to expertise. And from that perspective, one would hope that all online content would simply be a reflection of society and that the low barrier to entry would facilitate a more inclusive body of perspectives, knowledge, opinion, and analysis. There are, unfortunately, three factors that work against this: (1) online content creation and sharing is increasingly driven by capturing attention as more and more people use these mediums for monetization; (2) online content is used by governments, politicians, and supporters of politicians to influence and gain power; (3) access to online content is still far from ubiquitous.

In summary, the data used to create and train models is not set up to be verified and, as such, will likely contain many inaccuracies because so much content is created to leverage inaccuracies in order to gain influence, sales, and similar benefits. On top of that, replication mechanisms exacerbate the already small ratio between accurate and inaccurate content. As a result, the underlying models for generative AI will include many elements and relations between objects that will favor more extreme positions as the most likely objects to generate.

3.2.2 Communication in a connected world

The second element that affects how models are developed is how communication has evolved in a connected world. There are two key contexts to consider. The first is that the Internet at first moved us from access to media providers to access to broadband connectors, where many media sources became either free or ad-based, and an increased choice of sources could be accessed widely. Yet, mergers of companies that provide access to broadband internet and create content—such as ATT® and HBO®, Comcast® and NBCUniversal®, or Verizon® and AOL®/Yahoo®—followed as companies attempted to create strategic control points at both ends and so improve profitability.

A less charitable explanation is that they were attempting to protect content-creating assets among a flood of free and occasionally high-quality content, and not all these mergers have been equally successful. As a result, access to broadband is starting to merge with content supply both in terms of the supply itself and delivering select content at higher speeds, reducing another layer of independence. In addition, consolidation of power generally increases pricing to consumers and, therefore, exacerbates differential access across socio-economic classes.

Second, the way people place, interact with, and consume online content is predominantly anonymous and, unless you are famous, largely free of consequence as a result. Multiple parallel accounts can be created in seconds, nicknames are limited only by creativity, and comments can be left without a trace, mostly relying on the crowd to moderate and monitor. While social media companies have built impressive human and artificial workforces that flip through thousands of images and texts to spot illegal and harmful content, they neither can nor intend to keep up with inaccuracies.

While inaccuracies, misrepresentations, and lies are as old as, and central to, humanity, the ability to rapidly spread these without penalty is unparalleled. There are of course lots of defenses being put up, including identity verification and the ability to flag issues. However, companies understandably do not want to get into the business of truth, as that tends to be not very profitable. Furthermore, it is not clear to what extent these very large models provide any sort of filter or moderation of verified versus unverified content.

Third, another backdrop for how online communication has evolved is the COVID-19 pandemic. Essentially, a massive amount of communication that was previously in person moved online and, therefore, has become data to train generative AI models. Not only did people start to create and consume more online unverified sources (e.g., YouTube® viewership skyrocketed, see Stocking et al., 2020), but also they increasingly replaced social activities with spending time in generally signal-poor and signal-delayed online environments that restrict or inhibit learning (Kuhfeld et al., 2022). This too was moderated by access to the Internet, which was not uniformly distributed, and differences exacerbated as populations with lower incomes disproportionately suffered adverse financial effects from the pandemic and, with that, Internet access affordability.

In summary, generative AI models are most likely built by a specific slice of society that has access to devices and broadband infrastructure, resulting in a filtered and restricted participation in and applicability of the models. In addition, people interact with online content and contribute to the data that is used to build generative AI models in a largely uncontrolled and anonymized way, which is likely to exacerbate inaccuracies and inhibit learning. To take this one step further, creating and distributing viral content is not only used for product or service marketing, but is also increasingly used for political influence during legislative steps, to sway elections, and even to garner support during armed conflict. AI, including generative AI, is an increasingly important tool to reach audiences and serve them the desired or required content in a personalized way.

3.2.3 Personalization

Personalization or *individualization* are terms increasingly used to refer to experiences that are tailored to an individual's needs at a point in time. This can apply to just about anything but is most often referenced in the context of marketing, gaming, and learning. The basic idea is that value is delivered just in time, just enough, and just for you, and that this is done at scale in an automated fashion. Personalization can play out at several dimensions, including:

- **Time:** You receive value right at the moment when you need it, avoiding either being too late or carrying the overhead of unused value.
- **Complexity/ability:** The complexity of the content is targeted at or just above your level of complexity or understanding to maximize learning/consumption efficiency.
- **Topic:** The content topic itself is aligned with your interests to create a more resonating experience.
- **Volume:** The amount of material that you are working through is aligned with your ability to focus for a certain amount of time.

The promise of personalization is immense. You will learn at a far more advanced rate, never be bored playing a (digital) game, and only see advertising for things you care about. Furthermore, no resources are wasted on dead-end advertising or low-impact instruction. The most common frameworks that are applied in the context are *flow* (Csikszentmihalyi, 1990) and *zones of proximal development* (Vygotsky, 1978). Flow is essentially a highly enjoyable state of hyper focus and productivity, where time seems to pass unnoticed. Personalization is suspected to be one successful way to achieve that state. The zones of proximal development essentially describe the interplay between ability level and the challenge that an activity presents. When those two are not in balance, success on the activity is reduced because of boredom (skill level outpaces activity level) or anxiety (activity level outpaces skill level).

Generative AI is often heralded as the solution to developing personalization at scale. The idea is that while creating personalized experiences manually is prohibitively time intensive, AI can predict what the right personalization is for any person given sufficient data about the person and then automatically generate that environment. In addition, by doing this on the fly, the experience becomes highly interactive and responsive to your development. This has been a key tenet of the entertainment game industry, creating interactive, flow-like, personalized experiences within the context of a number of consecutive choices to solve a problem. Of course, most games are designed, built, and shipped as a whole rather than created on the fly and continuously adapted, though AI as part of streaming based gaming will undoubtedly change that.

There is an important flipside to personalization. As attractive as an experience is that is exactly right for you, you are also increasingly walking away from shared experiences and shared learning. Conversely, if, for example, topic interest becomes a driver for personalization, the logical endpoint is that you would never explore new topics since you are no longer exposed to them. In addition, and some might argue that this is already the case, the very definition of society changes where multiple realities are established concurrently with fewer opportunities to check those realities against each other and come to a more common understanding of what is true. You could argue that optimal personalization includes shared experiences as part of the thing we are trying to learn or do, but even those shared experiences are more and more replaced by simulations. Taking all that together, the interaction of AI and personalization could very well magnify existing differences while removing the opportunity to observe, analyze, and evaluate those differences.

3.2.4 Prompt engineering

Even just a year ago, the job of prompt engineer did not exist. Prompt engineers are people who specialize in writing the right kinds of prompts and do the right type of interrogation with AI engines to yield the most usable results. While broad accessibility to AI via prompt-based interfaces is a key strategic control point for the adoption of AI, it turns out that it is quite challenging to get useful results from these engines. LLMs can provide great first drafts for just about any written work, but few would recommend using these as final work products that meet standards for accuracy or completeness. As noted before, there are millions of specialized AI applications based on targeted models trained on specific data. These can often work very well autonomously and occasionally do not (e.g., inappropriate image identification, alleged discriminatory automated loan or credit decision-making processes).

A key tenet of AI is training the model *M,* and there is probably no better or more efficient way than to have experts directly interact with these engines to teach it what it needs to know to make useful predictions. A distant second is pulling all the expert knowledge from online sources, unfortunately with the baggage of lots of non-expert opinions, as discussed above. That is not to say that these non-expert opinions are not useful for certain generative AI applications, but the fact that prompt engineering has become a profession shows us two things: (1) these AI applications (still) need a lot of guidance and handholding to perform well, and (2) it requires more than just basic understanding to work effectively with these applications.

It is difficult not to notice the exceptional growth in the number of AI companies that either create platforms for the use of AI, provide consultancy to implement AI, or help build AI applications. Not only is this reserved for tech startups or the usual large technology companies, but we also see established, traditional consulting and technology consulting firms offering a wide range of services from robotic process automation to AI strategy development. Whether what is offered is valuable and will ultimately survive is a question better answered by others and in due time. However, the key is that this shows that there is a market for implementing and managing generative AI applications, that they are not ubiquitously accessible for companies, and that the required—perceived or actual—expertise is not widely available within the IT or R&D departments of many companies. On the other hand, if so many companies can spring up overnight, possibly the sophistication of the solutions they offer may not be as mature as the promise they hold.

In contrast to the data available to build models, the nature of communication, and the evolution to personalization, a gap in expertise may have a moderating effect requiring some level of human intervention. It could of course also exacerbate effects, as consultancies tend not to be incentivized according to the long-term outcomes of their recommended interventions, which are critical in the evaluation and appropriate use of AI applications. The remainder of this chapter will focus on the kinds of solutions that may help reduce or eliminate the effects of the factors described in this section.

3.3 Solutions

As we are delving into a range of solutions—or more accurately, recommendations for anyone implementing general generative AI applications or making use of existing ones—we will rely heavily on the basics of what is often referred to as "the scientific research method." These are not just important guardrails for researchers, but they generally serve us well to verify and validate knowledge and findings and, as a result, reduce the prevalence of adverse effects such as hate generated by generative AI. Before we do that, however, there are a few common aspects of AI that are important to discuss first: AI as a tool, the "torque" of AI, and some AI governance principles.

Foremost, AI is a tool, and nothing but a tool. And as is true for most tools, they can be used to construct or assemble things and they can be used to destroy or disassemble things. Sometimes constructing something can be valuable and contributory to society, and at other times those things are against the interests of others. The same is true for destroying things. Whether it be laws and regulations, weapons and arms, medical devices, or educational technologies, they all have in common with AI that they are tools that can be used (and removed) for good or bad. The question is to what extent society allows this tool to be used, and that is in part driven by regulations and in part by human values and whether, through our behavior, we assign value to AI solutions. If nobody clicked on Amazon® advertisements through AdSense on the webpages they visit, the market for predictive AI-based marketing would very quickly cease to exist.

The main concern then becomes to what extent people are aware of the value they assign to AI tools and, if aware that even their passive consumption may perpetuate adverse decisions, whether they would modify their behavior. The second concern is that different tools have different levels of "torque," meaning that even tools that spin fast do not necessarily have the power to affect movement in another object. Local ordinances may only affect a few thousand people and have low torque, whereas federal legislation or judicial decisions often affect most people and for generations to come. Larger, general generative AI applications at least have the potential to exert substantial torque in a connected world where scale and multiplicity are key goals. Yet, as argued before, it all depends on the application and (unmonitored) automation of AI and not necessarily the AI technology itself.

Basic governance of AI applications requires a few characteristics that are assumed to be present and that minimally can help protect both the user and the holder of the AI intellectual property. Without these, the solutions proposed here do not matter much:

- **Traceability:** The application or solution has to be fully traceable, meaning that there need to be mechanisms in place that allow the user to trace back why a certain decision or outcome was achieved and what factors played a role in that. In other words, black boxes with unspecified models are generally not helpful to either diagnose problems or to improve on the engine. Without traceability in place, it would be especially difficult to absolve the application provider from any adverse effects.
- **Intervenability:** The application has to have one or more kill switches built in to stop, reverse, and appeal decisions that were made automatically. This can be in the form of human review before a decision is final or ways to send results into an appeal process that involves humans.
- **Usability:** There need to be clearly stated terms of use and, where reasonably practicable, the application needs to prevent uses other than those intended. These terms and the claims about the application captured in the terms have to be based on formal research. New uses are of course encouraged to be explored, but they need to start in a controlled laboratory environment. When that is not possible, users should at the very least have a clear understanding that they are using the application in a way that was not designed.

This is not a list of principles. There are many of those published by many companies, small and large, and from a government perspective, the European Union has been the first out of the gate with regulations, first on data use and then on AI, that are intended to protect privacy, legality, and copyrights in addition to preventing discrimination on a range of characteristics (European Parliament, 2023). The US Executive Branch has issued an AI Bill of Rights (White House, 2022) along the same lines focusing on safety, effectiveness, discrimination prevention, privacy, and disclosure on use. Wherever the industry ends up and regulations are successfully enforced, the above three characteristics provide basic methods to achieve whatever set of principles is realized.

With all that in place, there are two things that can be done to improve the solutions that generative AI may issue: *validation* and *falsification*. Both will be discussed in turn, and each of these are based on basic scientific principles for assessing and gaining knowledge. We assume in the following that there are no experts present who we can just ask whether something is correct.

3.3.1 Validation

The first recommendation is to use *convergent validity* to check the stability of the solution. This could be done in a few ways, but the most practical would be to ask the application to generate a solution in a few different ways and see whether all of those lead to the same or similar outcome. Small changes in the ask should not lead to vastly different answers. This is not too dissimilar to k-class validation, where data is usually randomly divided into k sets and the analysis is done either on each of the k sets or, alternatively on all the data except one of the k sets (in turn), and consistency across the analyses is assessed.

The interrogation of the large language (or visual) model can be treated the same way—by asking it the same question in k different ways and analyzing the results for consistency. Conversely, one could also ask slightly similarly phrased questions with the goal of getting a different result. This would test the sensitivity of the model, and if the generated object or solution is not something different, then there is a problem with the sensitivity of the model, and there could be dominant positions that are overrepresented.

Practically speaking, and in relation to the topic of this book, one could ask an LLM to generate a statement on some controversial topic from the perspective of a neutral observer. Changing characteristics of the observer that are unrelated to the controversial topic should not affect the statement substantively. The ways to go about this are pretty much infinite. Subsequently, ask the application to generate the same statement on the controversial topic from the perspective of different observers, both neutral and less than neutral. The results should be appropriately different.

3.3.2 Falsification

The second method would be to *falsify* the results that the generative AI produces. This approach to scientific discovery was made popular by Karl Popper (1959) and basically argues that no theory can be proven, but only falsified. Not finding a counter-case that disproves a theory essentially means that the theory can be used provisionally until such counter evidence is found. The same could be applied to generative AI, arguing that the generated result cannot be proven to be accurate and then seeking counter-cases that show that a statement is, for example, not unique, not accurate, not part of generally accepted theory or practice, and so on.

In a practical sense, it forces the application and the user to think about conditions under which the generated statement, for example, would not be true, or under what circumstances this statement may be viewed as not coming from a neutral observer. Through those interrogations—including asking the interface of the AI application to come up with counter examples—the generation of hate and other adverse effects may be reduced.

3.4 Conclusion

General generative AI based on large language models and related visual sister models holds many promises. Yet, voices of concern are becoming increasingly prevalent, leading to the development of principles by companies and regulations by governments. One of those concerns is the potential for the generation of hate, discrimination, violation of privacy, and violation of copyright.

The starting notion in this chapter is that generative AI is a tool that can magnify already existing phenomena, including hate. Subsequently, we introduced the basic mechanics of generative AI, followed by four key factors that influence the way generative AI models and applications are created and the results that they produce. The main argument is that the way models are trained and the way we interact with those models and applications drives us into more extreme information inputs and, as a result, more extreme outputs.

There are a number of things that can be done to evaluate the tools themselves as well as their outputs. The key characteristics that tools need to have are traceability, intervenability, and usability terms, which in this context means that the appropriate and inappropriate uses of the application are clearly understood, stated, and verified through research. Alongside basic laws on privacy, copyright, and anti-discrimination, a framework for applications arises. In terms of evaluation of the application itself, two longstanding principles are to be applied: validation and falsification. Within the structure of these general generative models, there are many ways to assess both convergent and divergent validity by asking convergent and divergent questions and inspecting outcomes. Falsification takes this a step further in the quest to disprove anything generated by such applications.

It is important to stress the need for a much broader education on AI. It's certainly promising that computer science education has been in a state of hyper-growth, and even the Nation's Report Card is postponing its writing assessment by two to three years to appropriately modify the instrument to take the use of AI tools into account (NAGB, 2023). However, this field is growing extraordinarily rapidly, but AI is not a core component of most high school curricula, even if only within existing subjects. For something that appears to have become such a ubiquitous part of life, and already is present throughout much of the technology we consume, this is a gap. Without trying to argue for another cottage industry of AI coaches and trainers, a different view on the various elementary through tertiary curriculums appears warranted.

References

Csikszentmihalyi, M. (1990). *Flow: The psychology of optimal experience.* New York: Harper Perennial Modern Classics.

European Parliament (2023). EU AI Act: First regulation on artificial intelligence. https://www.europarl.europa.eu/news/en/headlines/society/20230601STO93804/eu-ai-act-first-regulation-on-artificial-intelligence

Kuhfeld, M., Soland, J., Lewis, K., & Morton, E. (2022). The pandemic has had devastating impact on learning. What will it take to help students catch up? https://www.brookings.edu/articles/the-pandemic-has-had-devastating-impacts-on-learning-what-will-it-take-to-help-students-catch-up/

NAGB (2023). National Assessment Governing Board calls on Congress to move the nation's report card to 2027. https://www.nagb.gov/news-and-events/news-releases/2023/governing-board-calls-on-congress-to-move-the-nations-report-card-to-2027.html

Popper, K. (1959). *The logic of scientific discovery.* London, UK: Routledge (2005 revised edition).

Stocking, G., van Kessel, P., Berthel, M., Matsa, K. E., & Khuzam, M. (2020). Many Americans get news on YouTube, where news organizations and independent producers thrive side by side. https://www.pewresearch.org/journalism/2020/09/28/many-americans-get-news-on-youtube-where-news-organizations-and-independent-producers-thrive-side-by-side/

Vygotsky, L. S. (1978). *Mind in society: The development of higher psychological processes.* Cambridge, MA: Harvard University Press.

White House (2022). Blueprint for an AI bill of rights. https://www.whitehouse.gov/wp-content/uploads/2022/10/Blueprint-for-an-AI-Bill-of-Rights.pdf

Chapter 4

Generative AI for Hate Speech Detection: Evaluation and Findings

Sagi Pendzel,[1] Tomer Wullach,[2] Amir Adler,[3,4]* and Einat Minkov[1]

[1]University of Haifa

[2]OriginAI

[3]Braude College of Engineering

[4]Massachusetts Institute of Technology

*Corresponding author

4.1 Introduction

Hate speech refers to the expression of hateful or violent attitudes based on group affiliation such as race, nationality, religion, or sexual orientation. In light of the increasing prevalence of hate speech on social media, there is a pressing need to develop automatic methods that detect hate speech manifestation at scale (Fortuna & Nunes, 2018). Automatic methods of natural language processing in general, and hate speech detection in particular, rely heavily on relevant datasets. While researchers have collected several datasets that contain hate speech samples, those resources are scarce. Furthermore, the difficulty in identifying hate speech on social media has led to the use of biased data sampling techniques, focusing on a specific subset of hateful terms or accounts. Consequently, relevant available datasets are limited in size, highly imbalanced, and exhibit topical and lexical biases. Several recent works have indicated these shortcomings and shown that classification models trained on those datasets merely memorize keywords, where this results in poor generalization (Wiegand, et al., 2019; Kennedy et al., 2020).

In this chapter, we describe a recent line of research which seeks to improve hate speech detection via the synthesis of large corpora of hate speech utterances (Wullach et al., 2021a). Indeed, it has been shown that augmenting labeled datasets with synthetic text sequences improves the generalization of hate speech detection using state-of-the-art pretrained large language models (LLMs) (Wullach et al., 2021a; 2021b). In general, we employ transformer-based language encoders like BERT (Devlin et al., 2019a), RoBERTa (Liu et al., 2019), and their variants as hate speech classifiers. These encoders have been pretrained on massive heterogeneous text corpora with the objective of encoding text semantics within a low-dimensional vector space. In order to perform text classification, the network parameters of the pretrained models are typically adapted to a target task using supervised training via a *fine-tuning* procedure (Devlin et al., 2019). Due to the deep language representations encoded in these LLMs, they typically achieve improved performance in low-resource classification settings (Kennedy et al., 2020). However, large volumes of high-quality labeled examples must be provided to achieve high model generalization (Gururangan et al., 2020).

In several recent works, we described a method for extending available manually curated hate speech datasets with large amounts of generated labeled examples. We generated a large number of synthetic text sequences using the LLM decoder of GPT-2 (Radford et al., 2019), having it tuned using human-labeled examples to generate hate (and non-hate) speech (Wullach et al., 2021a). We then augmented the existing gold-labeled datasets with large amounts of synthetic examples, increasing their size by several orders of magnitude. In experiments with pre-trained language models such as BERT, RoBERTa, and ALBERT (Lan et al., 2020), we observed substantial and consistent improvements when using synthetic data. Notably, we showed improved generalization in cross-dataset evaluation, simulating the realistic scenario where there is a distribution shift between the data that the model is trained and tested on.

In this chapter, we assess several additional, recently proposed LLMs, which have been specialized on the task of hate speech detection using additional amounts of relevant data. We examine whether incorporating large volumes of synthetic hate speech examples in further fine-tuning these models improve their generalization in the realistic cross-dataset evaluation setting. Our results show that this is indeed the case. In accordance with our previous findings (Wullach et al., 2021b), we find that fine-tuning the models using large amounts of synthetic examples often leads to dramatic improvements in recall.

In another experiment, we consider Toxigen, another corpus of synthetic hate speech sequences, which is targeted at representing implicit hate speech statements. We show that a mixture of the two corpora yields the best improvements in recall, probably resulting from increased data diversity.

Finally, we consider GPT-3.5 as a model of hate speech detection. While it is a proprietary model, GPT-3.5 is admittedly a very large language model, which has been trained using vast amounts of labeled and unlabeled data and has been tuned to process and generate text given human feedback with respect to multiple goals, one of which is presumably toxicity detection (Ye et al., 2023). Evaluating GPT-3.5 on our test sets reveals that it is recall oriented and yields the best recall as well as F1 (the harmonic mean of precision and recall) across all of the evaluated methods. Nevertheless, the performance of all methods is roughly in the same 'ballpark', reaching similar levels of recall. We attribute this to our dataset augmentation procedure.

It is important to note that we view that the challenge of automatic hate speech detection is far from being solved—the best models often fail to recognize some hate speech utterances, as reflected by lower-than-desired recall rates. And, while state-of-the-art models are sensitive to toxicity, prioritizing recall, precision is substantially lower. An open question of interest is whether and how data augmentation via speech synthesis can further enhance high-performing models like GPT-3.5 on the task of hate speech detection.

The rest of this chapter is organized as follows: Section 4.2 describes related work on LLMs adapted to hate speech detection, hate speech generation and other related research directions. Section 4.3 describes our recently proposed method for synthetic hate speech generation (Wullach et al., 2021a). The experimental setups for assessing hate speech detection using generated hate speech data are presented in Section 4.4, and the results are detailed in Section 4.5. Section 4.6 presents the application of GPT-3.5 as a hate detector, along with performance evaluation, followed by concluding remarks in Section 4.7.

4.2 Related work

This section first reviews recent content-based models which adapt large pre-trained language models to the task of hate speech detection using large amounts of related data. Our focus in this chapter is on text generation as a means of enriching the labeled data that is provided to such models. Accordingly, we then describe research efforts that use text generation for hate speech detection. Aiming to provide a broader view on the task of hate speech detection, we also refer the reader to several related works that combine semantic encodings of text with network information. This research direction is complementary to our work, and we believe that it holds promise for further improving hate and toxicity detection in social networks.

4.2.1 LLMs specialized for hate speech detection

Large language models (LLMs) are extensive transformer-based architectures which were trained to transform text into contextual semantic encodings given vast amounts of unlabeled text. LLMs may be further specialized to a particular domain and task by continued pre-training using related data or via fine-tuning on labeled task-related examples (Gururangan et al., 2020). It is non-trivial, however, to identify, obtain and employ relevant data. Below, we briefly describe several recent models, which enhance LLMs with relevant data either using extended pre-training or fine-tuning with the purpose of improving hate speech detection.

In our experiments, we examine the impact of further fine-tuning these specialized models using large amounts of synthetic examples. HateBERT (Caselli et al., 2020) is a specialized version of the BERT-base model (Devlin et al., 2019), which has been adapted to detect abusive language via pre-training. Concretely, extended pre-training was performed using more than a million posts from Reddit® communities which have been banned due to offensive, abusive, or hateful content.

HateXplain (Mathew et al., 2021) is another variant of the BERT-base model, which has been specialized to the tasks of hate speech detection and explanation via fine-tuning using a dedicated benchmark dataset. The HateXplain dataset includes approximately 20K posts sampled from Twitter® and Gab®, which are annotated with respect to multiple perspectives: whether a post is hateful, offensive, or normal; the target community that is victimized in the post; and the rationales or the specific portions of the post upon which the labeling decision is based.

ToxDect (Zhou et al., 2021) is another hate detection model which employs the RoBERTa-large model, a larger and more elaboratively pre-trained LLM, which is generally better performing than BERT (Liu et al., 2019). ToxDect utilized the Founta dataset (Fortuna & Nunes, 2018) for fine-tuning purposes, having the hateful and abusive classes merged into a single 'toxic' class. In order to mitigate biases in toxic language detection, an ensemble learning approach was employed, with the goal of identifying and reducing the importance of biased features in the final model. In general, the less bias a model is, the better it is expected to perform across different data distributions.

Finally, the Toxigen (Hartvigsen et al., 2022) model is the outcome of fine-tuning the specialized HateBERT model on large amounts of synthetic examples. Similar to our approach, the authors used a GPT model to generate hateful and non-hateful text sequences, resulting in the Toxigen dataset 2.2. Unlike our work, the Toxigen dataset was designed with the aim of representing implicit hate speech, mimicking tones and styles of hate speech directed at a large variety of social groups. In our experiments, we consider the fine-tuned Toxigen model in its final form as a task-specialized LLM and evaluate the Toxigen dataset as an alternative and complementary resource of synthetic examples. A more detailed description of their text generation approach follows.

4.2.2 Text generation for hate speech detection

Human-labeled datasets are generally of high relevance and quality, yet they are small and biased with respect to data distribution, where these fallbacks hamper learning generalization (Wiegand et al., 2019). Researchers have therefore attempted various ways of extending labeled datasets using automatic approaches.

One manner in which new sequences can be obtained is *back-translation*. Using this approach, labeled examples are automatically translated to another language, and are then back-translated to the source language. This method has been widely used to enhance text translation models, as it generates many aligned sentence pairs, which presumably preserve the original sentence meaning while introducing lexical variance (Beddiar et al., 2021).

However, the capacity of this method in generating new examples is limited. Instead, we opt for generating new text sequences which divert from the original dataset. Given labeled examples, we tuned a generative LLM, specifically a GPT-2 model, to synthesize class-dependent text sequences that are either hateful or non-hateful. In comparison to back-translation, this approach is not constrained to closely preserve the original texts and is therefore more scalable. In our work, we generated a corpus of synthetic text that is three orders of magnitude larger than the original datasets, reaching 2M sequences.

While text generation increases data diversity, it introduces some noise, either with respect to semantic relevance or syntax. Consequently, we observed that the augmentation of human-labeled datasets with synthetic examples results in substantial gains in recall, while precision is impaired (Wullach et al., 2021a; Wullach et al., 2021b). Considering that hate speech is a minority class, and that there are severe consequences of failing to identify hate speech, we argue that the utmost importance should be attributed to achieving high recall.

A few previous works used synthetic text sequences for related purposes. Similar to our approach, Anaby-Tavor et al. (2020) synthesized new examples from existing training data. They fine-tuned GPT-2 by prepending the class label to text samples, then generated new sentences conditioned on the class label. They rather focused on balancing multi-class datasets, however, generating up to several thousands of examples per class (Tepper et al., 2020).

More related to our task, Hartvigsen et al. (2022) generated synthetic hateful and neutral text sequences. Aiming at representing implicit hate speech, they used crowd sourcing to obtain implicit hate speech utterances, as well as neutral statements. The elicited examples were required to mention a variety of minority identity groups in order to mitigate lexical biases in the generated examples.

Employing GPT-3, they created a dataset of synthetic examples, named *ToxiGen,* which includes 274K synthetic examples, balanced across toxic and benign statements targeted at multiple minority groups. In our experiments, we show that also when using this resource for dataset augmentation, recall typically improves, supporting our general claims about the efficacy of employing data synthesis for fine-tuning LLMs.

In a recent study, Casula and Tonelli (2023) explored offensive language detection using generation-based data augmentation, suggested that while this approach can occasionally enhance model performance, its impact is inconsistent. In addition, they found that generative data augmentation can introduce unpredictable lexical biases. The experimental results that we report in this chapter are in line with their findings. While we do not study lexical biases, our experiments demonstrate high variance with respect to the impact of data augmentation across datasets and methods. Nevertheless, we do show that there are consistent and substantial improvements achieved in terms of recall using this approach.

In a related work (Wullach et al., 2022), which applied text generation in the context of hate speech detection, we demonstrated dramatic improvement of small hate speech classifiers, targeted at end devices of limited computation capacity, following training using synthetic examples. In another work of interest, researchers proposed to employ LLMs for the automatic generation of counter hate speech (Ashida & Komachi, 2022). They applied prompt engineering to generate counter speech using models such as GPT-2 and GPT-3, indicating that this approach forms a promising direction for combating hate speech online.

4.2.3 Contextual hate speech detection

In this chapter, we focus on content-based approaches to hate speech detection. This approach is arguably inherently limited, in that the texts posted on social media are inherently short and lack sufficient context information. The modeling of relevant context is crucial when rhetorical elements such as sarcasm are used.

Researchers have identified contextual evidence that can be used in determining text toxicity (Gao & Huang, 2017). One may refer to additional texts about the topic discussed or previous postings within the same thread (e.g., Pérez et al., 2023). In addition, information about the authors of the post, based on their previous posts or network information (Lotan & Minkov, 2023), may serve as meaningful evidence in inferring the text meaning as intended by them (Chakraborty et al., 2022; Lotan & Minkov, 2023). Our work is orthogonal to those efforts. Once LLMs are tuned to produce improved semantic encodings of the text for the task at hand, it is possible to integrate these encodings with additional evidence types using dedicated classifiers (Penzel et al., 2023). We believe this to be a promising direction of future research.

4.3 Synthetic hate speech generation: Method and the MegaSpeech corpus

In our work, we proposed to exploit existing gold-labeled datasets, which are limited in size, for the generation of large amounts of related, pseudo-labeled, synthetic text sequences (Wullach et al., 2021a). More formally, given a dataset d^i that consists of hate and non-hate labeled examples $\{d^i_h, d^i_{nh}\}$, generating additional class-conditioned synthetic text sequences is desired. While various generative language models may be used, our work utilized the model of GPT-2 (764M parameters). Notably, larger and improved generative models exist today which have produced better text sequences, of improved semantic and syntactic quality (Ye et al., 2023). The application of the framework to those models is a direction of future work.

The approach is based on the following principles:

- In order to bias the model towards the genre of micro-posts, hate speech, and the topics and terms that characterize each dataset, we continue training the GPT model from its distribution checkpoint, serving it with the labeled text sequences. Concretely, we adapt distinct models per dataset and class—that is, for each dataset d^i, we obtain two models, G^i_h (hate speech) and G^i_{nh} (non-hate).
- In text synthesis, we provide no prompt to the respective GPT model—that is, the token sequences are generated unconditionally, starting from the empty string. Similar to the labeled datasets, we generate sequences that are relatively short, up to 30 tokens.
- Presumably, not all of the text sequences generated by G^i_h are hateful. We utilize the labeled examples d^i for fine-tuning a classifier (BERT) on hate detection and apply the resulting classifier to the sequences generate by G^i_h. Only those sequences that are perceived as hateful by the model, for which the prediction confidence scores are high, are maintained. In our experiments, we set the threshold to 0.7, discarding about two-thirds of the generated hate speech sequences.
- Finally, we augment the labeled examples d^i with an equal number of hate and non-hate synthetic examples.

The MegaSpeech corpus

Applying this procedure to the datasets described in Table 4.1, we created a large resource of synthetic hateful and non-hateful examples. Specifically, we generated 200K text sequences per dataset: 100k per the hate speech class and 100k per the neutral class. It is important to point out that a subset (20%) of each dataset was excluded for both text generation and evaluation purposes, comprising our test

Table 4.1 The experimental hate speech datasets

Dataset	Source	Size (K)	Hate class ratio
DV	(Davidson et al., 2017)	6	0.24
FT	(Founta et al., 2018)	53	0.11
WS	(Waseem and Hovy, 2016)	13	0.15
SF (StormFront)	(de Gibert et al., 2018)	9.6	0.11
SE (SemEval)	(Basile et al., 2019)	10	0.40

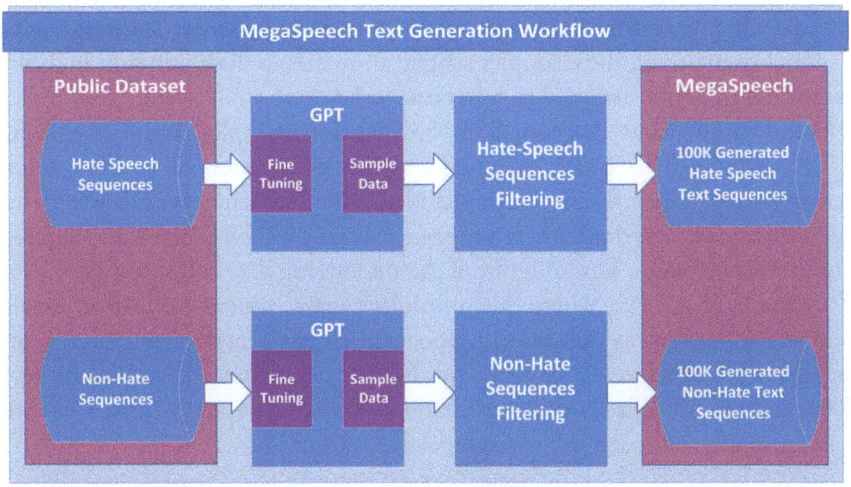

Figure 4.1 The text generation workflow, performed using the method described in Section 4.3 and each one of the five baseline public datasets in Table 4.1 (200K per dataset), resulted in a total of 1M generated text sequences, which make up the MegaSpeech corpus (Wullach et al., 2021a).

sets. The resulting corpus, named MegaSpeech, includes 1M sequences overall. Figure 4.1 provides an illustration of the MegaSpeech corpus generation process.

4.4 Experiments

We wish to assess whether and to what extent the generated synthetic data is sufficiently relevant and diverse for improving the generalization of pretrained LLMs on the hate detection task. Compared with our previous work (Wullach et al., 2021b), our current experiments include multiple state-of-the-art LLMs which were specialized for hate speech detection, where we show that the synthetic examples can be used to enhance them further. Our evaluation is focused on a cross-dataset setup, testing the generalization of the models across data distributions. Throughout this work, performance is reported in terms of precision, recall, and F1 with respect to the hate class. Considering that hate speech is a minority class within the general data stream in social media, and that the harm caused by hate speech is high, we place emphasis on recall (Wullach et al., 2021a).

4.4.1 Datasets

Table 4.1 provides details about the experimental datasets. Some of the datasets originally used a fine annotation scheme—for example, distinguishing between hate speech and abusive language. Since we perform transfer learning across datasets, we maintain the examples strictly annotated as hate and non-hate and discard the examples assigned to other categories.

As shown, the datasets are small (6–53K labeled examples) and skewed, with as little as 1–6K hate speech examples available per dataset. All of the datasets include tweets, except for SF, which includes individual sentences extracted from the StormFront Web domain. It has been previously shown that these datasets exhibit various biases, stemming from the underlying data collection procedure (Wiegand et al., 2019), where this prohibits generalization. Additional details about these datasets, as well as examples of the tweets generated per dataset, are available in Wullach et al. (2021a). All datasets were randomly split into train (80%) and test (20%) sets, while maintaining similar class proportions. Only the train examples were used in the sequence generation process.

4.4.2 Experimental setup

Models. In our previous experiments (Wullach et al., 2021b), the popular RoBERTa model (Liu et al., 2019) yielded comparable or preferable hate detection results compared with the models of BERT and ALBERT (Lan et al., 2020). Here, we consider RoBERTa-Toxicity, a variant of RoBERTa which has been fine-tuned on the Jigsaw toxic online comment classification datasets, encompassing approximately 2M toxic and benign comments.* In preliminary experiments, this model yielded comparable and sometimes better results than the benchmark version of RoBERTa. In the experiments, we further evaluate the performance of specialized hate speech LLMs described in Section 4.2. All

* Concretely, the model was fine-tuned using the English parts of multiple Jigsaw datasets: Jigsaw 2018, https://www.kaggle.com/c/jigsaw-toxic-comment-classification-challenge; Jigsaw 2019, https://www.kaggle.com/c/jigsaw-unintended-bias-in-toxicity-classification; and Jigsaw 2020, https://www.kaggle.com/c/jigsaw-multilingual-toxic-comment-classification

models were applied using their public implementations, which are available on the HuggingFace platform.*

A cross-dataset evaluation setup. In applying hate speech detection models, it is likely that the target distribution of hate speech differs or varies over time from the train set distribution. A realistic evaluation of hate speech detection models must therefore test their generalization in conditions of transfer learning, having the models trained and tested using examples drawn from different datasets (Wiegand et al., 2019).

As expected, we observed steep degradation in performance of LLMs trained and tested across dataset pairs. We further showed that augmenting the labeled datasets with a large number of synthetic examples improves cross-dataset generalization (Wullach et al., 2021a). Along these lines, we consider here a cross-dataset evaluation setup. Similar to our previous work (Wullach et al., 2021b), we opt for a resource-inclusive cross-dataset learning and evaluation strategy, where we fine-tune the various models using the labeled examples of multiple (4) datasets, then apply the adapted models to predict the labels of the remaining held-out dataset. As shown by us and other researchers (Antypas & Camacho-Collados, 2023), this training strategy yields better generalization compared with a procedure that uses a homogeneous dataset in training.

Considering the cross-dataset evaluation setup as proxy to hate speech detection 'in the wild', we wish to gauge the potential benefit of using synthetic examples for learning more effective models. Accordingly, we report our results for the following experimental sets:

- *4-vs-1.* Provided with 5 datasets, we perform and report five experiments. In each experiment, the specified LLM is trained using the labeled examples of 4 datasets and tested on the labeled examples of the remaining held-out dataset.
- *4-vs-1: Gen.* For each of the experiments above, we fine-tune the same LLM using the same labeled examples, incorporating an additional 240K synthetic examples. The added examples were randomly selected from the MegaSpeech corpus. As described in Section 4.3, each synthetic example was generated so as to match the language of a given dataset. In selecting the random example, we maintain a balance across source dataset and class. The models fine-tuned using the augmented datasets are tested on the labeled examples of the held-out dataset, allowing a direct comparison with the non-augmented fine-tuning experiments.

* RoBERTa-Toxicity: https://huggingface.co/s-nlp/roberta_toxicity_classifier; HateBERT: https://huggingface.co/GroNLP/hateBERT; ToxDect: https://huggingface.co/Xuhui/ToxDect-roberta-large; Toxigen: https://huggingface.co/tomh/toxigen_hatebert; HateXplain: https://huggingface.co/Hate-speech-CNERG/bert-base-uncased-hatexplain

Implementation details. In both sets of experiments, we split the training examples into stratified train (90%) and validation (10%) sets, fine-tuning the parameters to values that optimize the cross-entropy loss on the validation examples. Each experiment was conducted up to a maximum of 3 training epochs, randomly shuffling the training examples. Evaluations were conducted at intervals of 0.25 epoch, employing an early stopping mechanism. In practice, the majority of experiments terminated after 0.75 epochs. A mini-batch size of 32 was employed in combination with the Adam optimizer, initialized with a learning rate of 2e-5 and 200 warm-up steps. The experiments were conducted using a NVIDIA® Tesla® P100 GPU and 16GB RAM as the implementation environment.

4.5 Experimental results

4.5.1 *Main findings*

Table 4.2 shows our results without and with train data augmentation, applying the 4-vs-1 cross-dataset experimental setup using the various models. Our examination of the results focuses on the impact of train set augmentation with a large number of synthetic examples on test set performance. In general, we observe mixed trends in the improvement rates across target datasets and methods. Substantial improvements in all metrics are observed in most of the experiments when the WhiteStorm dataset is set as the test set distribution. When SemEval is the set-aside dataset, we observe high increase in recall performance, alongside moderate decrease in precision, where the overall impact on F1 performance is positive. For other datasets, the results differ more significantly depending on the methods employed. Indeed, a related work recently showed that data augmentation results may be inconsistent (Casula & Tonelli, 2023). Questions regarding the factors that affect learning improvements using synthetic examples in concrete cases remain open.

Table 4.2 Detailed Cross-Dataset (4-vs-1) Results Reported in Terms of Precision, Recall, and F1 with Respect to the Hate Speech Class[a]

	4-vs-1			4-vs-1: Gen (240K)		
	Precision	Recall	F1	Precision	Recall	F1
FT						
RoBERTa-Tox.	**0.673**	0.424	**0.521**	0.397	**0.569**	0.467
ToxiGen	0.313	0.325	0.319	0.439	0.421	0.430
HateXplain	0.561	0.358	0.437	0.471	0.500	0.485
ToxDect	0.552	0.473	0.509	0.514	0.445	0.477
HateBERT	0.508	0.464	0.485	0.373	0.536	0.440

SF						
RoBERTa-Tox.	0.597	0.627	0.612	0.468	0.742	0.574
ToxiGen	0.525	0.456	0.488	0.449	0.632	0.525
HateXplain	0.559	0.680	**0.614**	0.470	0.739	0.574
ToxDect	**0.599**	0.566	0.582	0.388	0.781	0.519
HateBERT	0.479	0.792	0.597	0.396	**0.797**	0.529
DV						
RoBERTa-Tox.	0.762	0.820	**0.790**	0.692	0.691	0.692
ToxiGen	**0.867**	0.369	0.517	0.698	0.557	0.620
HateXplain	0.721	0.720	0.720	0.633	0.663	0.648
ToxDect	0.647	0.835	0.729	0.631	0.741	0.682
HateBERT	0.713	**0.853**	0.776	0.680	0.764	0.719
SE						
RoBERTa-Tox.	0.642	0.472	0.544	0.539	0.743	0.625
ToxiGen	**0.665**	0.319	0.432	0.545	0.633	0.585
HateXplain	0.659	0.446	0.532	0.555	0.688	0.614
ToxDect	0.576	0.678	0.623	0.517	0.739	0.608
HateBERT	0.622	0.657	**0.639**	0.539	**0.764**	0.632
WS						
RoBERTa-Tox.	0.861	0.673	0.756	0.853	0.856	0.854
ToxiGen	0.770	0.478	0.590	0.881	0.790	0.833
HateXplain	**0.891**	0.659	0.758	0.848	0.865	0.856
ToxDect	0.625	0.844	0.719	0.831	0.902	**0.865**
HateBERT	0.791	0.891	0.838	0.753	**0.919**	0.828
Average improvement using the generated examples, per model:						
RoBERTa-Tox.				–17.8%	24.3%	-0.2%
ToxiGen				0.6%	56.5%	27.8%
HateXplain				–13.0%	25.2%	4.6%
ToxDect				–4.3%	7.3%	-1.1%
HateBERT				–13.3%	5.0%	-6.1%
Overall average improvement using the generated examples:						
				–9.6%	23.7%	5.0%

[a] The table shows the results of learning models using the original labeled datasets, training the models using 4/5 datasets and evaluating them on the remaining set-aside dataset (4-vs-1). The table further shows the results of learning and evaluating the models using the same datasets, having the training datasets augmented with 240K synthetic examples, generated at equal proportions across source dataset and class (4-vs-1: Gen).

A higher-level view of the results is provided at the bottom of Table 4.2, showing a summary of the improvement rates with respect to each metric, averaged across the experiments, per method. This summary illustrates the experimental results with greater clarity. On average, data augmentation leads to improved recall. Recall rates improved by a striking ratio of 24% or more on average using most of the models. On the other hand, precision decreased in most cases, yet more moderately, reaching a decrease of 17.8% at the worst case. Accordingly, the average improvement in terms of F1 performance ranged between –6.1% and 27.8% across models. A yet broader summary of the results is included in the bottom line of Table 4.2, averaging the improvement rates with respect to both experiment and model. It is shown that overall, recall improved to a great extent (23.7%) at the cost of reduced precision (–9.6%), resulting in overall increase in terms of F1 (5.0%).

Thus, this set of experiments shows similar trends to the results that we observed in our previous studies (Wullach et al., 2021a; Wullach et al., 2021b). We believe that data augmentation introduces lexical diversity into the training datasets, leading to improved recall in learning from the augmented datasets. On the other hand, the potentially lower quality or relevance of the artificially generated examples could reduce precision. It is important to note that the F1 metric attributes equal importance to precision and recall performance. To the extent that detecting as large a number of hate speech instances as possible is flagged as top priority, recall is of higher importance in practice. To that end, dataset augmentation via generation serves to significantly increase recall rates. It is important that the methods evaluated in this paper have already been specialized on the task of hate speech detection using additional dedicated data. Hence, the reported results corroborate our previous findings, showing that data augmentation can boost recall rates also using task-specialized models.

4.5.2 MegaSpeech vs. ToxiGen: Experiments using different synthetic example distributions

To assess the impact of text synthesis on hate speech detection performance more broadly, we conducted additional experiments, varying and comparing data augmentation results using different resources of generated examples. Concretely, we consider the ToxiGen corpus as an alternative resource of generated hate and non-hate speech examples. As described in Section 4.2, the ToxiGen corpus was generated using the GPT-3 model. Unlike the MegaSpeech corpus, which expands existing labeled datasets by means of text generation, ToxiGen was initialized with a relatively small number of human-authored texts that articulate implicit hate speech towards a variety of minority social groups. Hence, the text sequences within ToxiGen are similarly intended to portray implicit hate speech, applying to multiple targets.

In another set of experiments, we assess hate speech performance using the two sources of synthetic examples, MegaSpeech and Toxigen. For simplicity, we set the learning model of choice to RoBERTa-Toxicity. We maintain the 4-vs-1 dataset evaluation setup. That is, the labeled training and test examples remain the same as in our main experiments. For consistency in training set size, we limit the number of synthetic examples to 240K in all experiments. We drew synthetic examples from the Toxigen corpus randomly and in a stratified fashion, ensuring equal proportions of synthetic examples considered as hateful and non-hateful, as well as similar proportions of text sequences with respect to the various targets, as represented in the Toxigen corpus.

Our experimental results are reported in Table 4.3. For convenience, the table repeats our baseline results as reported in Table 4.2. These results used the RoBERTa-Toxicity model fine-tuned with labeled examples (termed *No aug.*). The table further repeats our results using the labeled datasets augmented with synthetic examples from the MegaSpeech corpus (labeled *MegaSpeech*). Alongside those results, produced in our main experiments, the table displays the results using the alternative pool of examples drawn from the ToxiGen corpus for train set augmentation (*ToxiGen*). Finally, we report the results of mixing synthetic examples from the two corpora (*Both*). In this subsequent experiment, we kept the training set size constant, where rather than incorporating 240K examples from a single source, we obtain 120K synthetic examples from each of the MegaSpeech and ToxiGen corpora. The pool of synthetic examples in this setup was selected randomly and in a stratified fashion with respect to example label, origin dataset (MegaSpeech) or target (ToxiGen).

There are several findings that arise from the results presented in Table 4.3. The bottom part of the table shows the average improvement in precision, recall and F1 across all datasets, having the synthetic examples drawn from either MegaSpeech, ToxiGen, or their balanced mixture. This summary of the results shows similar trends following dataset augmentation for both types of synthetic examples. Specifically, recall rises significantly in both cases, improving by 24.3% and 21.4% on average using MegaSpeech and ToxiGen examples, respectively. In both setups, a decrease in precision is incurred due to data augmentation. Overall, there is greater decrease in precision using the ToxiGen (–29.7%) vs. the MegaSpeech examples (–17.8%).

We conjecture that ToxiGen presents data distribution that is more remotely different from the test set distribution compared with MegaSpeech. Possibly, a larger gap between train and test distributions hurts precision, while the increased diversity among the training examples benefits recall. As in our main results, the

Table 4.3 Detailed Cross-Dataset (4-vs-1) Results Reported in Terms of Precision, Recall, and F1 with Respect to the Hate Speech Class[a]

	Precision	Recall	F1
FT			
No augmentation	**0.673**	0.424	**0.521**
+ generated examples: MegaSpeech	0.397	0.569	0.467
+ generated examples: ToxiGen	0.332	0.491	0.396
+ generated examples: Mixed	0.356	**0.606**	0.449
SF			
No augmentation	**0.597**	0.627	**0.612**
+ generated examples: MegaSpeech	0.468	0.742	0.574
+ generated examples: ToxiGen	0.179	**0.945**	0.301
+ generated examples: Mixed	0.185	0.936	0.309
DV			
No augmentation	**0.762**	0.820	**0.79**
+ generated examples: MegaSpeech	0.692	0.691	0.692
+ generated examples: ToxiGen	0.658	**0.850**	0.742
+ generated examples: Mixed	0.664	0.778	0.716
SE			
No augmentation	**0.642**	0.472	0.544
+ generated examples: MegaSpeech	0.539	**0.743**	**0.625**
+ generated examples: ToxiGen	0.619	0.535	0.574
+ generated examples: Mixed	0.575	0.663	0.616
WS			
No augmentation	**0.861**	0.673	0.756
+ generated examples: MegaSpeech	0.853	**0.856**	**0.854**
+ generated examples: ToxiGen	0.768	0.830	0.798
+ generated examples: Mixed	0.760	0.842	0.799
Average improvement			
MegaSpeech	**–17.8%**	24.3%	**–0.2%**
ToxiGen	–29.7%	21.4%	–14.0%
Mixed	–30.2%	**30.53%**	–10.8%

[a] For each target dataset, the table repeats the results reported in Table 4.2, using the RoBERTa-Toxicity model, without and with data augmentation using synthetic examples drawn from our MegaSpeech corpus. In addition, the table shows the results of data augmentation using the same number (240K) of examples drawn from ToxiGen, an alternative corpus of generated hateful and non-hateful text sequences. And the results of data augmentation where an equal number of examples (120K) is drawn from each source (Mixed).

factors that affect performance gains (or losses) following data augmentation remain unclear and are a subject of interest for future inspection and research.

Another encouraging result that arises from Table 4.3 is that the combination of synthetic examples from the two sources yields the highest increase in recall, reaching 30.5% versus 24.3% or 21.4% using the same number of synthetic examples drawn from a single resource. This result supports our conjecture by which increasing train set diversity leads to improved recall in hate speech detection.

4.6 GPT as a hate detector

So far, we have examined the performance of popular LLMs that have been specialized for hate speech detection. Recently, there have been advances in even larger language models that are pretrained on significantly more text data. These models have also been adapted to generate text that aligns with specific user quality criteria (Ye et al., 2023). Remarkably, these models have been shown to perform a variety of text processing tasks when adequate prompts are provided, even in zero-shot settings, where no explicit examples are provided (Ouyang et al., 2022). Along these lines, researchers have shown that generative LLMs can be used for text labeling, or classification—for example, when the classification task is phrased as text completion (Chiu et al., 2022; Wang et al., 2021).

Next, we gauge the performance of such a model on our task of hate speech detection, applying a recent GPT-3.5 model which has been tuned to follow instructions (Ouyang et al., 2022) as a hate detection classifier to our experimental labeled test sets. It is important that this and similar GPT models are attributed high sensitivity to toxic language (Ye et al., 2023; Deshpande et al., 2023). It is a significant question whether such models yield hate speech performance that is nearly perfect at best, or very high at least.

As detailed below, our experiments show that this is not the case. Furthermore, comparing hate speech performance using a GPT-3.5 model and the other LLMS evaluated in this work shows that while the GPT model is generally superior, the latter smaller models deliver comparable or better performance in some cases. While we do not evaluate it here, a following research question is whether augmenting the data that very large language models are trained on using data generation at large scale can improve their performance on this task.

Experimental setup. We report our results using 'text-davinci-003', a GPT-3.5 series model (Brown et al., 2020) which was designed for instruction-following tasks. This choice is motivated by preliminary experiments in which we manually assessed various recent GPT model variants and found this model to deliver the most sensible results on a set of reference labeled examples. While other related models may yield different results (Ye et al., 2023), systematically optimizing the selection among the existing GPT model variants is beyond the scope of this work.

We phrased the prompt in a manner typical to common practice in instructing the model to perform a text classification task (Ouyang et al., 2022). The prompt was phrased such that it first defined the task, instructing the model to perform as a 'hate speech classification system'. Then it detailed standard procedural text categorization directives, including the requested format of the response. Finally, the target categories were described in natural language: 'the semantics of the provided text is hateful', versus, 'the semantics of the provided text is non-hateful'. While we experimented with few-shot learning, we found that zero-shot learning, where no examples are provided in addition to this prompt, yielded comparable or better performance. We therefore report our results using a zero-shot classification setting.

Results. Table 4.4 shows hate speech detection results using the GPT-3.5 model. In order to minimize computational costs, we applied and report the performance of the model on 20% randomly selected examples of each test set.

It is apparent from the table that this model has been trained to be sensitive to toxicity. In each of the individual experiments, recall performance of this model is higher than its precision performance. Overall, across the experiments, recall ranges between 0.61 and 0.96, whereas precision ranges between 0.48 and 0.69. We find that this affirms the high importance attributed to detecting text sequences that are potentially hateful.

In order to allow direct comparison with the other LLMs evaluated in this work, Table 4.4 repeats relevant results using the various LLMs that are included in Table 4.2. Maintaining our focus on recall performance, we consider the models that were fine-tuned using the synthetic examples, as data augmentation achieves higher recall rates. While the DaVinci model is evaluated on 20% of the examples, and the other models are evaluated on the full test sets, we believe that the comparison shows general trends of interest. As shown, the GPT-3.5 model achieves the best performance in most of the experiments.

However, it is striking that the smaller LLMs achieve higher performance in some cases. Specifically, HateBERT, a variant of BERT, which is smaller by orders of magnitude than GPT-3.5, yields the best recall performance in two-fifths of the experiments. (It is interesting that these are the two experiments in which the largest improvements were obtained following data augmentation, as reported in Table 4.2.)

Overall, the following insights arise from Table 4.4: First, it shows that state-of-the-art LLMs, which show unprecedented capabilities of natural language

Table 4.4 Cross-Dataset (4-vs-1) Results Reported in Terms of Precision, Recall, and F1 with Respect to the Hate Speech Class[a]

FT

Text-DaVinci	0.503	**0.609**	**0.551**
RoBERTa-Tox.	0.397	0.569	0.467
ToxiGen	0.439	0.421	0.430
HateXplain	0.471	0.500	0.485
ToxDect	**0.514**	0.445	0.477
HateBERT	0.373	0.536	0.440

SF

Text-DaVinci	**0.483**	**0.835**	**0.612**
RoBERTa-Tox.	0.468	0.742	0.574
ToxiGen	0.449	0.632	0.525
HateXplain	0.470	0.739	0.574
ToxDect	0.388	0.781	0.519
HateBERT	0.396	0.797	0.529

DV

Text-DaVinci	0.609	**0.957**	**0.744**
RoBERTa-Tox.	0.692	0.691	0.692
ToxiGen	**0.698**	0.557	0.620
HateXplain	0.633	0.663	0.648
ToxDect	0.631	0.741	0.682
HateBERT	0.680	0.764	0.719

SE

Text-DaVinci	**0.632**	0.745	**0.684**
RoBERTa-Tox.	0.539	0.743	0.625
ToxiGen	0.545	0.633	0.585
HateXplain	0.555	0.688	0.614
ToxDect	0.517	0.739	0.608
HateBERT	0.539	**0.764**	0.632

(continues on next page)

Table 4.4 (*continued*)

WS

Text-DaVinci	0.690	0.845	0.761
RoBERTa-Tox.	0.853	0.856	0.854
ToxiGen	**0.881**	0.790	0.833
HateXplain	0.848	0.865	0.856
ToxDect	0.831	0.902	**0.865**
HateBERT	0.753	**0.919**	0.828

[a] For each target dataset, the table repeats the results using the various LLMs, which we fine-tuned using the other four labeled datasets, augmented with 240K synthetic examples drawn from the MegaSpeech corpus, as reported in Table 4.2. The top line of results for each of the target datasets show the evaluation of Text-DaVinci, a recent GPT-3.5 model that has been adapted to follow instructions in natural language. The prompt used to elicit class labels using Text DaVinci is described above.

understanding, still struggle in identifying hate as intended or perceived in human-authored texts. Thus, despite recent advancements, hate speech detection remains an open, pending problem. Second, we find it encouraging that relatively small models sometimes yield hate speech detection performance that surpasses models like GPT-3.5. Considering the improvements in recall performance that we observed following data augmentation in fine-tuning these models, we believe that further scaling the data that models like the recent variants of GPT are trained on by means of targeted text generation holds promise for improving state-of-the-art performance on this task.

4.7 Conclusion

This work evaluated several large transformer-based language models that have been specialized for the task of hate speech detection using task-related data. The key findings are that augmenting training data for those hate speech classifiers with generated examples leads to substantial gains in recall, at the cost of some precision loss. This indicates that the synthetic data introduces useful lexical diversity, while potentially adding some noise. Overall F1 scores still tend to improve. Among the models tested, the large generative model GPT-3.5 showed strong hate speech detection capabilities even in a zero-shot setting, although smaller specialized models like HateBERT were competitive in some cases.

As future research, we believe that extending and enhancing data-generation efforts using state-of-the-art generative LLMs may yield even higher-quality synthetic text sequences. Scaling up these efforts may also support enhanced training of very large language models to various semantic phenomena, including hate speech.

References

Anaby-Tavor, A., Carmeli, B., Goldbraich, E., Kantor, A., Kour, G., Shlomov, S., Tepper, N., & Zwerdling, N. (2020). Do not have enough data? Deep learning to the rescue! In *The AAAI Conference on Artificial Intelligence* (AAAI).

Antypas, D., & Camacho-Collados, J. (2023). Robust hate speech detection in social media: A cross-dataset empirical evaluation. In *The 7th Workshop on Online Abuse and Harms* (WOAH).

Ashida, M., & Komachi, M. (2022). Towards automatic generation of messages countering online hate speech and microaggressions. In *Proceedings of the Sixth Workshop on Online Abuse and Harms* (WOAH) (pp. 11–23). Seattle, WA (Hybrid): Association for Computational Linguistics.

Basile, V., Bosco, C., Fersini, E., Nozza, D., Patti, V., Pardo, F. M. R., Rosso, P., & Sanguinetti, M. (2019). Semeval-2019 task 5: Multilingual detection of hate speech against immigrants and women in Twitter. In *Proceedings of the 13th International Workshop on Semantic Evaluation.*

Beddiar, D. R., Jahan, M. S., and Oussalah, M. (2021). Data expansion using back translation and paraphrasing for hate speech detection. *Online Social Networks and Media, 24,* 100153. *arXiv:2106.04681v1* [cs.CL]

Brown, T., Mann, B., Ryder, N., Subbiah, M., Kaplan, J. D., Dhariwal, P., Neelakantan, A., Shyam, P., Sastry, G., Askell, A., Agarwal, S., Herbert-Voss, A., Krueger, G., Henighan, T., Child, R., Ramesh, A., Ziegler, D., Wu, J., Winter, C., . . . Amodei, D. (2020). Language models are few-shot learners. In H. Larochelle, M. Ranzato, R. Hadsell, M. Balcan, & H. Lin (Eds.), *Advances in Neural Information Processing Systems, 33,* (pp. 1877–1901). Curran Associates, Inc.

Caselli, T., Basile, V., Mitrovic, J., & Granitzer, M. (2020). HateBERT: Retraining BERT for abusive language detection in English. *CoRR*, abs/2010 .12472.

Casula, C., & Tonelli, S. (2023). Generation-based data augmentation for offensive language detection: Is it worth it? In *Proceedings of the 17th Conference of the European Chapter of the Association for Computational Linguistics,* pp. 3351–3369.

Chakraborty, S., Dutta, P., Roychowdhury, S., & Mukherjee, A. (2022). CRUSH: Contextually regularized and user anchored self-supervised hate speech detection. In *Findings of the Association for Computational Linguistics:* NAACL 2022.

Chiu, K., Collins, A., & Alexander, R. (2021). Detecting hate speech with GPT-3. *ArXiv*. /abs/2103.12407

Davidson, T., Warmsley, D., Macy, M., & Weber, I. (2017). Automated hate speech detection and the problem of offensive language. In *Eleventh International AAAI Conference on Web and Social Media* (ICWSM).

de Gibert, O., Perez, N., García-Pablos, A., & Cuadros, M. (2018). Hate speech dataset from a white supremacy forum. *arXiv preprint arXiv:1809.04444.*

Deshpande, A., Murahari, V., Rajpurohit, T., Kalyan, A., & Narasimhan, K. (2023). Toxicity in ChatGPT: Analyzing persona-assigned language models. *CoRR*, abs/2304.05335.

Devlin, J., Chang, M.-W., Lee, K., & Toutanova, K. (2019). BERT: Pre-training of deep bidirectional transformers for language understanding. In *NAACL-HLT.*

Fortuna, P., & Nunes, S. (2018). A survey on automatic detection of hate speech in text. *ACM Computing Surveys* (CSUR), *51*(4), 1–30.

Founta, A. M., Djouvas, C., Chatzakou, D., Leontiadis, I., Blackburn, J., Stringhini, G., Vakali, A., Sirivianos, M., & Kourtellis, N. (2018). Large scale crowdsourcing and characterization of Twitter abusive behavior. In *International AAAI Conference on Web and Social Media.*

Gao, L., & Huang, R. (2017). Detecting online hate speech using context aware models. In *Proceedings of the International Conference Recent Advances in Natural Language Processing* (RANLP).

Gururangan, S., Marasović, A., Swayamdipta, S., Lo, K., Beltagy, I., Downey, D., & Smith, N. A. (2020). Don't stop pretraining: Adapt language models to domains and tasks. In *Proceedings of the Annual Meeting of the Association for Computational Linguistics* (ACL).

Hartvigsen, T., Gabriel, S., Palangi, H., Sap, M., Ray, D., & Kamar, E. (2022). ToxiGen: A large-scale machine-generated dataset for adversarial and implicit hate speech detection. In *Proceedings of the Annual Meeting of the Association of Computational Linguistics* (ACL).

Kennedy, B., Jin, X., Mostafazadeh Davani, A., Dehghani, M., & Ren, X. (2020). Contextualizing hate speech classifiers with post-hoc explanation. In *Proceedings of the Annual Meeting of the Association for Computational Linguistics* (ACL).

Lan, Z., Chen, M., Goodman, S., Gimpel, K., Sharma, P., & Soricut, R. (2020). ALBERT: A lite BERT for self-supervised learning of language representations. In *International Conference on Learning Representations* (ICLR).

Liu, Y., Ott, M., Goyal, N., Du, J., Joshi, M., Chen, D., Levy, O., Lewis, M., Zettlemoyer, L., & Stoyanov, V. (2019). RoBERTa: A robustly optimized BERT pretraining approach. *arXiv preprint arXiv:1907.11692.*

Lotan, N., & Minkov, E. (2023). Social world knowledge: Modeling and applications. *PLOS ONE, 18*(7), e0283700. https://doi.org/10.1371/journal.pone.0283700

Mathew, B., Saha, P., Yimam, S.M., Biemann, C., Goyal, P., & Mukherjee, A. (2020). HateXplain: A benchmark dataset for explainable hate speech detection. *AAAI Conference on Artificial Intelligence.* doi: https://doi.org/10.48550/arXiv.2012.10289

Ouyang, L., Wu, J., Jiang, X., Almeida, D., Wainwright, C. L., Mishkin, P., Zhang, C., Agarwal, S., Slama, K., Ray, A., Schulman, J., Hilton, J., Kelton, F., Miller, L., Simens, M., Askell, A., Welinder, P., Christiano, P. F., Leike, J., & Lowe, R. (2022). Training language models to follow instructions with human feedback. *NeurIPS.* https://doi.org/10.48550/arXiv.2203.02155

Penzel, S., Lotan, N., Zoizner, A., & Minkov, E. (2023). Detecting and characterizing political incivility on social media. *arXiv preprint arXiv:2305.14964*

Pérez, J. M., Luque, F. M., Zayat, D., Kondratzky, M., Moro, A., Serrati, P. S., Zajac, J., Miguel, P., Debandi, N., Gravano, A., & Cotik, V. (2023). Assessing the impact of contextual information in hate speech detection. *IEEE Access, 11,* 30575–30590.

Radford, A., Wu, J., Child, R., Luan, D., Amodei, D., & Sutskever, I. (2019). Language models are unsupervised multitask learners. *OpenAI Blog, 1*(8), 9.

Tepper, N., Goldbraich, E., Zwerdling, N., Kour, G., Anaby Tavor, A., & Carmeli, B. (2020). Balancing via generation for multi-class text classification improvement. In *Findings of the Association for Computational Linguistics:* EMNLP 2020.

Wang, S., Liu, Y., Xu, Y., Zhu, C., & Zeng, M. (2021). Want to reduce labeling cost? GPT-3 can help. In *Findings of the Association for Computational Linguistics:* EMNLP 2021, (pp. 4195–4205), Punta Cana, Dominican Republic. Association for Computational Linguistics.

Waseem, Z., & Hovy, D. (2016). Hateful symbols or hateful people? Predictive features for hate speech detection on Twitter. In *Proceedings of the NAACL Student Research Workshop.* https://aclanthology.org/N16-2013; doi: 10.18653/v1/N16-2013

Wiegand, M., Ruppenhofer, J., & Kleinbauer, T. (2019). Detection of abusive language: The problem of biased datasets. In *Proceedings of the 2019 Conference of the North American Chapter of the Association for Computational Linguistics: Human Language Technologies, 1.*

Wullach, T., Adler, A., & Minkov, E. (2021a). Towards hate speech detection at large via deep generative modeling. *IEEE Internet Computing, 25*(2), 48–57.

Wullach, T., Adler, A., & Minkov, E. (2021b). Fight fire with fire: Fine-tuning hate detectors using large samples of generated hate speech. In *Findings of the Association for Computational Linguistics:* EMNLP 2021.

Wullach, T., Adler, A., & Minkov, E. (2022). Character-level hypernetworks for hate speech detection. *Expert Systems with Applications, 205,* 117571.

Ye, J., Chen, X., Xu, N., Zu, C., Shao, Z., Liu, S., Cui, Y., Zhou, Z., Gong, C., Shen, Y., Zhou, J., Chen, S., Gui, T., Zhang, Q., & Huang, X. (2023). A comprehensive capability analysis of GPT-3 and GPT-3.5 series models. *ArXiv. /abs/2303.10420*

Zhou, X., Sap, M., Swayamdipta, S., Choi, Y., & Smith, N. A. (2021). Challenges in automated debiasing for toxic language detection. In *Proceedings of the 16th Conference of the European Chapter of the Association for Computational Linguistics* (pp. 3143–3155).

Chapter 5

Best Practices and Key Considerations for Artificial Intelligence Regulation

Patricia de Sá Freire* and Ana Donner Abreu

Federal University of Santa Catalina, Brazil

*Corresponding author

5.1 Introduction

The rise of artificial intelligence (AI) and generative artificial intelligence (GAI) represents a significant technological milestone in today's digital world. However, as this technology evolves, critical challenges also emerge, not only in the technological sphere but also in organizational, legal, cultural, and international relations contexts. The academic literature and the global community recognize the need to regulate AI and GAI to address major problems related to the increase of online hate speech and the spread of false information on social media, seeking to hold individuals and institutions that promote intelligent systems accountable for these activities.

This chapter aims to contribute to the creation of a healthier and safer digital environment by conducting a critical analysis of best practices for the development of GAI in a way that mitigates the risks associated with the automation of the dissemination of hate speech and misinformation on social media. To this end, we describe the scenarios provoked by the rapid advancement of AI applications as designed by the latest research, we discuss the challenges of controlling and monitoring them, and we examine the recognized positive and negative impacts on society. Finally, we analyze the challenges to applying the five identified categories of best practices, and we offer eight key considerations for creating effective regulation of generative AI that promotes a safer and more ethical digital environment.

5.2 Theoretical foundation

The term *artificial intelligence* (AI), coined by McCarthy (1995), represents a collection of mathematical and statistical algorithms that execute processes at super speed using a huge volume of data at the same time (Goeman Jr., 2022). Current AI systems perform ultra-fast processing on information bases that contain data in the trillions that humans would not be capable of seeing, evaluating, and processing adequately (Goeman Jr., 2022).

From virtual assistants that simplify daily tasks to the creation of innovative art, AI has the potential to positively revolutionize the way we interact with technology. In reality, there is practically no sector that is not being impacted by the use of AI. Finance, government, logistics, law, health, communication, and security are examples of sectors that are benefiting from the use of AI and its optimization and prediction algorithms of a mathematical and statistical nature (Goeman Jr., 2022).

To draw an analogy, the emergence of generative AI (GAI) with its linguistic and dialogical capacity demonstrates its ability with ChatGPT® (Generative Pretrained Transformer—third-generation generative pretrained transformers), which is based on large language models (LLMs). These natural language processing models can understand and generate language similar to human language, have many parameters, and are trained with large volumes of data that allow for unique use cases, generating responses in dialogs/conversations, explaining complex subjects, concepts, or themes, as well as generating new codes (Eke, 2023).

At this point, Scott's (2023) warning about the massive transformations that will happen in society with the arrival of this technology seems pertinent. Even positioning himself as an optimist regarding the future use of GAI, the author highlights the need to reflect on the consequences of the choices that society will make about its use. By doing so, it is possible to develop models that empower and amplify human needs, ensuring a positive impact on the use of technology.

The applications of this technology are found in systems, apps, software, search engines, social networks, and more. Beyond its use for generating text automatically, including chatbots, virtual assistants, and even the creation of journalistic content (ChatGPT–OpenAI®), generative AI is being utilized for automatic translation through platforms like Google® Translate, which employs this technology to translate texts between different languages with high quality.

In addition, in the creative industry, GAI is inspiring artists and designers to create innovative works, exploring new frontiers in music, visual art, and film (Clarke, 2022). An example of an application in this field of art creation, such as images, videos, and music, is the technology DeepArt.io. On the positive side, there is Grammarly®, the assisted writing tool that helps improve grammar and text style, or virtual assistants such as Apple® Siri® or Google Assistant for integration with users through conversations. In medicine, for example, AI accelerates the process of researching new drugs and improving disease diagnosis, significantly reducing the risks, time, and costs involved in these processes.

The applications of GAI have indeed provided remarkable benefits in various fields, positively transforming many aspects of our society. Such references corroborate the perception of the positive applications of GAI, identifying how it has provided significant benefits in various areas, improving efficiency, creativity, and convenience in our daily lives.

However, when analyzing the risks associated with the use of GAI, it is important to consider solid data and evidence related to hate speech and misinformation. The proliferation of online misinformation has been widely documented, with studies indicating that fake news has the potential to spread six times faster than true news (Vosoughi, 2018). Moreover, GAI is increasingly used in the creation of deepfakes, with falsified videos that can deceive even the most attentive eyes (Saylor & Harris, 2023).

In highlighting hate speech, social networks have faced increasing challenges as they have given voice to the intrinsic aspect of human nature, widely studied by psychology. Psychological studies, such as those by Philip Zimbardo on the Stanford Prison Experiment in 1971,* have demonstrated that, under certain circumstances and in the absence of social control, people can exhibit harmful and even cruel behaviors. The application of this understanding to the era of social networks suggests that when there are no significant barriers to inhibit these negative impulses, individuals may feel entitled to vent their pains and hatred in a harmful and aggressive way online, contributing to the spread of hate speech. Therefore, social control plays a crucial role in moderating human behavior, especially in the digital environment, as, in the context of GAI, it can be used to automatically generate hate messages and disseminate them on a large scale, creating a toxic online environment (ADL, 2023).

* https://www.prisonexp.org/

Adding to this serious negative impact of the use of GAI, it is also used to affect the way people access information online. Machine learning algorithms in search engines are designed to personalize the content that is shown to the user. The way social media feeds are organized is also dictated by these algorithmic predictions. These deployed algorithms decide what people see and in what order (Flaxman et al., 2016).

This scenario has led to evaluations of the economic, legal, and social impacts of its use. There are numerous documents and reports with different scopes, conducted by universities, governments, and multilateral organizations. One of them is the AI Index Annual Report by the Human-Centered AI Institute (HAI, 2021) of Stanford University, which lists the ethical challenges and a set of recommendations for the use of GAI.

Another is the Coordinated Plan for Artificial Intelligence of the European Union (European Commission, 2021). The plan outlines a coordinated approach to maximizing the benefits and addressing the challenges brought about by AI, detailing seven objectives, including funding startups, investing in various research centers of excellence, supporting master's and doctoral degrees in AI, creating common European data spaces, and developing ethical guidelines with a global perspective. This document is the work of the European Commission on Artificial Intelligence, which was created for the development of independent strategies to regulate AI-based solutions that are becoming increasingly common. In fact, the European Parliament passed the Europe AI Act on June 16, 2023 (Del Sesto et al., 2023; European Parliament, 2023).

This same document defined a set of ethical norms to guide the development of AI on the continent, with the premise that every decision made by an algorithm needs to be checked and explained. Moreover, the EU considers that reliable and safe GAI applications must take into account aspects of people, safety, privacy, transparency, diversity, social and environmental well-being, and accountability (European Commission, 2022). Such references lead to the necessity of constructing a regulatory framework for the use of GAI that seeks to find a normative balance to foster and promote the development of a human-centered technology (Goemann Jr., 2022).

Of course, while GAI offers numerous positive opportunities for use, its implementation must be carefully considered and regulated to minimize its risks and ensure a healthier and safer digital environment for all. As we celebrate the achievements of GAI, it is imperative that we consider the risks associated with its use, especially regarding hate speech and the spread of misinformation. The same technology that brings us positive experiences can also be exploited for harmful purposes, highlighting the importance of regulations as well as practices to ensure that GAI is a beneficial and not a harmful force in our ever-evolving digital society.

5.3 Best practices for a healthy and secure digital environment

There are several authors who contribute significantly to the study of best practices for GAI for a healthy and secure digital environment. Among these, we identify Gebru et al. (2021), researchers in artificial intelligence ethics. The authors are known for their work in identifying biases in artificial intelligence systems, as well as for promoting transparency in artificial intelligence and responsibility in AI research. In their work titled "Datasheets for Datasets," the authors propose the creation of datasheets for datasets used in AI, increasing transparency and understanding of the limitations of the data.

The work of Joanna Bryson (2018), a researcher in AI and computer ethics, focuses on ethics in the field of AI, human-machine interaction, and governance of AI systems. Bryson discusses the importance of establishing clear ethical boundaries in the autonomy of robots and AI systems. Her text is clear as to:

> *Robots should not be described as people, nor should they be given legal or moral responsibility for their actions. Robots are entirely our property. We determine their goals and behavior, directly or indirectly, by specifying their intelligence or how their intelligence is acquired. By humanizing them, we not only further dehumanize real people, but we also encourage poor human decision-making in the allocation of resources and responsibilities. This is true at both the individual and institutional levels.*

And Kate Crawford (2013) corroborates this when discussing how the use of big data can perpetuate prejudices and social biases, and she proposes approaches to mitigate these problems. Crawford explores issues of ethics and justice in AI and data science. Her work includes critical analyses of AI algorithms and their influence on society.

Another notable contribution to the discussion of ethics in AI came with the book *Algorithms of Oppression: How Search Engines Reinforce Racism* by Safiya Umoja Noble (2018), a professor and author who addresses issues of prejudice and social justice in AI and internet search technology. This book examines how search algorithms can perpetuate biases and discrimination, with a focus on Internet search.

These authors, among others, have been contributing significantly to the understanding of necessary best practices for ethics in AI, providing valuable insights on how to create a healthier and safer digital environment. Their research is widely cited and influential in the field of AI ethics.

From these discussions, which have been going on for some time, some practical initiatives have been generated around the world. Let's recall the experiences being carried out by companies like Google and Meta/Facebook® in using GAI to make their search filters more effective and, among other things, recognize people's facial features, make personalized recommendations through algorithms, and automatically eliminate offensive content (Goeman Jr., 2022). This initiative is extremely significant since Internet platforms today represent a central place where public discussions are held (Latonero, 2018), expanding their scope and their impact on the formation of collective opinions. A significant proportion of speech and expression happens online (Balkin, 2017).

When it comes to AI, certain characteristics of this intelligent technology, such as opacity, complexity, and autonomy of some algorithms, make it difficult to establish the cause between the operation of a program and its results (Goeman Jr., 2022). The role of algorithms responsible for personalizing information, as well as those involved in online content moderation, is largely opaque. There is a challenge for Internet companies to provide transparency in these processes and be held accountable (UNESCO, 2023). This document from UNESCO discusses transparency in AI systems, focusing on the importance of transparency for accountability and trust in AI platforms. It highlights the need for clear and meaningful transparency, not just in terms of quantity but also in quality. The document also mentions the challenges in defining and implementing transparency in algorithmic systems, such as internet fragmentation and ineffectiveness in addressing digital harms. It emphasizes the need for a multilevel approach to transparency throughout the AI system lifecycle, considering ethical impacts, explainability, and potential sharing of code or datasets in critical situations. Meta/Facebook, for example, has an independent board to review content moderation decisions and provide greater transparency and opportunities for redress when dealing with offensive content.

From a review directed to the theme, we recognize some practices that stand out for the importance of multidisciplinary and collaborative approaches to mitigate the risks associated with AI and GAI and promote a healthier and safer digital environment. For this work, we have categorized practices into five categories: organizational, technological, legal, cultural, and international cooperation, as listed below.

5.3.1 *Organizational practices*

Transparency and accountability are fundamental to building a healthy and safe digital environment. Organizations such as OpenAI (OpenAI, 2023) have stood out in promoting transparency by publishing information about their generative AI models and practices. This means that the public and the research community can understand how these systems work, assess their impacts, and ensure that organizations are accountable for their actions in the creation and use of AI. The European Commission also emphasizes the importance of transparency in its Ethical Guidelines for Trustworthy and Transparent AI (AI Ethics Guidelines for Trustworthy AI, European Commission, 2019), encouraging practices that foster public trust in technology.

Ethical training is a cornerstone for AI developers and organizations working with GAI technologies. Companies like Google® (Google, n.d.) are investing in ethical training programs to ensure that their developers understand the ethical and social implications of their projects. This helps prevent the creation of systems that could inadvertently harm society or reinforce biases. Ethical training also encourages the creation of more responsible technologies that are sensitive to human concerns. In the United States, the widely cited NIST AI Risk Management Framework was developed in 2023 (NIST, 2023) to help organizations deal with mitigating possible AI risks.

5.3.2 Technological practices

Content moderation has come to play a vital role in promoting a healthy and safe digital environment, as evidenced by platforms such as Meta/Facebook® (Facebook, n.d.) that employ content moderation algorithms to identify and remove harmful content such as hate speech and disinformation. These algorithms help protect users from unwanted exposure to harmful content and contribute to promoting constructive and respectful online discussions.

Automated AI-based fact-checking is a valuable tool for combating the spread of false and dishonest information. Organizations like Full Fact (Full Fact, 2021) develop systems that can identify misleading statements and provide accurate information to users. This helps improve the quality of information available online and reduce the impact of misinformation.

5.3.3 Cultural practices

Promoting media literacy and teaching critical media skills, as UNESCO (n.d.) aims to do, is crucial in empowering people to discern truthful information from false and to recognize hate speech. This helps individuals become informed consumers of digital content and contribute to a healthier online environment.

Raising awareness about ethics in AI, promoted by organizations such as the Institute for Ethics in AI at the University of Oxford (Oxford, 2024), stimulates critical discussions about the social, ethical, and political impacts of AI. This helps raise awareness among developers, researchers, and society in general to consider the ethical implications in their work.

5.3.4 Legal practices

In the United States, the White House Office of Science and Technology Policy recently developed the Blueprint for an AI Bill of Rights (White House, n.d.) to serve as a way to reduce possible harmful effects from AI systems. A significant practice is beginning to emerge in Canada, which has a principles-based approach to regulating AI, focusing on equality, privacy, and accountability. And, as previously mentioned, Europe passed the Europe AI Act in 2023 to address similar issues.

Also, strict laws against hate speech, such as the NetzDG in Germany (NetzDG, n.d.), are essential to tackle the growing problem of online hate speech. These laws establish clear guidelines and legal responsibilities for online platforms, encouraging the prompt removal of harmful content and the protection of user rights.

Specifically in Brazil, the Brazilian Artificial Intelligence Strategy—EBIA, instituted by Ordinance MCTI No. 4,979 of July 13, 2021 (MCTI, 2021), takes on the role of guiding the actions of the Brazilian State in favor of the development of actions, in its various aspects, that encourage research, innovation, and the development of solutions in AI as well as its conscious, ethical use in favor of a better future. Aligned with the Organisation for Economic Co-operation and Development (OECD) guidelines endorsed by Brazil, the EBIA is based on the five principles defined by the organization for responsible management of AI systems—namely: (1) inclusive growth, sustainable development, and well-being; (2) human-centered values and equity; (3) transparency and explainability; (4) robustness, safety, and protection; and (5) accountability.

While there is not yet specific legislation to regulate AI or GAI, the Brazilian Federal Senate is currently considering Bill 2338/2023 (Brazil, 2023) for the creation of the Regulatory Framework for Artificial Intelligence. Kaufman (2023) considers the project a good starting point, but suggests that it still needs to reduce compliance risks and better specify user rights to be perfected.

However, there are some laws and regulations that can serve as foundations for the creation of this legal framework, such as Law No. 13.709, known as the General Data Protection Law (LGPD), enacted by the National Congress of Brazil on August 14, 2018, which establishes principles for the treatment of personal data, which is relevant, as many generative AI systems use personal data (Brazil, 2018). There is also Law No. 12.965, known as the Civil Rights Framework for the Internet, enacted by the National Congress of Brazil on April 23, 2014, which establishes principles such as net neutrality and platform responsibility for illegal content (Brazil, 2014). These two laws could be expanded to include specific provisions related to AI—for instance, LGPD could address transparency and accountability with the use of individual data by AI, and the Civil Rights Framework for the Internet could be extended to address issues related to disinformation and hate speech generated by AI.

5.3.5 *International cooperation practices*

The pursuit of global regulatory standards for AI, including the regulation of GAI by the United Nations, indicates that, in parallel with regulatory practices, priority should be given to international cooperation practices, as the movement must be global (Azouley, 2018). In this way, global standards aim to establish common guidelines that can be followed by countries and organizations around the world. This promotes consistency and international cooperation in addressing ethical and legal issues related to AI.

The sharing of best practices, as promoted by the Global Network Initiative,* allows technology companies to learn from each other and collaborate in mitigating risks and promoting a safer digital environment.

5.4 Final considerations

It is not surprising that the Internet is still a space where, among other things, misinformation, hate speech, and propaganda of violence and war are also conveyed. On the other hand, initiatives have been recorded on all continents to monitor and control the automatic proliferation of this evil, as seen among the good practices listed. As a result of this movement and of the pressure from governments to regulate the content posted on their platforms, social media companies and various technological platforms have been investing in finding solutions to address some of these issues (Citron & Pasquale, 2014).

Some governments require platforms to monitor and remove content without waiting for requests based on national authorities' laws. The Council of the European Union (2017) explicitly expects Internet platforms to develop new technologies and tools to improve the detection and automatic removal of content that incites such acts. This demand on Internet platforms has generated the exercise of good practices that drive the use of automated systems for content moderation (Andersen, 2018).

However, the good practices mentioned are still initial and raise doubts and uncertainties about their scope and guarantees. Private entities, which have the legal right to make their own decisions about the limits of content moderation, for example, have expressed concern that governments may violate freedom of speech rights by delegating to platforms the removal of offensive but legal speech, avoiding process and accountability (Keller, 2018).

In summary, regulation and international consensus are expected, as the dimension of the Internet crosses continental borders. However, it is appropriate to conclude some key points that should be taken into consideration by legislators to create regulations about AI and its consequent GAI, as follows.

A clear definition of generative AI is fundamental to establishing the groundwork for regulation. This enables lawmakers and authorities to understand exactly what is being regulated and how to categorize different types of generative AI

* https://globalnetworkinitiative.org/

based on risk. Clear definitions help avoid ambiguity and ensure that regulations are applied consistently.

Transparency is essential for public trust in generative AI. Requiring developers and platforms to disclose the use of AI in online content helps users understand when they are interacting with automated systems. This also allows for independent assessments of potential biases and drives accountability for all involved parties (European Commission, 2021).

Assigning responsibility to both AI developers and platforms is another point to consider to ensure that all stakeholders are held accountable for their actions. This is especially important when it comes to the dissemination of hate speech and misinformation, as it prevents malicious actors from evading responsibility (NetzDG, n.d.)

Requiring ethical and social impact assessments when developing and deploying generative AI systems helps anticipate and mitigate potential negative consequences. This encourages a more responsible approach to AI development and ensures that systems are designed with societal and ethical impacts in mind (Jobin et al., 2019).

Promoting education and awareness about AI and its negative impacts is essential to empower individuals to understand and make informed decisions about its use. This contributes to a safer digital environment and enables people to identify and resist hate speech and misinformation (UNESCO, 2021).

International cooperation with organizations and other countries is crucial because many problems related to generative AI are global. Working together facilitates the exchange of best practices, coordination in addressing transnational threats, and the development of a unified approach to regulating generative AI.

It is essential to ensure that regulations consider the protection of human rights, such as freedom of speech, while addressing abuses of generative AI. This requires a delicate balance to avoid undue censorship while protecting individuals' fundamental rights (European Commission, 2021).

Continuous improvement of the legislation itself should be allowed. The law should be adaptable and flexible to keep pace with the rapid advancement of technology and changes in threats. This ensures that regulations remain relevant and effective over time as generative AI evolves (Floridi et al., 2018).

These key points should be considered for the creation of effective regulation of generative AI that promotes a safer and more ethical digital environment.

5.5 Conclusion and contribution

From the results achieved in this study, we can conclude that we are at a crucial moment for the creation and implementation of effective regulations that can guide the development and responsible use of artificial intelligence and generative artificial intelligence. The lack of specific legislation for these technologies is a challenge, but also an opportunity to build a solid regulatory framework adapted to the needs of society.

In Brazil, Bill 2338/2023 in particular is an important step in this direction, but as Kaufman (2023) points out, there is still room for improvement, especially regarding the protection of users' rights and the minimization of compliance risks. This reinforces the need for a broad and participatory debate that includes not only legislators and experts but also civil society, so that a consensus can be reached on how these technologies should be regulated.

Furthermore, international cooperation is essential to address the global challenges that AI and GAI present. The exchange of best practices and the construction of a unified approach to regulating these technologies are fundamental to ensuring that we can reap the benefits of AI and GAI while minimizing their risks.

In summary, this chapter seeks to contribute to the debate on the regulation of AI and GAI, highlighting the importance of legal practices and international cooperation and presenting key points that should be considered by legislators to create effective regulations adapted to the needs of society.

This chapter's contribution to the understanding of the necessary regulation of technologies based on AI and GAI is fundamental, especially by identifying the essential points that must be considered by legislators. These points serve as a guide for creating effective regulations adapted to the needs of society, ensuring that we can reap the benefits of these technologies while minimizing their risks. For future research, it would be interesting to explore the practical applicability of these points in different contexts and jurisdictions, as well as to analyze specific cases of AI and GAI regulation in different countries. Furthermore, it is essential to investigate the ethical and social implications of these technologies, seeking to understand how they can affect society as a whole and how we can ensure that their development and use are conducted in an ethical and responsible manner.

References

ADL (2023). Online hate and harassment: The American experience 2023. https://www.adl.org/sites/default/files/pdfs/2023-06/Online-Hate-and-Harassmen-2023_0.pdf

Andersen, R. (2018). Automated content moderation: Technical and ethical considerations. In *Proceedings of the 2018 CHI Conference on Human Factors in Computing Systems* (pp. 1–12). https://dl.acm.org/doi/proceedings/10.1145/3173574?tocHeading=heading5

Azouley, A. (2018). Towards an ethics of artificial intelligence. New Technologies: Where To? UN Chronicle, *LV* (3&4).

Balkin, J. M. (2007). Digital speech and democratic culture: A theory of freedom of expression for the information society. *Yale Law Journal, 116*(6), 1168–1220. https://doi.org/10.2307/20455645

Brazil (2014). Law No. 12.965 of April 23, 2014 (Establishment of principles, guarantees, rights and obligations for the use of the Internet in Brazil) https://www.wipo.int/wipolex/en/legislation/details/15514

Brazil (2018, last updated 2020). Brazilian General Data Protection Law (LGPD, English translation). IAPP Resource Center. https://iapp.org/resources/article/brazilian-data-protection-law-lgpd-english-translation/

Brazil (2023). Brazil: Introduced Bill No. 2338 of 2023 regulating the use of artificial intelligence, including consumer protection regulation. https://digitalpolicyalert.org/event/11239-introduced-bill-no-2338-of-2023-regulating-the-use-of-artificial-intelligence-including-consumer-protection-regulation

Bryson, J. J. (2018). Robots should be slaves. In A. H. Leaver (Ed.), *The robotics divide: A new frontier in the 21st century?* (pp. 53–66). Routledge.

Citron, D. K., & Pasquale, F. A. (2014). The scored society: Due process for automated predictions. *Washington Law Review, 89*(1), 1–27.

Clarke, L. (2022, November 12). When AI can make art—What does it mean for creativity? *The Guardian.*

Crawford, K. (2013). The hidden biases in big data. *Harvard Business Review,* April 1.

Del Sesto, R. W., Síes, A., & Cave, P. (2023). European Parliament adopts position on Artificial Intelligence Act. Morgan Lewis. www.morganlewis.com

European Commission (2019). Ethics guidelines for trustworthy AI. https://digital-strategy.ec.europa.eu/en/library/ethics-guidelines-trustworthy-ai

European Commission (2021). Artificial Intelligence Act. https://eur-lex.europa.eu/legal-content/EN/TXT/?uri=CELEX%3A52021PC0206

European Parliament (2023). Artificial Intelligence Act: Deal on comprehensive rules for trustworthy AI. http://www.europarl.europa.eu

Eke, C. (2023). Generative artificial intelligence: An analysis of ChatGPT. *Brazilian Journal of Informatics in Education, 31*(1), 1–15. https://doi.org/10.5753/cbie.wie.2023.1.15

Facebook (n.d.). Facebook's community standards. https://transparency.fb.com/pt-br/policies/community-standards/

Flaxman, S., Goel, S., & Rao, J. M. (March 22, 2016). Filter bubbles, echo chambers, and online news consumption. *Public Opinion Quarterly, 80,* Special Issue, pp. 298–320. https://ssrn.com/abstract=2363701 or http://dx.doi.org/10.2139/ssrn.2363701

Floridi, L., Cowls, J., Beltrametti, M., Chatila, R., Chazerand, P., Dignum, V., Luetge, C., Madelin, R., Pagallo, U., Rossi, R., Shafer, B., Valcke, P., & Haase, C. (2018). AI4People—An ethical framework for a good AI society: Opportunities, risks, principles, and recommendations. *Minds and Machines, 28*(4), 689–707. https://pubmed.ncbi.nlm.nih.gov/30930541/

Full Fact (2021). How does automated fact-checking work? https://fullfact.org/blog/2021/jul/how-does-automated-fact-checking-work/

Gebru, T., Morgenstern, J., Vecchione, B., Vaughan, J.W., Wallach, H., Daumé III, H., Crawford, K., et al. (2021). Datasheets for datasets. *arXiv:1803.09010v8* [cs.DB]

Global Network Initiative (n.d.). https://globalnetworkinitiative.org/

Goemann Jr., G. R. (2022). *Artificial intelligence and its ambivalences.* Rio de Janeiro, Brazil: Alta Books Publisher.

GoogleAI (n.d.). ResponsibleAIpractices. https://ai.google/responsibility/responsible-ai-practices

HAI (2022). Stanford Institute for Human-Centered Artificial Intelligence AI Index 2022 Annual Report. Stanford University. https://aiindex.stanford.edu/ai-index-report-2022/

Institute for Ethics in AI (n.d.). University of Oxford. https://www.oxford-aiethics.ox.ac.uk/

Jobin, A., Ienca, M., & Vayena, E. (2019). The global landscape of AI ethics guidelines. *Nature Machine Intelligence, 1*(9), 389–399.

Kaufman, D. (2023, June 22). The fear of artificial intelligence. *O medo da Inteligência Artificial.* O GLOBO.

Keller, P. (2018). Content moderation and the U.S. Communications Decency Act. In *Proceedings of the 2018 CHI Conference on Human Factors in Computing Systems,* (pp. 1–12). ACM. https://crsreports.congress.gov/product/pdf/R/R46662.

Latonero, M. (2018). The digital transformation of public discourse and collective action: Case studies from the Arab Spring to the present. Annenberg School for Communication & Journalism, University of Southern California.

McCarthy, J. (1995). What has AI in common with philosophy? In *Proceedings of the 14th International Joint Conference on Artificial Intelligence* (IJCAI-95) (pp. 1038–1045). Montreal, Quebec, Canada: Morgan Kaufmann Publishers.

NetzDG (n.d.) Network Enforcement Act. https://www.gesetze-im-internet.de/netzdg/

MCTI (2021). Ordinance No. 4,979, of July 13, 2021, the Brazilian Strategy for Artificial Intelligence—EBIA. Brazilian Ministry of Science, Technology and Innovations. https://www.gov.br/mcti/pt-br/acompanhe-o-mcti/transformacaodigital/inteligencia-artificial

NIST (2023). AI risk management framework. National Institute of Standards and Technology. https://www.nist.gov/itl/ai-risk-management-framework

Noble, S. U. (2018). *Algorithms of oppression: How search engines reinforce racism.* New York: NYU Press.

OpenAI (April 5, 2023). OpenAI's Commitment to Safety. https://openai.com/blog/our-approach-to-ai-safety

Oxford (2024). Institute for ethics in AI. https://www.schwarzmancentre.ox.ac.uk/ethicsinai

Saylor, K. M., Harris, L. A. (2023). Deep fakes and national security. Congressional Research Service. https://crsreports.congress.gov/product/pdf/IF/IF11333

Scott, M. (2023). The future of AI Generative: A reflection on the consequences of choices. *Journal of Artificial Intelligence, 31*(1), 1–15. https://doi.org/10.5753/cbie.wie.2023.1.15

The Council of the European Union. (2017). European Council meeting conclusions. https://data.consilium.europa.eu/doc/document/ST-8-2017-INIT/en/pdf

Vosoughi, S., Roy, D., & Aral, S. (2018). The spread of true and false news online. *Science.* https://doi.org/aap9559

UNESCO (2021). UNESCO member states adopt the first ever global agreement on the ethics of artificial intelligence. https://en.unesco.org/news/unesco-member-states-adopt-first-ever-global-agreement-ethics-artificial-intelligence.

UNESCO (n.d., latest update November 2023). Media and information literacy. https://www.unesco.org/en/media-information-literacy/about

UNESCO (2023). Multilevel and meaningful transparency in algorithmic systems: Developing concrete criteria to guide institutional and legal reforms. https://www.unesco.org/en/articles/multilevel-and-meaningful-transparency-algorithmic-systems-developing-concrete-criteria-guide

White House (n.d.) Blueprint for an AI Bill of Rights: Making automated systems work for the American people. https://www.whitehouse.gov/ostp/ai-bill-of-rights/

Chapter 6

The Use of Generative Artificial Intelligence (GenAI) Capabilities for Early Detection of Threats in the Digital Environment: The Good Side of GenAI

Edyta Skarzynska and Joanna Paliszkiewicz*

Warsaw University of Life Sciences—SGGW, Poland

*Corresponding author

6.1 Introduction

In today's society, which is increasingly globalized and centered around information technology, growing cyber threats pose a challenge to organizations, institutions, and individuals (Bove, 2023). A cyberattack can attack nearly every aspect of our lives, from personal information and privacy to national security and economic stability. As our dependence on information technology grows, so does our vulnerability to cyber threats. A cyberattack is any attempt to access, alter, or delete data or computer systems without authorization, as well as any action aimed at disrupting the normal functioning of digital infrastructure. These attacks are carried out by hackers, cybercriminals, terrorist organizations, and sometimes even nation-states. The motivation for such actions can be financial gain, industrial espionage, or political or ideological activities. The consequences of such attacks can be catastrophic and include loss of data, financial losses, and even threats to human life.

Cyber threats are ubiquitous, and attackers constantly improve their skills and tools (Marr, 2021). As a result, it is necessary to adapt and expand defense strategies against cyberattacks constantly. Adequate cyber risk management and early detection of threats are key elements in maintaining security in the digital environment.

In this rapidly changing situation, generative artificial intelligence (GAI) is increasingly important in cybersecurity (Tlili et al., 2023; Adetayo, 2023). GAI is an area of artificial intelligence that focuses on creating systems capable of generating new content, including text, images, audio, and more (Radford et al., 2019). GAI technologies are profoundly impacting many industries (De et al., 2022). These technologies, driven by big data, have accelerated the rapid evolution of pre-trained foundational models, including conversational artificial intelligence systems. Such models unlock enormous potential to revolutionize applications, from customer service to content generation.

However, GAI can also be important in cybersecurity through its ability to analyze data, identify patterns, and detect unknown threats (Floridi & Cowls, 2019; Florek-Paszkowska et al., 2021). In cybersecurity, GAI could analyze network traffic, identify unexpected patterns and behaviors, and detect attacks early (Du et al., 2023). Traditional threat monitoring and detection methods relied on rules and known signatures, limiting them in detecting new, unknown threats. GAI, with its ability to perform machine learning and large-scale data analysis, can significantly improve the detection of attacks, including those that were previously difficult to identify.

However, GAI is not just for detecting attacks. It can also predict attacker behavior, analyze cybersecurity trends, and develop defense strategies against future threats. It is worth noting that GAI can continuously learn and adapt to the changing cybersecurity landscape, which is crucial in the fight against increasingly sophisticated attacks.

This chapter will discuss various ways to use GAI to prevent cyberattacks and respond to high-probability emergencies. We will present practical solutions and strategies that allow early detection of threats to the digital environment and effective counter-attacks. As technology evolves and becomes more advanced and accessible, GAI is a promising tool in the fight against threats in a dynamic cyber environment.

6.2 Generative Artificial Intelligence (GAI) in the Fight Against Threats

GAI is a powerful tool that can be used for early detection of threats in the digital environment. However, at the same time, it risks being used for hate, disinformation, and manipulation (Korzynski et al., 2023). Therefore, it is important to focus on developing detection technology, education, and international cooperation to combat these threats. The future of early detection of digital threats will depend on our actions and commitment to ensuring a safe and hate-free online environment.

Log and data analysis using GAI is an indispensable tool in the field of cyber security. GAI can process vast amounts of information, including system logs, security data, network traffic, and many other data sources, allowing it to detect potential threats efficiently and effectively. GAI analyzes this data to look for disturbing patterns, anomalies, and behaviors that may indicate attempted attacks or security breaches (Norori et al., 2021).

GAI systems can sift through vast amounts of content, including text, images, and videos, in search of hateful, extremist, or potentially harmful content (Moravec et al., 2020). This enables rapid response to potential threats, which is key to preventing cyberattacks and minimizing the impact of incidents. One of GAI's main strengths is its ability to identify new and unknown threats, which is especially important for zero-day attacks that do not yet have available signatures or known patterns. This allows organizations to be better prepared for the changing cybersecurity landscape.

GAI can also provide real-time data to monitor and respond to ongoing threats. It automatically generates alerts and reports on detected anomalies, enabling security teams to take immediate defensive action. With its ability to effectively analyze logs and data, GAI helps organizations secure their systems against attacks, minimizing the risk of data loss, security breaches, and IT disruptions (Rana et al., 2022). In a world of increasingly sophisticated cyber threats, GAI is becoming a key component of cyber security strategies.

Generating attack signatures by GAI represents an important step in the evolution of the cybersecurity field. Attack signatures are sets of hallmarks that identify specific threats and malware. Traditionally, these signatures were created manually by security analysts based on information about known attacks.

However, as attacks evolve and become more complex, the manual creation of signatures must be improved (Piotrowski, 2023). GAI uses machine learning techniques to automatically generate attack signatures based on analysis of a range of data, such as system logs, message content, network traffic, and more. The process involves extracting characteristics of a specific type of attack or malicious behavior, which enables the automatic identification of these threats.

One of the main strengths of GAI's attack signature generation is its ability to identify new and unknown threats. Traditional methods rely on prior knowledge of known attacks, which means they cannot detect zero-day attacks—those that have not been previously identified and have no signatures available. GAI can analyze new behavioral patterns and characteristics to detect such attacks (Eke, 2023). Generating attack signatures is scalable and can be applied to different types of data and systems (Teubner et al., 2023). GAI can also provide these signatures in real time, enabling immediate response to detected threats.

Finally, GAI reduces the workload of security analysts, who no longer have to create attack signatures manually. Instead, they can focus on more advanced tasks and strategic aspects of cybersecurity. GAI's generation of attack signatures is a step forward in threat detection, allowing organizations to better prepare for the changing cybersecurity landscape and more effectively protect their assets and data from attacks.

Phishing detection by GAI is an effective way to defend against one of the most common threats in the digital environment. Phishing is an insidious technique that cybercriminals use to phish for sensitive information such as passwords, credit card numbers, and personal information by impersonating trusted sources. Phishing attacks can take many forms, including fake emails, websites, text messages, and social media messages (Varsha, 2023). The consequences of such attacks can be severe, leading to data loss, theft of financial resources, and invasion of privacy (Oduro et al., 2022).

GAI has become a key tool in combating phishing. GAI uses advanced machine learning techniques to analyze message content and identify caesuras specific to phishing attempts. GAI helps combat phishing by analyzing the content of emails, text messages, and other communications to look for caesuras characteristic of phishing attempts, such as requests for sensitive information or links to suspicious sites (Mazurek & Malagocka, 2019; Piotrowski, 2023). It can detect attempts to impersonate known and trusted companies or institutions, a common practice in phishing.

GAI can analyze URLs in the content of messages and identify fake or suspicious web domains that can be used to redirect victims to phishing sites. It can also analyze attachments and files for malware or data capture attempts (Nasir et al., 2021). Examining sender behavior, including message frequency, communication patterns, and other characteristics that may indicate phishing attempts, is possible. GAI works in real time, enabling rapid response to phishing attempts and generating alerts, and by automating the phishing detection process, analysts can focus on more advanced tasks and tracking advanced attacks. GAI can be continuously improved and adapted to new phishing techniques and trends. By using GAI in phishing detection, organizations can protect their employees and customers more effectively from such attacks (Eke, 2023). This tool makes it possible to detect phishing attempts early and minimize the risks associated with these attacks, which is a key component of a cybersecurity strategy.

Social media monitoring by GAI is important to cyber security and online reputation protection strategies. Social media has become integral to online life, providing platforms for communication, content sharing, and networking (Teubner et al., 2023).

However, they are also a hotbed for various threats, including misinformation, reputation attacks, fake profiles, cyberbullying, and more (Rana et al., 2022). GAI is being used to monitor and respond to these threats effectively by analyzing vast amounts of data published on social media to look for disturbing patterns and behaviors that may indicate threats (Stahl, 2021). These systems can monitor user activity on social media, discussion forums, and other online platforms, identifying behaviors that suggest potential threats (Moravec et al., 2020; Freelon et al., 2022). This could include attempts at bullying, causing conflict, or spreading hateful content.

At the same time, however, GAI can also create erroneous and malicious information. The hope, though, is that by analyzing content published on social media, sources of information can be verified, and potential cases of misinformation and false information can be detected (Wach et al., 2023). GAI could detect reputational attacks and monitor comments, posts, and mentions on social media to identify attempts to damage the reputation of companies, institutions, or individuals (Dwivedi et al., 2023; Palladino, 2022; Kietzmann et al., 2020; Jones-Jang et al., 2021; Androniceanu et al., 2022).

Detecting distributed denial of service (DDoS) attacks using GAI is a key component of cybersecurity strategies used by organizations and ISPs, for whom DDoS attacks pose a tough challenge (Du et al., 2023). Attackers seek to overwhelm servers and networks, leading to decreased availability of online services and potential financial losses. Therefore, there is an urgent need to detect and defend against these attacks effectively. GAI is becoming a key tool in combating DDoS attacks, as it can accurately analyze network traffic to look for disturbing patterns that may indicate DDoS attacks and detect traffic patterns that differ from normal behavior, indicating attempted attacks.

Attackers often change tactics to avoid detection (Illia et al., 2023). GAI is flexible, can adapt to new attack methods and can distinguish between a DDoS attack and an increase in natural traffic, thus minimizing false alarms. GAI can be integrated with defense systems to automatically implement defense strategies, such as redirecting attacker traffic, and it generates alerts and reports on detected attacks, allowing for effective monitoring and response to threats (Garibay et al., 2023). By using GAI in detecting DDoS attacks, organizations can more effectively defend against these types of threats and minimize the impact of attacks on the availability of online services. This tool is becoming a key component of cyber security strategies in an era of increasing numbers of DDoS attacks with increasing severity.

Predicting the behavior of cyber criminals using GAI is a modern and advanced technique in cybersecurity. It allows identifying potential threats and preparing to defend against them. In this context, predicting the behavior of cyber criminals is becoming a key component of cyber security strategies. GAI is a tool that enables organizations to predict and respond to such behavior (Eliot, 2023; Piotrowski, 2023).

GAI can analyze large amounts of historical data on attacks, techniques, targets, and tactics of cybercriminals. Based on this data, it can identify patterns and trends in attacker behavior. It can extract caesuras specific to certain criminal groups, allowing it to identify their digital signatures. Attackers are constantly adapting their methods and tactics, and GAI can study and track changes in criminal behavior and new trends in cybercrime. Based on analysis of historical data and ongoing monitoring, it is possible to identify attempted attacks before they are executed, and it can analyze criminals' publications and communications for information on their motivations, which helps understand why they attack and what targets are important to them. GAI can automatically generate alerts on potential threats and recommendations for defensive actions. By using GAI to predict the behavior of cybercriminals, organizations can more effectively prepare to defend against threats and minimize the risk of attacks. This tool enables a more proactive approach to cybersecurity and improves an organization's ability to anticipate and respond to new and advanced attacks.

GAI is an advanced technology revolutionizing the approach to data analysis and report generation in cybersecurity. GAI can analyze data from various sources, such as system logs, network traffic, email messages, or social media content, to identify potential threats. Generating reports and analysis by GAI to detect threats is an important part of a cybersecurity strategy (Li et al., 2023). GAI can analyze huge amounts of data, processing vast amounts that would be difficult or impossible for humans to analyze quickly. GAI analyzes data to look for anomalies or disturbing patterns or behaviors that may indicate attacks or security breaches and automatically generates alerts when such patterns or behaviors are detected, enabling security teams to take immediate defensive action (Greshake et al., 2023).

GAI operates in real time, allowing for real-time monitoring of digital behavior and situations, and it can be adapted to different types of data and systems, enabling organizations to monitor multiple aspects of cybersecurity simultaneously (MaungMaung & Kiya, 2023)—reports and analyses generated from processed data, providing relevant information and insights for security and management teams. By using GAI in generating reports and analysis, organizations can more effectively monitor their digital environment, detect threats, and take appropriate defensive actions (Chan, 2023).

Automating threat response is one of the most important steps in building an effective cybersecurity strategy. Rapid response is key in an environment where cyberattacks are increasingly sophisticated and intense. GAI is becoming a central component of this strategy, enabling the automation of many aspects of defense operations. It analyzes real-time data and network traffic to detect troubling patterns and security incidents. It automatically generates alerts when threats are detected, enabling security teams to respond quickly and classify threats based on data analysis to determine their priority and importance (Du et al., 2023).

Generating recommendations for defensive actions, such as blocking network traffic associated with an attack or isolating infected devices, is possible. GAI can identify intrusion attempts and unauthorized access attempts, generate alerts, and implement appropriate security measures, and it can be customized for different types of data and systems, allowing organizations to monitor multiple aspects of cyber security simultaneously (MaungMaung & Kiya, 2023). Automating threat response using GAI allows organizations to minimize response time to security incidents, which is crucial in combating attacks.

6.3 The future of early threat detection in the digital environment

While GAI has great potential for cybersecurity, there are more secure solutions. There are challenges to overcome—for instance, understanding threats, protecting against malicious data, entering protection mode, and controlling AI.

Understanding threats in the context of the future of early threat detection in the digital environment is crucial in an era in which our lives are increasingly intertwined with technology (Du et al., 2023). The digital environment, which includes the Internet, information systems, and networked devices, is becoming an integral part of our daily lives. However, at the same time, it is becoming a field in which numerous threats are developing that can have serious consequences for our privacy, security, and stability (Karim, 2023).

One key aspect is understanding the changing role of data. Data has become a key component of the digital world, and its value is enormous. As the flow of information increases, the dangers of inappropriate use are also growing. Theft of personal data, attacks on companies and institutions, and disinformation campaigns are examples of what can happen when data falls into the wrong hands. Therefore, early detection of threats in the digital environment is essential to staying safe. The added value is anticipating potential attacks and responding to them before they cause significant damage. Online behavior monitoring and analysis systems and artificial intelligence technologies are key to identifying suspicious activity and catching previously unknown threats.

Education and awareness are also extremely important in understanding the risks in the digital environment (Cooper, 2023). People should understand what risks online activities entail, what practices can help minimize those risks, and what consequences come with inappropriate use of technology. This task is for individual users as well as educational institutions, companies, and governments, which should support educational initiatives and awareness campaigns.

In the context of the future, new technologies such as the Internet of Things (IoT), artificial intelligence, and 5G will create new opportunities and risks. Therefore, investing in research and development of new digital security tools and strategies is important. A proactive approach is key to understanding threats in the future of early digital threat detection. We cannot wait until we are attacked but must act in advance to protect our data, privacy, and the stability of our digital world. This requires cooperation between the public and private sectors and continuous monitoring and adaptation to the changing cybersecurity landscape.

Protecting against harmful data in the context of the future of early threat detection in the digital environment is becoming increasingly critical as our dependence on data continues to grow (Du et al., 2023). In the digital age, data is inextricably linked to our personal and professional lives. However, the dangers of using data in harmful and illegal ways are also growing at the same time. Harmful data includes various types of information, such as malicious software (malware), fake websites, personal data stolen by cybercriminals, misinformation, and false information that can mislead or manipulate people. Protecting this data is becoming a priority, as its misuse can lead to financial losses, violations of privacy, and even threats to democracy and society (Dwivedi et al., 2023).

Early detection of malicious data threats is critical. With the right tools and technologies, such as online behavior monitoring systems, data analytics, and artificial intelligence, suspicious activity and dangerous content can be detected before they cause significant damage. Examples of such activities include detecting phishing, an attempted online scam involving phishing for sensitive information, or detecting malware in real time. In parallel with the technical aspect of protecting from malicious data, promoting awareness and education among Internet users is crucial. People need to understand the risks of different types of malicious data and what security practices they should follow. This also includes verifying information sources, thinking critically, and distinguishing fake content from real content (Das, 2023).

In the context of the future, developing more advanced tools and technologies to protect malicious data will be essential. Cybercriminals are constantly improving their methods, so we must constantly improve our defenses. In addition, international cooperation is becoming increasingly important, as malicious data threats know no borders. In conclusion, protecting malicious data in the context of the future is a challenge that requires both advanced technology and public awareness (Du et al., 2023). Early detection of threats, education, and cooperation are key to maintaining security in a digital environment that is becoming increasingly complex and challenging.

Moving into protection mode against the backdrop of the future of early detection of threats in the digital environment is becoming a key element in ensuring online security. This is due to the need to respond quickly to growing threats in a digital world that is increasingly complex and dynamic (Li & Liao, 2023). Protection mode is a process in which organizations and users proactively prepare to defend against potential threats and respond to them rapidly and coordinatedly. It is an approach that assumes that threats are unavoidable but that they can be minimized and their impact limited by taking appropriate precautions.

In terms of the future, moving into protection mode will be based on several key elements. The first is constant awareness of the different types of threats in the digital environment (Cooper, 2023). This means that organizations and individual users must stay informed about new types of attacks, techniques used by cybercriminals, and current risks (Blasingame & Liu, 2023). Organizations and users must invest in digital security training and education. Good practices, procedures, and techniques for responding to attacks should be known and implemented at all levels (Du et al., 2023). Early detection of threats relies on advanced tools and technologies. Online behavior monitoring systems, data analytics, and artificial intelligence can detect disturbing activity and suspicious behavior in real time (Wach et al., 2023).

Organizations and individuals should develop detailed plans to respond to various attack scenarios. The added value is that the response is quick, coordinated, and effective to minimize damage. In today's global digital environment, collaboration is key. Organizations should collaborate with other institutions, companies, and governments to share threat information and work together for security.

It is worth emphasizing that going into protection mode does not mean you have to live in constant fear. It is a preventive approach that allows us to focus on proactively and effectively responding to threats instead of avoiding them. In this way, we can enjoy the benefits of the digital world while maintaining our security and privacy. Going into protection mode will become even more important in the future in the face of growing threats and increasingly sophisticated attack techniques.

GAI has great potential for content creation, but at the same time, it carries challenges of abuse and potential threats to society (Amariles & Baquero, 2023). GAI can be used to create textual and multimedia content (Cooper, 2023). It is a tool that can be used to entertain, educate, and create valuable information. However, there is a risk that it can be used to spread disinformation and spam, manipulate public opinion, and create harmful content (Chan, 2023). The control of GAI in the context of the future is based on several key elements:

monitoring and detection, regulation and ethics, education and awareness, technology, and innovation.

It is necessary to continuously monitor GAI activity on the network to detect content or behavior that may pose a threat (Scharth, 2022). Content analysis technologies and content verification algorithms are key tools in the early detection process. Creating regulations and ethical rules regarding the use of GAI is key. Organizations and online platforms should adopt appropriate guidelines and regulations to control how GAI is used and what the restrictions are (Blasingame & Liu, 2023). Educating users so that they understand the potential risks of GAI and know how to recognize them is critical. This helps build more critical thinking toward the information generated by GAI. At the same time, developing advanced technological tools, such as algorithms to detect harmful or manipulative content, is essential to control GAI effectively.

In the context of the future, continuing to work on GAI control will be crucial as these technologies evolve, and with them will come new threats (Wach et al., 2023). Striking a balance between harnessing the potential of GAI and controlling its operation is a challenge that will be important for the security and stability of the digital environment. However, developing technologies and strategies for early detection of threats in the digital environment will continue to be a key area of focus. GAI has tremendous potential to be used in the fight against hateful content and cyber threats, subject to proper oversight and regulation (Cooper, 2023). It is important to continue researching and developing tools that help detect threats early while protecting Internet users' freedom of speech and privacy. Combating threats in the digital environment will be a long-term process that requires the involvement of various sectors of society.

6.4 Summary

Intelligent security systems based on GAI are key in the fight against growing cyber threats. With the ability to analyze data, detect patterns, and respond in real time, GAI can help organizations and individuals prevent attacks and minimize the impact of cyber threats. As technology evolves, GAI becomes an increasingly indispensable cybersecurity tool. However, there are still many challenges to overcome before we can realize the full potential of GAI in cybersecurity. It is worth investing in researching and developing this technology to keep in step with evolving threats and protect our digital future. By analyzing large amounts of data in real time, GAI is able to detect disturbing patterns and anomalies that may indicate attempted attacks or other security breaches. In addition, GAI can identify potential security vulnerabilities and predict the evolution of threats, allowing for more proactive defense measures.

While traditional security analysis and response methods remain important, integrating GAI into a cybersecurity strategy opens up new possibilities and allows organizations to adapt to increasingly sophisticated attacks. Working with GAI is becoming essential for organizations to effectively protect their assets, data, and reputation from the growing cyber threat. It is worthwhile to continue researching this area and investing in developing and implementing GAI technologies as part of a digital security strategy.

References

Adetayo, A. J. (2023). Artificial intelligence chatbots in academic libraries: The rise of ChatGPT. *Library Hi Tech News.*

Amariles, D. R., & Baquero, P. M. (2023). Promises and limits of law for a human-centric artificial intelligence. *Computer Law & Security Review, 48*, 1–9.

Androniceanu, A., Georgescu, I., & Sabie, O.-M. (2022). The impact of digitalization on public administration, economic development, and well-being in the EU countries. *Central European Public Administration Review, 20*(1), 7–29.

Blasingame, Z., & Liu, C. (2023). Diffusion models for stronger face morphing attacks. *arXiv preprint arXiv:2301. 04218.*

Bove, T. (2023). Bill Gates says ChatGPT will 'change our world' but it doesn't mean your job is at risk. https://fortune. com/2023/02/10/bill-gates-chatgpt-jobs-chatbot-microsoft-google-bard-bing/

Chan, A. (2023). GPT-3 and InstructGPT: Technological dystopianism, utopianism, and "contextual" perspectives in AI ethics and industry. *AI and Ethics, 3*(1), 53–64.

Cooper, G. (2023). Examining science education in ChatGPT: An exploratory study of generative artificial intelligence. *Journal of Science Education and Technology, 32*(3), 444–452.

Das, D. (2023). Understanding the choice of human resource and the artificial intelligence: "Strategic behavior" and the existence of industry equilibrium. *Journal of Economic Studies, 50*(2), 234–267. https://dx.doi.org/10.2139/ssrn.3868734

De, S., Bermudez-Edo, M., Xu, H., & Cai, Z. (2022). Deep generative models in the industrial internet of things: A survey. *IEEE Transactions on Industrial Informatics, 18*(9), 5728–5737.

Du, H., Wang, J., Niyato, D., Kang, J., Xiong, Z., & Kim, D. I. (2023). AI-generated incentive mechanism and full-duplex semantic communications for information sharing. *IEEE Journal on Selected Areas in Communications.* 28 Jun 2023. arXiv:2303.01896v2 [eess.SP]

Dwivedi, Y. K., Kshetri, N., Hughes, L., Slade, E. L., Jeyaraj, A., Kar, A. K., Baabdullah, A. M., Koohang, A., Raghavan, V., Ahuja, M., Albanna, H., Albashrawi, M. A., Al-Busaidi, A. S., Balakrishnan, J., Barlette, Y., Basu, S., Bose, I., Brooks, L., Buhalis, D. . . . Wright, R. (2023). So what if ChatGPT wrote it? Multidisciplinary perspectives on opportunities, challenges and implications of generative conversational AI for research, practice and policy. *International Journal of Information Management, 71.* https://doi.org/10.1016/j.ijinfomgt.2023.102642

Eke, D. O. (2023). ChatGPT and the rise of generative AI: Threat to academic integrity? *Journal of Responsible Technology, 13.*

Eliot, L. (2023). Generative AI ChatGPT as masterful manipulator of humans, worrying AI ethics and AI law. Forbes. https://www.forbes.com/sites/lanceeliot/2023/03/01/generative-ai-chatgpt-as-masterful-manipulator-of-humans-worrying-ai-ethics-and-ai-law/?sh=74d194521d66

Florek-Paszkowska, A., Ujwary-Gil, A., & Godlewska-Dzioboń, B. (2021). Business innovation and critical success factors in the era of digital transformation and turbulent times. *Journal of Entrepreneurship, Management, and Innovation, 17*(4), 7–28.

Floridi, L., & Cowls, J. (2019). A unified framework of five principles for AI in society. *Harvard Data Science Review, 1*(1).

Freelon, D., Bossetta, M., Wells, C., Lukito, J., Xia, Y., & Adams, K. (2022). Black trolls matter: Racial and ideological asymmetries in social media disinformation. *Social Science Computer Review, 40*(3), 560–578.

Garibay, O. O., Winslow, B., Andolina, S., Antona, M., Bodenschatz, A., Coursaris, C., Falco, G., Fiore, S. M., Garibay, I., Grieman, K., Havens, J. C., Jirotka, M., Kacorri, H., Karwowski, W, Kider, J., Konstan, J., Koon, S., Lopez-Gonzalez, M., Maifeld-Carucci, I. . . . Xu, W. (2023). Six human-centered artificial intelligence grand challenges. *International Journal of Human-Computer Interaction, 39*(3), 391–437.

Greshake, K., Abdelnabi, S., Mishra, S., Endres, C., Holz, T., & Fritz, M. (2023). More than you've asked for: A comprehensive analysis of novel prompt injection threats to application-integrated large language models. *arXiv preprint arXiv:2302. 12173.*

Illia, L., Colleoni, E., & Zyglidopoulos, S. (2023). Ethical implications of text generation in the age of artificial intelligence. *Business Ethics, the Environment & Responsibility, 32*(1), 201–210.

Jones-Jang, S. M., Mortensen, T., & Liu, J. (2021). Does media literacy help identification of fake news? Information literacy helps, but other literacies don't. *American Behavioral Scientist, 65*(2), 371–388.

Karim, R. (2023). ChatGPT: Old AI problems in a new guise, new problems in disguise. Monash Lens. https://lens.monash.edu/@politics-society/2023/02/13/1385448/chatgpt-old-ai-problems-in-a-new-guise-new-problems-in-disguise

Kietzmann, J., Lee, L. W., McCarthy, I. P., & Kietzmann, T. (2020). Deepfakes: Trick or treat? *Business Horizons, 63*(2), 135–146.

Korzynski, P., Mazurek, G., Altmann, A., Ejdys, J., Kazlauskaite, R., Paliszkiewicz, J., Wach, K., & Ziemba, E. (2023) Generative artificial intelligence as a new context for management theories: Analysis of ChatGPT. *Central European Management Journal, 31*(1).

Li, H., Guo, D., Fan, W., Xu, M., & Song, Y. (2023). Multi-step jailbreaking privacy attacks on ChatGPT. *arXiv preprint arXiv:2304. 05197.*

Li, X., & Liao, H. (2023). A large-scale group decision making method based on spatial information aggregation and empathetic relationships of experts. *Information Sciences, 632*, 503–515.

MaungMaung, A., & Kiya, H. (2023). Generative model-based attack on learnable image encryption for privacy-preserving deep learning. *arXiv preprint arXiv:2303. 05036.*

Marr, B. (2021). What are the negative impacts of artificial intelligence (AI)? Bernard Marr & Co. https://bernardmarr.com/what-are-the-negative-impacts-of-artificial-intelligence-ai/

Mazurek, G., & Malagocka, K. (2019). Perception of privacy and data protection in the context of the development of artificial intelligence. *Journal of Management Analytics, 6* (4), 344–364.

Moravec, P. L., Kim, A., & Dennis A. R. (2020). Appealing to sense and sensibility: System 1 and System 2 interventions for fake news on social media. *Information Systems Research, 31*(3), 987–1006.

Nasir, J. A., Khan, O. S., & Varlamis, I. (2021). Fake news detection: A hybrid CNN-RNN based deep learning approach. *International Journal of Information Management Data Insights, 1*(1).

Norori, N., Hu, Q., Aellen, F. M., Faraci, F. D., & Tzovara, A. (2021). Addressing bias in big data and AI for health care: A call for open science. *Patterns, 2*(10), 100347.

Oduro, S., Moss, E., & Metcalf, J. (2022). Obligations to assess: Recent trends in AI accountability regulations. *Patterns, 3*(11), 100608.

Palladino, N. (2022). A 'biased' emerging governance regime for artificial intelligence? How AI ethics get skewed moving from principles to practices. *Telecommunications Policy, 47*(5). DOI: 10. 1016/j. telpol. 2022. 102479.

Piotrowski, D. (2023). Privacy frontiers in customers' relations with banks. *Economics and Business Review, 23*(1), 119–141.

Radford, A., Wu, J., Child, R., Luan, D., Amodei, D., & Sutskever, I. (2019). Language models are unsupervised multitask learners. *OpenAI Blog, 1*(8).

Rana, N. P., Chatterjee, S., Dwivedi, Y. K., & Akter, S. (2022). Understanding dark side of artificial intelligence (AI) integrated business analytics: Assessing firm's operational inefficiency and competitiveness. *European Journal of Information Systems, 31*(3), 364–387.

Scharth, M. (2022). The ChatGPT chatbot is blowing people away with its writing skills. The University of Sydney. https://www.sydney.edu.au/news-opinion/news/2022/12/08/the-chatgpt-chatbot-is-blowing-people-away-with-its-writing-skil.html

Stahl, B. C. (2021). Artificial intelligence for a better future: An ecosystem perspective on the ethics of AI and emerging digital technologies. Springer *Nature.* https://link.springer.com/book/10.1007/978-3-030-69978-9

Teubner, T., Flath, C. M., Weinhardt, C., van der Aalst, W., & Hinz, O. (2023). Welcome to the era of ChatGPT et al. *Business & Information Systems Engineering, 65*(2), 95–101.

Tlili, A., Shehata, B., Adarkwah, M. A., Bozkurt, A., Hickey, D. T., Huang, R., & Agyemang, B. (2023). What if the devil is my guardian angel: ChatGPT as a case study of using chatbots in education. *Smart Learning Environments, 10*(1).

Varsha, P. S. (2023). How can we manage biases in artificial intelligence systems—A systematic literature review. *International Journal of Information Management Data Insights, 3*(1).

Wach, K., Duong, C. D., Ejdys, J., Kazlauskaitė, R., Korzynski, P., Mazurek, G., Paliszkiewicz, J., & Ziemba, E (2023). The dark side of generative artificial intelligence: A critical analysis of controversies and risks of ChatGPT. *Entrepreneurial Business and Economics Review, 11*(2), 7–24.

Chapter 7

Unwanted Psychological Diagnoses: Discriminative Dangers of Generative AI

Mirko Farina,[1]* Xiao Yu,[2] and Andrea Lavazza[3]

[1]Institute for Digital Economy and Artificial Systems: Xiamen University, China, and Lomonosov Moscow State University, Russia

[2]Sichuan Center for Digital Development, China

[3]Centro Universitario Internazionale, Arezzo and University of Pavia, Italy

*Corresponding author

7.1 Generative AI and why it matters to healthcare

Machine learning (ML) is a branch of artificial intelligence (AI) that focuses on using data and algorithms to mimic the way humans learn. ML does so by unearthing patterns from data and by providing key insights about them (LeCun et al., 2015). Because of that quality, one can legitimately consider ML as the heavy lifter of the AI world (Farina, Karimov et al. 2022; Farina, Gorb et al., 2022).

Generative AI (GAI) can be considered as an extension of machine learning. GAI can learn to generate data (via ML), but it can also turn around to critique and refine such data, thereby transforming them into something actionable (Farina & Lavazza, 2023; Farina, 2023). GAI has, for these reasons, the potential to transform and revolutionize our interactions with machines and computers, potentially unlocking uncharted territories across various industries and domains (Brynjolfsson et al., 2023).

GAI has a long and rich history. One can argue that the origin of GAI can be traced back to the mid-20th century, when researchers and scientists embarked on a mission to create intelligent machines.* More specifically, in the early 1930s, Georges Artsrouni and Petr Smirnov-Troyanskii patented a device called 'the mechanical brain', which had facilities for retrieving and printing stored information. The device was multipurpose. The inventors suggested applications 'such as the automatic production of railway timetables, of telephone directories, of commercial telegraph codes, of banking statements, and even of anthropometric records' (Hutchins, 2004, p. 13). However, the mechanical brain became famous as a mechanical multilingual dictionary.†

A few decades later, Joseph Weizenbaum (1966) created the first chatbot, ELIZA, which could simulate conversations with a psychotherapist. Shortly after that, in 1968, another computer scientist, Terry Winograd, developed SHRDLU, a natural language–understanding program that could manipulate and reason out of a world of blocks according to instructions from a user (Winograd, 1972).

However, it was not until the 1980s that more significant progress was achieved in the field, and these were due to two fundamental innovations: (1) the introduction of Bayesian network causal analysis in computer science (see Pearl, 2000, for a review), which offered the possibility to represent uncertainty through statistical techniques; and (2) the development of neural networks (such as recurrent neural networks [RRNs]; Jordan, 1986) or convolutional neural networks (CNNs; LeCun et al., 1989), which could learn from data and evolve over time.

Taking full advantage of these important innovations, Bengio et al. (2003) famously published a paper which suggested a method to model language using feed-forward neural networks. The paper opened the door to the creation and development of sophisticated AI applications (such as voice-powered personal assistants).

In 2012, Krizhevsky et al. designed the AlexNet CNN architecture (see also Krizhevsky et al., 2017), pioneering a new way of automatically training neural networks. However, it was not until the advent of variational autoencoders (VAEs; Kingma & Welling, 2013) and generative adversarial networks (Goodfellow et al., 2014) that GAI's true potential began to manifest.

VAEs learn the underlying distribution of input data and can generate new data (say, images) by sampling from the learnt latent distribution. These models consist of two parts: an encoder that transforms input data into a latent space,

* Some may push its origins back to the 17th century, with the ideas of Descartes and Leibniz and the need to develop a universal, philosophical and 'logical' language.

† The source is a report by the Estonian newspaper *Vaba Maa*, which was reproduced (in Russian) in the proceedings of a conference on MT held in Tallin in 1962.

and a decoder that reconstructs the original data. In the generation process only the decoder part of VAE is used.

Generative adversarial networks (GANs) were developed in 2014. The architecture of GANs consists of two neural networks: a *generator* network that generates data (say, images) from noise, and a *discriminator* network that determines whether the generated data is real or fake. The generator network is trained to produce, for instance, images that can fool the discriminator network into believing that they are real, while the discriminator network is trained to differentiate between the real and generated images. Through this adversarial training process, the generator network becomes better at generating more realistic images that closely resemble real images.

Since the creation of VAEs and GANs, GAI has proliferated and been leveraged to produce a plethora of things, ranging from videos to music and literature. In 2017, Vaswani et al. developed the concept of transformers and inspired researchers to look into the development of AI tools that could automatically parse unlabeled text into large language models (LLMs).

In 2018, Devlin et al. developed Bidirectional Encoder Representations from Transformers (BERT), which, unlike previous deep learning models, has already been pre-trained and therefore has in-built representations of the words and sentences as well as underlying semantic relations through which they connect. This was a very important step in the development of modern GAI tools, as it paved the way for more reliable and effective content generation in LLMs, opening the door to releases of models (such as generative pre-trained transformers [GPT®] and subsequent versions, e.g., GPT-4) which are capable of effortlessly composing original texts—in a coherent manner and with minimal overlapping with existing works—or translating them between different languages (Farina, 2023).

GAI (and ML) have since then found profitable applications in various sectors, including healthcare (Darcy et al., 2016; Farina & Lavazza, 2021), education (Jarke & Breiter, 2019), finance (Ryman-Tubb et al., 2018; Farina et al., 2024), criminal justice (Ryberg & Roberts, 2022), marketing (Coyle & Weller, 2020), and entertainment (Bilow, 2022; Ciancarini et al., 2023).

In this contribution, we will look at the potential applications of ML (Deo, 2015; Obermeyer & Emanuel, 2016) and GAI tools in the field of medicine (Alamir & Alghamdi, 2022; Morley et al., 2023). The application of modern GAI tools (such as ChatGPT®-3.5/4) can help healthcare organizations achieve the goals of the *quadruple aim* as described in Bodenheimer and Sinsky (2014). That is, it can contribute to enhancing patient/consumer experience, expanding population health, improving the work life of healthcare providers while reducing the cost of care (see also Lenharo, 2023). In our chapter, however, we will focus mostly on the ethical and moral dimension of this fascinating debate. We note here that our contribution is non-axiological and non-normative in character.

Specifically, in Section 2, we review the possible benefits arising from the application of GAI in the medical practice. These are mostly found in diagnostics, in optimization of medical resources, and in disease screening, as well as in the improvement of patient engagement and in the construction of voice-based electronic medical records (in line with the goals of the quadruple aim described above).

In Section 3, we describe the potential dangers and pitfalls surrounding the large-scale application of this technology. These dangers and pitfalls are mostly concerned with security issues, biases, and oversight.

In Section 4, we focus on our case study (unwanted psychological diagnoses), which further illustrates problems related to the application of AI tools in medicine. Through the discussion of this case study, we highlight a series of ethical and moral considerations, which we believe should be addressed with urgency by researchers, practitioners, and decision-makers.

Finally, in Section 5, we summarize what we have achieved and discuss possible future research directions.

7.2 Generative AI in healthcare: Potential benefits

In many fields, as we noted above, the development of machine learning and of various GAI tools has been indispensable in solving complex problems. This is also true for medicine, where AI technology is expected to deeply transform the medical sector during the next 20 years* (see also Stoumpos et al., 2023). More specifically, GAI tools could provide valuable prognostic and diagnostic information, which could improve the relationship between the doctor and the patient. They could also help with management of scarce resources (e.g., medical personnel), as well as with the construction of digital medical records (from users' speech via speech recognition technology), which could save much time for doctors. In this section, we will discuss all these benefits in turn, starting from the capacity to provide quick and helpful diagnostic and prognostic information.

GAI tools can certainly improve diagnostic accuracy. Arrhythmia detection from electrocardiogram (ECG) recordings is typically performed by expert technicians or by cardiologists. Rajpurkar et al. (2017) developed an algorithm which exceeded the performance of board-certified cardiologists in detecting diverse types of cardiac arrhythmias from ECGs. The authors trained a 34-layer CNN architecture capable of detecting 12 types of arrhythmia on a sample of 29,163 subjects. The results obtained from the model were 'tested on 336 records against six board-certified cardiologists, yielding an aggregate positive predictive value of

* https://www.mckinsey.com/industries/healthcare/our-insights/what-to-expect-in-us-healthcare-in-2023-and-beyond

0.80 compared to 0.72 in cardiologists and aggregate sensitivity of 0.78 compared to 0.72 in cardiologists' (see Haq et al., 2021, p. 914).

More recently, building and expanding on those earlier results, Hannun et al. (2019) developed a deep neural network (DNN) with the intent of classifying '12 rhythm classes using 91,232 single-lead ECGs from 53,549 patients who used a single-lead ambulatory ECG monitoring device' (p. 65). After validation against a control test dataset compiled by a committee of board-certified cardiologists, the aforesaid model achieved a significantly higher positive predictive value and sensitivity (0.837) than that displayed by the cardiologists themselves (0.780).

In addition, Esteva et al. (2017) trained a CNN model to detect and diagnose skin cancers. The model runs on a dataset of 129,450 skin images. The CNN model managed to achieve a performance on par with that of certified and practicing dermatologists, thereby demonstrating that it could effectively diagnose skin cancers.

GAI tools can also improve prognostic accuracy. For example, Kather et al. (2019) used ML techniques to predict the survival and molecular alternations in gastrointestinal and liver cancer.

The use of these AI tools, in combination with human doctors, could make both the diagnoses and the prognoses more accurate and even more acceptable by the patients, as they will provide not only an empirically informed—yet phenomenological—interpretation of the findings, but also an absolutely objective analysis of the results at hand. These are just two ways in which AI tools could be beneficial for the medical profession.

Another way in which these tools could help doctors would be through the management of scarce resources (e.g., medical personnel), especially at times of emergency (think about scenarios similar to the one faced by public health systems across the world at the onset of the COVID-19 pandemic). GAI tools could well extend the reach of doctors and, by extensions, of hospitals and healthcare institutions broadly conceived, by providing relatively low-cost instruments for dealing with non-emergency situations. For instance, chatbots could be set up to answer common questions in reception, or to perform easy tasks under relatively light supervision (such as scans, content-based image retrievals, image annotations; see Obermeyer & Emanuel, 2016) in radiology or anatomical pathology, thereby performing much routine medical work, allowing the doctors to be more aptly reallocated into sectors where humans are so far irreplaceable.

And yet, GAI tools could also contribute, in line with the goals of the quadruple aim described above, to the construction of voice-based electronic medical records. Voice electronic medical record systems could save doctors quite a bit of time in their daily practice and allow patients to enjoy a fuller and better experience with the specialist (Payne et al., 2018). It is well known that doctors spent a lot of time (between 3 and 5 hours per day)* checking medical records. Logging large amounts of clinically irrelevant data results in less meaningful communication with patients and even less time for careful and thorough medical diagnoses.

For these reasons, voice electronic medical record systems (developed, for instance, by iFly-Tek in China) were put into operation by some hospitals (for example, the Chinese Academy of Medical Sciences & Peking Union Medical College). This resulted in many benefits. The doctors could efficiently and almost effortlessly complete digital medical records, and the patients were able to enjoy better medical care and access their medical records by simply printing the documents converted from the voice electronic medical records (Kong et al., 2019).

There are many other ways in which GAI tools could benefit the medical profession (see Sohail, 2023, and Peng et al., 2023, for helpful insights)—for instance, through the adoption of medical robots guided or supervised by chatbots or even with predictions in drug discovery applications. However, owing to the limits of space, we will skip their analysis here and will focus instead on the potentially nefarious effects that this forthcoming AI revolution may bring about in the medical profession.

7.3 Generative AI in healthcare: Pitfalls and open challenges

Biological systems are indeed very complex (holistic) entities, with multiple interrelated elements, not merely reducible to a set of mechanical (formal) inputs and outputs. Thus, the key to extracting the most valid, biologically meaningful interpretation of any medical findings is the integration process between all the resources at hand (the doctors, the infrastructure in which they operate, the culture and the community in which they are immersed, and the tools—the technology—which they use). Albeit deep learning algorithms are quite capable of operating with multiplatform data, their full integration in a human, holistically driven milieu is computationally nontrivial and does present challenges.

In this section, building and expanding on this initial observation, we look into potential issues that threaten to undermine the meaningful application of GAI in medicine, hence balancing the positive outlook we sketched in the previous section with some realistic concerns, which we believe deserve much attention by both professionals (practitioners) and decision-makers. We do so with respect to three main areas, domains, or categories: security, biases, and oversight.

Security and privacy concerns should be discussed in parallel to the full implementation of GAI in medicine. Patient healthcare data are very valuable and

* https://www.kevinmd.com/2022/04/how-much-time-do-physicians-spend-in-the-ehr.html

should be protected unconditionally (Singh et al., 2021). This is why, without direct informed consent by patients, collecting and using patient data should, we believe, be categorically forbidden. However, even if consent is given, a number of issues still arise. These are mostly concerned with risks related to data leakage or data breaches (Bloudoff-Indelicato, 2015).

Healthcare institutions and related parties are particularly vulnerable to data breaches and ransomware attacks. A 2023 IBM Security report shows a 15% increase over three years in costs for data breaches.* Data leakage (voluntarily, for commercial purposes, or involuntarily, driven, say, by the incompetence of system administrators) is therefore a very serious issue for the field. In addition, the sharing of private health data to train and use AI tools constitutes another significant downside in terms of privacy, which requires focus and care by decision makers. Training AI algorithms requires access to enormous amounts of private data, and the use of GAI tools risks the exposure of such data.

Furthermore, the tools may memorize and retain the information on which they have been trained (Dar et al., 2023). As a matter of fact, a series of studies (e.g., Price & Nicholson, 2021) demonstrated that AI tools can sometimes re-identify individuals even if the data has been effectively anonymized. More worryingly perhaps, in some instances, it was shown that GAI tools could not only re-identify the individual but could also make informed guesses about the individual's non-health condition (Price & Nicholson, 2021).

As happens with other issues concerning general privacy, many states worldwide are trying to regulate the use of such tools and therefore somehow protect individuals' privacy in healthcare; however, we are still a long way from the development of supranational binding regulations. As the use of AI in healthcare expands, all parties involved in the process should be aware of the risks underlying the use of these tools and therefore collectively act towards the protection of the public.

Besides issues with personal security, the application of GAI tools in healthcare has recently raised many concerns about the potential biases underlying the algorithms governing the functioning of such tools (Lancet Regional Health, 2023). A few studies (e.g., Obermeyer et al., 2019; Vartan, 2019; Confalonieri et al., 2022) found race-based discrepancies, which were due to the lack of training data for minority populations. In a recent report, Bhatt et al. (2022) also emphasized the need to reassess the sensitivity of clinical algorithms to make sure it is well understood 'how race is used and justified'.

To help ensure that all patients receive the care they need, the American Medical Association (Henry, 2023) also identified a series of key points for the

* https://www.ibm.com/reports/data-breach?utm_content=SRCWW&p1=Search&p4=43700072379268622&p5=p

use of AI in healthcare. Those points are essentially suggestions for the use of population-representative data and contains recommendations to avoid explicit and implicit biases and to maximize transparency. To this extent, the AMA encourages the use of human-machine partnerships (augmented AI) rather than of fully autonomous GAI tools.

However, it should also be noted that, if appropriately used, GAI tools have the potential to actually reduce the prevalence of bias in medicine. This is because, if properly trained and not constrained by external forces, such tools can include a broader (hence fairer) range of inputs in their datasets. So, when physicians 'forget' to prescribe adequate pain medication or order a necessary laboratory test for Black or Hispanic subjects, the GAI tool might come in and question that decision, ultimately leading to a more equitable form of care for all.

Lastly, another open challenge remains to be discussed in this section. This is the issue of oversight (Meskó & Topol, 2023). A number of studies (e.g., Lal et al., 2022) have already called for the implementation of revised ethical approaches towards GAI tools. Such approaches should be underpinned by a broader vision on research and by a proactive stance on oversight, which should aim at creating a new regulatory category for GAI tools, while providing regulatory guidance or assistance (possibly supranational and multipolar) for companies and healthcare organizations (Vayena & Blasimme, 2022; Finlayson et al., 2021). This means that human oversight should be required by law, and this could be ultimately aimed at improving the accuracy and quality of the answers produced by GAI tools.

7.4 Case study: Unwanted psychological diagnoses

In addition to the technical opportunities examined so far, clinical evidence seems to converge in creating the possibility of mass health screenings. This opens the door to unwanted psychological diagnoses—that is, in a general sense, diagnoses conducted remotely through new digital medical tools, without the knowledge of the individual being examined.

With respect to the above, a first general premise is that the burden, both personal and social, produced by psychiatric disorders and the difficulty of having accurate early diagnoses seems to justify the use of new digital tools, even in place of care provided directly by physicians.

Second, it appears that clinical data in the classical sense are less predictive of the development of psychiatric disorders than other biographical and contextual information that is indirect and much easier to obtain.

Third, automation, as it were, of diagnosis and treatment in psychology and psychiatry seems to have some drawbacks, but these appear to be outweighed by the advantages offered by AI tools for the clinical practice.

Fourth, precisely based on the technical possibilities offered by the new AI tools in fields other than medicine, applications capable of making screenings and evaluations based on elements provided voluntarily or involuntarily by the individuals examined are being proposed and disseminated.

In what follows, we'll consider these premises in turn with the intent of understanding what the perspective of unwanted psychological diagnoses might be. This will be followed by a discussion of possible applications, weighing the benefits and risks of such practices.

The first premise is that the burden of mental illness is growing. Arias et al. (2022, p. 1) estimated 'that 418 million disability-adjusted life years (DALYs) could be attributable to mental disorders in 2019 (16% of global DALYs)—a more than three-fold increase compared to conventional estimates. The economic value associated with this burden is estimated at about USD 5 trillion. At a regional level, the losses could account for between 4% of gross domestic product in Eastern sub-Saharan Africa and 8% in high-income North America'.

We also know that patients with psychiatric disorders are more likely to develop other organic diseases and experience premature mortality (Plana-Ripoll et al., 2019). The COVID pandemic that has affected the entire planet since 2020 has exacerbated the spread of some psychiatric disorders because of measures to restrict social contacts, the general climate of fear and threat, and the difficulty of accessing diagnosis and treatment due to the shift in health care attention to those affected by the virus (Penninx et al., 2022).

It therefore comes as no surprise that methods to identify psychiatric disorders at an early, even asymptomatic, stage and more effective individualized treatments are being sought. A review of recent meta-analyses of randomized controlled trials of psychotherapies and pharmacotherapies for the main mental disorders in adults showed that, 'after more than half a century of research, thousands of RCTs and millions of invested funds, the effect sizes of psychotherapies and pharmacotherapies for mental disorders are limited, suggesting a ceiling effect for treatment research as presently conducted. A paradigm shift in research seems to be required to achieve further progress' (Leichsenring et al., 2022, p. 133).

The second premise follows from the studies that are trying to answer the challenges laid out above about mental illness. In particular, we know that most lifetime psychiatric disorders can be diagnosed clinically from 10 to 24 years of age, but symptoms that occur for years before the illness is full blown are hardly observed, thus losing the opportunity for prevention and early intervention (Kessler et al., 2005).

A recent study (de Lacy et al., 2023) used 160 candidate predictors across multiple domains of human function to predict mental illness. They ranged from developmental aspects (prenatal exposures to substances, pregnancy, and infant history) and cognitive domains (educational history including IQ and discipline issues, traits, and cognitive aspects); to the behavioral domain (marijuana use to distress tolerance), the social domain (parent demographic, race, social experience and skills), and even to the physiological one (characteristics, medical history, functional connectivity—46 metrics). In the study the authors used three machine learning algorithms optimized with a novel artificial intelligence meta-learning technique to predict individual cases of anxiety, depression, attention deficit, disruptive behaviors and post-traumatic stress. The authors found that 'across all five conditions, psychosocial and psychometric constructs were more important final predictors than neural metrics of brain function' (p. 11).

The third premise concerns the effective counterarguments made to the possible objections against the massive use of artificial intelligence. It is generally believed that, especially in the field of psychology, direct interaction with a physician is essential and cannot be delegated to artificial intelligence. However, it must be considered that in some rather widespread conditions, such as depression or autism, patients find it difficult to leave their homes and relate to other people, physicians in particular. Minerva and Giubilini (2023) attest that soldiers are more likely to talk about post-traumatic stress to virtual interviewers than to human doctors. In addition, patients with digital tools have less fear of disclosing their illness, which can lead to social stigma.

On the other hand, the lack of healthcare practitioners has a negative impact because many people who need care cannot get it, while simple apps that can be installed on smartphones can at least partially make up for this. Still, some digital devices are proving more effective than the best psychologists and psychiatrists—for example, in the accuracy with which they detect suicidal tendencies in patients (Walsh et al., 2017).

Finally, the fourth premise ties in with some of the points made above. Personal sensing (or digital phenotyping), natural language processing, and chatbots are new tools capable of detecting at least some symptoms of mental disorders at a distance and without the need for complex or expensive equipment (Minerva & Giubilini, 2023). Personal sensing is the use of digital data to measure and monitor the mental state of individuals. AI can analyze material posted on social media, medical records, and other data, looking for changes in behavior that can be traced to mental health issues (Valentine et al., 2023).

Natural language processing algorithms track language use in chats, emails, and social media posts looking for patterns that may be connected with psychiatric disorders such as anxiety or depression (Zhou et al., 2022). Chatbots can also detect mental issues by asking questions directly to the human interlocutor, just as physicians do. The chatbot can ask about the individual's mood, stress levels or sleep patterns and then recommend therapies or refer directly to a psychologist (Pham et al., 2022).

Recently, ChatGPT-3.5 has been shown to be very good at evaluating 100 clinical case vignettes in both diagnosis and prognosis as well as in management and counseling (D'Souza et al., 2023). The authors claim that, 'It is evident from our study that ChatGPT 3.5 has appreciable knowledge and interpretation skills in Psychiatry. Thus, ChatGPT 3.5 undoubtedly has the potential to transform the field of Medicine and we emphasize its utility in Psychiatry' (p. 103770).

Based on these premises, it is plausible to infer that unwanted psychological diagnoses may become one of the most important issues in the future of digital medicine. Think of the case of automated tests for admission to colleges of excellence proposed as a (partial replacement) for tests conducted by human supervisors (Lira et al., 2023). The idea is that certain personal qualities can predict college success. To assess these personal characteristics, many universities have introduced holistic reviews of applicants by evaluating essays describing extracurricular and work experiences.

However, the assessment of personal qualities made by college staff is often opaque and inefficient. In the study introduced above, the authors identified the presence/absence of seven personal qualities (prosocial purposes, leadership, learning, goal pursuit, intrinsic motivation, teamwork, and perseverance) in 313 essays. Then they 'fine-tuned pre-trained language models with these ratings, which successfully reproduced human codes across demographic subgroups. Last, in a national sample (*N* = 309,594), computer-generated scores collectively demonstrated incremental validity for predicting 6-year college graduation' (Lira et al., 2023).

If certain personal qualities are reliable predictors of success in college, other personality aspects and specific behaviors that are also predictors or proxies of psychiatric disorders may also be considered as predictors of failure and, more importantly perhaps, of potential drawbacks for the college admitting individuals who manifest such personality aspects and behaviors.

It is not only universities and private companies that could resort to unwanted psychological diagnoses. Large-scale psychiatric diagnoses unbeknownst, initially, to the population involved could become widespread in other areas as well. As it turns out, mental illness is a heavy burden on the individual and society, but diagnoses are often late or never arrive in some individuals' lives. Moreover, the earlier the diagnosis, the more effective treatment can be enabled. If one respects the privacy of the individual and his or her freedom to undertake treatment or not, the decision to initiate indirect mass screenings using AI could be judged acceptable from a cost-benefit perspective at the aggregate level.

There is indeed an element of paternalism in deciding to make diagnoses without the consent of the individuals concerned, who would see their right to sign an informed consent for the test violated, albeit indirectly. On the other hand, it can be argued that the autonomy of the individual being tested without their knowledge is first diminished, because their data are being used for an unauthorized purpose, and then increased because they are offered a chance to know whether they need treatment, and their life may improve as a result.

By itself, if the subject's data are public, making a psychiatric diagnosis indirectly does not constitute a violation of existing norms if its result is not disclosed to anyone and is not used to discriminate against the individuals themselves. However, the mere existence of a diagnosis, even if not disclosed, creates pressure on the subject receiving it to undergo treatment. Given the nature of psychiatric disorders, which are often never truly permanently curable, this would also create the risk that the individual diagnosed without their authorization would potentially remain discriminated against or looked upon with suspicion in at least some sphere, at least the one in which the diagnosis was made.

Another related issue is that of incidental findings. Given the ease of implementing various functions in AI programs, it cannot be ruled out that companies, institutions, and states—when using algorithms to do personnel selection, admissions testing, or security checks—will also come across profiles of potential antisocial personality or other disorders with behavioural fallout. How should they deal with this? In general, medical practice is to have subjects choose in advance whether to be alerted to incidental findings—for example, the discovery of a cyst in a kidney. But it remains at the discretion of the physician in full awareness of his or her professional duties to warn the individual of the risks they face—for example, when a tumour is discovered.

In the case of psychiatric disorders, there is also a component of preventing hostile acts that the ill person might perform against other people. Therefore, those who find incidental findings of potential signs of a serious mental disorder should also consider whether to make unwanted psychological diagnoses known in some way. The step, however, is short to making such diagnoses widespread, so as to reduce incidents in which severely disturbed people commit serious crimes (Farina, Levin, & Lavazza, 2023; Lavazza, Levin, & Farina, 2023; Levin, Farina, & Lavazza, 2021). However, it is important to point out that the threat of danger and criminality posed by people with mental disorders is lower than thought by the non-expert public (Ghiasi et al., 2023).

7.5 Conclusion

Ultimately, the rapid advancement of artificial intelligence, particularly of algorithms based on ML and LLMs (GAI tools), opens up the possibility of making many processes in medicine more accurate, efficient, and rapid (as outlined in Section 2 above). However, this AI revolution (Lavazza & Farina, 2023a,b; Farina & Karimov, 2022) may also create a series of problems and issues in the profession as well as in society (see also Farina et al., 2024). One phenomenon of particular importance is what we have called 'unwanted psychological diagnoses' (Section 4), which could lead to many ethical and moral dilemmas.

In addition, there is the still unresolved issue of sparse database. A recent study (Bertl et al., 2022) found several problems (including small sample sizes, possibilities of bias, lack of evaluation in production) underlying the algorithms on which these GAI tools rely. Furthermore, one could argue that predictive systems in psychiatry should take into account the relevance of social and environmental factors on the presentation and development of disorders, the so-called *externalist perspective* on mental disorders (Starke et al., 2023), which such tools generally lack.

Despite these latter critical considerations, the push for the use of GAI tools in the profession is likely to increase (Cheng et al., 2023). Two elements may contribute to the possible spread of indirect prognoses and diagnoses of individuals' mental health based on the data and traces left by them in digital environments. The first element is the technical possibility opened up for the first time to conduct automated diagnoses (and prognoses) without the active participation of the individual. The second is what we may call *therapeutic culture*—in brief, the idea that people's emotional states are key elements of their identity and that they should be shaped through expert support.

Obviously, one cannot prohibit the use of the tools made available by artificial intelligence or oppose the therapeutic culture as such. What can be spread, however, is the realization that a perspective of mental health as a positive condition that can be achieved solely with AI tools is unrealistic. As recently stated, 'AI predictions may contribute to unnecessary institutionalization, undermine patients' credibility about their own experiences, and in extreme cases, contribute to decisions to remove a patient's right to make their own treatment decisions' (McCradden et al., 2023, p. 573).

So, we recommend the development of clinical and cultural frameworks that recognize that there is no widespread agreement on what a mental health condition is for everyone. In essence, we feel there is a need to promote the idea that mental health is a multidimensional (time-varying) process, as opposed to a classic, stabilized nosography. Recognizing this point would make it possible to counter the phenomenon of unwanted psychological diagnoses with GAI tools, which we described in Section 4.

The awareness of the risks we have described in this paper should thus lead to careful surveillance of potential abuses as well as to the identification of suitable tools to limit an era of psychiatric control, even if motivated by the best of intentions.

References

Alamir, M., & Alghamdi, M. (2022). The role of generative adversarial network in medical image analysis: An in-depth survey. *ACM Computing Surveys, 55*(5), 1–36.

Arias, D., Saxena, S., & Verguet, S. (2022). Quantifying the global burden of mental disorders and their economic value. *EClinicalMedicine, 54,* 1–10.

Bengio, Y., Ducharme, R., Vincent, P., & Jauvin, C. (2003). A neural probabilistic language model. *Journal of Machine Learning, 3,* 1137–1155.

Bertl, M., Ross, P., & Draheim, D. (2022). A survey on AI and decision support systems in psychiatry—Uncovering a dilemma. *Expert Systems with Applications, 202,* 117464.

Bhatt, J., Nelson, H., Veroff, D., Chang, C., & Overmann, J. (2022). Rethinking when and how to use race appropriately in care delivery. Deloitte Insights. https://www2.deloitte.com/us/en/insights/industry/health-care/racial-bias-health-care-algorithms.html

Bilow, S. (2022). The ever-growing importance of AI and machine learning in media and entertainment. *SMPTE Motion Imaging Journal, 131*(3), 6.

Bloudoff-Indelicato, M. (2015). Threat of interim data leaks prompts call for international rules. *Nature Medicine, 21*(3), 200–201.

Bodenheimer, T., & Sinsky, C. (2014). From triple to quadruple aim: Care of the patient requires care of the provider. *The Annals of Family Medicine, 12*(6), 573–576.

Brynjolfsson, E., Li., D., & Raymond, L. (2023). *Generative AI at work.* National Bureau of Economic Research, Working Paper 31161. http://www.nber.org/papers/w31161

Cheng, S. W., Chang, C. W., Chang, W. J., Wang, H. W., Liang, C. S., Kishimoto, T., Pei-Chen Chang, J., Kuo, J. S., Su, K.-P. (2023). The now and future of ChatGPT and GPT in psychiatry. *Psychiatry and Clinical Neurosciences, 11*(7), 1–5.

Ciancarini, P., Farina, M., Okonicha, O., Smirnova, M., & Succi, G. (2023). Software as story telling: A systematic literature review. *Computer Science Review, 47,* 100517. doi: 10.1016/j.cosrev.2022.100517

Combi, C. (2017). Editorial from the new editor-in-chief: Artificial intelligence in medicine and the forthcoming challenges. *Artificial Intelligence in Medicine, 100*(76), 37–39.

Confalonieri, R., Lucchesi, F., Maffei, G., & Catuara-Solarz, S. (2022). A unified framework for managing sex and gender bias in AI models for healthcare. In D. Cirillo, S. Catuara-Solarz, & E. Guney (Eds.), *Sex and gender bias in technology and artificial intelligence* (pp. 179–204). Academic Press.

Coyle, D., & Weller, A. (2020). "Explaining" machine learning reveals policy challenges. *Science, 368*(6498), 1433–1434.

Dar, S. U. H., Ghanaat, A., Kahmann, J., Ayx, I., Papavassiliou, T., Schoenberg, S. O., & Engelhardt, S. (2023). Investigating data memorization in 3D latent diffusion models for medical image synthesis. *arXiv preprint arXiv:2307.01148*

Darcy, A. M., Louie, A. K., & Roberts, L. W. (2016). Machine learning and the profession of medicine. *JAMA, 315*(6), 551–552.

De Bruijne, M. (2016). Machine learning approaches in medical image analysis: From detection to diagnosis. *Medical Image Analysis, 33,* 94–97.

de Lacy, N., Ramshaw, M. J., McCauley, E., Kerr, K. F., Kaufman, J., & Nathan Kutz, J. (2023). Predicting individual cases of major adolescent psychiatric conditions with artificial intelligence. *Translational Psychiatry, 13*(1), 314.

Deo, R. C. (2015). Machine learning in medicine. *Circulation, 132*(20), 1920–1930.

Devlin, J., Chang, M. W., Lee, K., & Toutanova, K. (2018). BERT: Pre-training of deep bidirectional transformers for language understanding. *arXiv preprint arXiv:1810.04805*

D'Souza, R. F., Amanullah, S., Mathew, M., & Surapaneni, K. M. (2023). Appraising the performance of ChatGPT in psychiatry using 100 clinical case vignettes. *Asian Journal of Psychiatry*, 103770.

Esteva, A., Kuprel, B., Novoa, R. A., Ko, J., Swetter, S. M., Blau, H. M., & Thrun, S. (2017). Dermatologist-level classification of skin cancer with deep neural networks. *Nature, 542*(7639), 115–118.

Farina, M. (2023). Chat GPT in smart home systems: Prospects, risks, and benefits. *Journal of Smart Environments and Green Computing, 3,* 37–43. https://segcjournal.com/article/view/5831

Farina, M., Gorb, A., Kruglov, A., & Succi, G. (2022). Technologies for GQM-based metrics recommender systems: A systematic literature review. *IEEE Access, 10,* 23098–23111. doi: 10.1109/ACCESS.2022.3152397

Farina, M., Karimov, A., Zhdanov, P., & Lavazza, A. (2022). AI and society: A virtue ethics approach. *AI & Society.* https://doi.org/10.1007/s00146-022-01545-5

Farina, M., & Lavazza, A. (2021). The meaning of freedom after Covid-19. *History and Philosophy of the Life Sciences, 43*(3), doi: https://doi.org/10.1007/s40656-020-00354-7

Farina, M., & Lavazza, A. (2023). ChatGPT in society: Emerging issues. *Frontiers in Artificial Intelligence, 6,* 1130913. https://doi.org/10.3389/frai.2023.1130913

Farina, M., Lavazza, A., Sartori, G., & Pedrycz, W. (2024). Machine learning in human creativity: Status and perspectives. *AI & Society.* https://doi.org/10.1007/s00146-023-01836-5

Farina, M., Levin, S., & Lavazza, A., (2023). Pushing the boundaries of the quarantine model: Philosophical concerns and policy implications. *Diametros,* https://diametros.uj.edu.pl/diametros/article/view/1892/1751

Farina, M., Yu, X., & Lavazza, A. (2024). Ethical considerations and policy interventions concerning the impact of ChatGPT in the economy and in society. *AI and Ethics.* https://doi.org/10.1007/s43681-023-00405-2

Finlayson, S. G., Subbaswamy, A., Singh, K., Bowers, J., Kupke, A., Zittrain, J., Kohane, I. S., & Saria, S. (2021). The clinician and dataset shift in artificial intelligence. *New England Journal of Medicine, 385*(3), 283–286.

Furedi, F. (2004). *Therapy culture: Cultivating vulnerability in an uncertain age.* New York: Routledge.

Ghiasi, N., Azhar, Y., & Singh, J. (Last update March 2023). *Psychiatric illness and criminality.* Treasure Island, FL: StatPearls Publishing. https://www.ncbi.nlm.nih.gov/books/NBK537064/

Goodfellow, I., Pouget-Abadie, J., Mirza, M., Xu, B., Warde-Farley, D., Ozair, S., Courville, A., & Bengio, Y. (2014). https://arxiv.org/abs/1406.2661

Hannun, A. Y., Rajpurkar, P., Haghpanahi, M., Tison, G. H., Bourn, C., Turakhia, M. P., & Ng, A. Y. (2019). Cardiologist-level arrhythmia detection and classification in ambulatory electrocardiograms using a deep neural network. *Nature Medicine, 25*(1), 65–69. https://doi.org/10.1038/s41591-018-0268-3

Haq, I. U., Haq, I., & Xu, B. (2021). Artificial intelligence in personalized cardiovascular medicine and cardiovascular imaging. *Cardiovascular Diagnosis and Therapy, 11*(3), 911.

Henry, T. A. (2021). 7 tips for responsible use of health care AI. American Medical Association (AMA). https://www.ama-assn.org/practice-management/digital/7-tips-responsible-use-health-care-ai

Hutchins, J. (2004). Two precursors of machine translation: Artsrouni and Trojanskij. *International Journal of Translation, 16*(1), 11–31.

Jarke, J., & Breiter, A. (2019) Editorial: The datafication of education. *Learning, Media and Technology, 44*(1), 1–6. https://doi.org/10.1080/17439884.2019.1573833

Jo, T., Nho, K., & Saykin, A. J. (2019). Deep learning in Alzheimer's disease: Diagnostic classification and prognostic prediction using neuroimaging data. *Frontiers in Aging Neuroscience, 11,* 220.

Jordan, M. I. (1986). Serial order: A parallel distributed processing approach. ICS Report 8604. *Institute for Cognitive Science.* La Jolla, CA: University of California–San Diego.

Kather, J., Pearson, A., Halama, N., Jäger, D., Krause, J., Loosen, S. H., Marx, A., Boor, P., Tacke, F., Neumann, U. P., Grabsch, H. I., Yoshikawa, T., Brenner, H., Chang-Claude, J., Hoffmeister, M., & Trautwein, C. (2019). Deep learning can predict microsatellite instability directly from histology in gastrointestinal cancer. *Nature Medicine, 25*(7). https://doi.org/10.1038/s41591-019-0462-y

Kessler, R. C., Berglund, P., Demler, O., Jin, R., Merikangas, K. R., & Walters, E. E. (2005). Lifetime prevalence and age-of-onset distributions of DSM-IV disorders in the National Comorbidity Survey Replication. *Archives of General Psychiatry, 62*(6), 593–602.

Kingma, D. P., & Welling, M. (2013). Auto-encoding variational Bayes. *arXiv preprint arXiv:1312.6114*

Kong, X., Ai, B., Kong, Y., Su, L., Ning, Y., Howard, N., Gong, S., Li, C., Wang, J., Lee, W. T., Wang, J., Kong, Y., Wang, J., & Fang, Y. (2019). Artificial intelligence: A key to relieve China's insufficient and unequally distributed medical resources. *American Journal of Translational Research, 11*(5), 2632.

Kong, X., Feng, M., & Wang, R. (2015). The current status and challenges of establishment and utilization of medical big data in China. *European Geriatric Medicine, 6*(6), 515–517.

Krizhevsky, A., Sutskever, I., & Hinton, G. E. (2012). Imagenet classification with deep convolutional neural networks. *Advances in Neural Information Processing Systems, 25,* 1–9.

Krizhevsky, A., Sutskever, I., & Hinton, G. E. (2017). ImageNet classification with deep convolutional neural networks. *Communications of the ACM, 60*(6), 84–90.

Lal, A., Dang, J., Nabzdyk, C., Gajic, O., & Herasevich, V. (2022). Regulatory oversight and ethical concerns surrounding software as medical device (SaMD) and digital twin technology in healthcare. *Annals of Translational Medicine, 10*(18), 1–7.

Lancet Regional Health (2023). Embracing generative AI in health care. *The Lancet Regional Health–Europe, 30,* 100677. https://doi.org/10.1016/j.lanepe.2023.100677

Lavazza, A., Levin, S., & Farina, M., (2023). The quarantine model and its limits. *Philosophia.* https://doi.org/10.1007/s11406-023-00683-4

Lavazza, A., & Farina, M. (2023a). Leveraging autonomous weapon systems: realism and humanitarianism in modern warfare. *Technology in Society,* https://doi.org/10.1016/j.techsoc.2023.102322

Lavazza, A., & Farina, M. (2023b). Infosphere, datafication, and decision-making processes in the AI era. *Topoi, 42,* 843–856. https://link.springer.com/article/10.1007/s11245-023-09919-0

LeCun, Y., Bengio, Y., & Hinton, G. (2015). Deep learning. *Nature, 521*(7553), 436–444.

LeCun, Y., Boser, B., Denker, J. S., Henderson, D., Howard, R. E., Hubbard, W., & Jackel, L. D. (1989). Backpropagation applied to handwritten zip code recognition. *Neural Computation, 1*(4), 541–551.

Leichsenring, F., Steinert, C., Rabung, S., & Ioannidis, J. P. (2022). The efficacy of psychotherapies and pharmacotherapies for mental disorders in adults: An umbrella review and meta-analytic evaluation of recent meta-analyses. *World Psychiatry, 21*(1), 133–145.

Lenharo, M. (2023). An AI revolution is brewing in medicine. What will it look like? Emerging generalist models could overcome some limitations of first-generation machine-learning tools for clinical use. *Nature, 622,* 686–688.

Levin, S., Farina, M., & Lavazza, A. (2021). Dealing with criminal behavior: The inaccuracy of the quarantine analogy. *Criminal Law and Philosophy.* doi: 10.1007/s11572-021-09608-2

Lira, B., Gardner, M., Quirk, A., Stone, C., Rao, A., Ungar, L., Hutt, S., Hickman, L., D'Mello, S. K., & Duckworth, A. L. (2023). Using artificial intelligence to assess personal qualities in college admissions. *Science Advances, 9*(41), eadg9405.

Luedde, T. (2019). Deep learning microsatellite instability directly from histology in gastrointestinal cancer. *Nature Medicine, 25,* 1054–1056. doi: 10.1038/s41591-019-0462-y

Mamoshina, P., Vieira, A., Putin, E., & Zhavoronkov, A. (2016). Applications of deep learning in biomedicine. *Molecular Pharmaceutics, 13*(5), 1445–1454.

McCradden, M., Hui, K., & Buchman, D. Z. (2023). Evidence, ethics and the promise of artificial intelligence in psychiatry. *Journal of Medical Ethics, 49*(8), 573–579.

Meskó, B., & Topol, E. J. (2023). The imperative for regulatory oversight of large language models (or generative AI) in healthcare. *NPJ Digital Medicine, 6*(1), 120.

Minerva, F., & Giubilini, A. (2023). Is AI the future of mental healthcare? *Topoi, 42,* 809–817. https://doi.org/10.1007/s11245-023-09932-3

Morley, J., DeVito, N. J., & Zhang, J. (2023). Generative AI for medical research. *BMJ, 382.*

Obermeyer, Z., & Emanuel, E. J. (2016). Predicting the future—Big data, machine learning, and clinical medicine. *The New England Journal of Medicine, 375*(13), 1216.

Obermeyer, Z., Powers, B., Vogeli, C., & Mullainathan, S. (2019). Dissecting racial bias in an algorithm used to manage the health of populations. *Science, 366*(6464), 447–453.

Payne, T. H., Alonso, W. D., Markiel, J. A., Lybarger, K., & White, A. A. (2018). Using voice to create hospital progress notes: Description of a mobile application and supporting system integrated with a commercial electronic health record. *Journal of Biomedical Informatics, 77,* 91–96.

Pearl, J. (2000). *Causality: Models, reasoning, and inference.* Cambridge, UK: Cambridge University Press.

Peng, Y., Rousseau, J. F., Shortliffe, E. H., & Weng, C. (2023). AI-generated text may have a role in evidence-based medicine. *Nature Medicine, 29,* 1593–1594.

Penninx, B. W., Benros, M. E., Klein, R. S., & Vinkers, C. H. (2022). How COVID-19 shaped mental health: From infection to pandemic effects. *Nature Medicine, 28*(10), 2027–2037.

Pham, K. T., Nabizadeh, A., & Selek, S. (2022). Artificial intelligence and chatbots in psychiatry. *Psychiatric Quarterly, 93*(1), 249–253.

Plana-Ripoll, O., Pedersen, C. B., Agerbo, E., Holtz, Y., Erlangsen, A., Canudas-Romo, V., Andersen, P. K., Charlson, F. J., Christensen, M. K., Erskine, H. E., Ferrari, A. J., Iburg, K. M., Momen, N., Mortensen, P. B., Nordentoft, M., Santomauro, D. F., Scott, J. G., Whiteford, H. A., Weye, N., McGrath, J. J., . . . Laursen, T. M. (2019). Comprehensive analysis of mortality-related health metrics associated with mental disorders: A nationwide, register-based cohort study. *Lancet, 394*(10211), 1827–1835. https://doi.org/10.1016/S0140-6736(19)32316-5

Price, W., & Nicholson, I. I. (2021). Problematic interactions between AI and health privacy. *Utah Law Review, 4,* 925–936.

Rajpurkar, P., Hannun, A. Y., Haghpanahi, M., Bourn, C., & Ng, A. Y. (2017). Cardiologist-level arrhythmia detection with convolutional neural networks. *arXiv preprint arXiv:1707.01836*

Ryberg, J., & Roberts, J. V. (2022). *Sentencing and artificial intelligence.* Oxford, UK: Oxford University Press.

Ryman-Tubb, N. F., Krause, P., & Garn, W. (2018). How artificial intelligence and machine learning research impacts payment card fraud detection: A survey and industry benchmark. *Engineering Applications of Artificial Intelligence, 76,* 130–157.

Singh, A. K., Anand, A., Lv, Z., Ko, H., & Mohan, A. (2021). A survey on healthcare data: A security perspective. *ACM Transactions on Multimedia Computing Communications and Applications, 17*(2s), 1–26.

Sohail, S. S. (2023). A promising start and not a panacea: ChatGPT's early impact and potential in medical science and biomedical engineering research. *Annals of Biomedical Engineering,* 1–5.

Starke, G., D'Imperio, A., & Ienca, M. (2023). Out of their minds? Externalist challenges for using AI in forensic psychiatry. *Frontiers in Psychiatry, 14.*

Stoumpos, A. I., Kitsios, F., & Talias, M. A. (2023). Digital transformation in healthcare: Technology acceptance and its applications. *International Journal of Environmental Research and Public Health, 20*(4), 3407.

Valentine, L., D'Alfonso, S., Lederman, R. (2023). Recommender systems for mental health apps: Advantages and ethical challenges. *AI & Society, 38*(4), 1627–1638.

Vartan, S. (2019). Racial bias found in a major health care risk algorithm. *Scientific American, 24.*

Vaswani, A., Shazeer, N., Parmar, N., Uszkoreit, J., Jones, L., Gomez, A. N., Kaiser, L., & Polosukhin, I. (2017). Attention is all you need. *Advances in Neural Information Processing Systems, 30.*

Vayena, E., & Blasimme, A. (2022). A systemic approach to the oversight of machine learning clinical translation. *The American Journal of Bioethics, 22*(5), 23–25.

Walsh, C. G., Ribeiro, J. D., & Franklin, J. C. (2017). Predicting risk of suicide attempts over time through machine learning. *Clinical Psychological Science, 5*(3), 457–469.

Weizenbaum, J. (1966). ELIZA—A computer program for the study of natural language communication between man and machine. *Communications of the ACM, 9*(1), 36–45. https://doi.org/10.1145/365153.365168

Winograd, T. (1972). *Understanding natural language.* Cambridge, MA: Academic Press.

Yue, W., Wang, Z., Chen, H., Payne, A., & Liu, X. (2018). Machine learning with applications in breast cancer diagnosis and prognosis. *Designs, 2*(2), 13. doi: 10.3390/designs2020013

Zhou, B., Yang, G., Shi, Z., & Ma, S. (2022). Natural language processing for smart healthcare. *IEEE Reviews in Biomedical Engineering*, doi: 10.1109/RBME .2022.3210270

Chapter 8

The Changing Landscape of the World Influenced by the Impact of Technology Driven by Artificial Intelligence

Moti Zwilling,[1*] Idit Yutav Sohlberg,[1] and Avi Zigdon[2]

[1]Department of Economics and Business Administration, Ariel University, Israel

[2]Department of Health Systems Management, School of Health Sciences, Ariel University, Israel

*Corresponding author

8.1 Introduction

8.1.1 General

Over the past 10 years, artificial intelligence (AI) has been used in an increasing number of applications and technologies to enhance performance and make better decisions (Duan et al., 2019). In fact, people frequently use AI programs without realizing it. Examples include using smart cleaning robots, navigation apps, stock market investing, retail purchases, and computer security detection tools while using a computer. As AI has grown over the past 10 years, it has begun to change a wide range of industries, including healthcare, finance, and more (Bughin et al., 2017). The use of smart algorithms to boost productivity across a wide range of industries and applications in automation are two of the most prominent changes in our society (Parker & Grote, 2022). While these developments created opportunities for workers to find new jobs, they also raised concerns about job displacement (Engel & Dahlhaus, 2022).

Furthermore, the reliance on AI has compelled managers and staff to continuously learn new skills and embrace AI-based technologies, some of which are being used to carry out repetitive tasks that have historically been completed by humans. The integration of AI into the workplace has also defined the future job market and led to the further development of new workplace skills, such as data analysis, problem-solving, and creative thinking.

8.1.2 AI and healthcare

The emergence of AI has also made it possible to have significant effects on medical services and treatments, including personalized treatment plans, diagnostic tools for a variety of illnesses, and predictive analysis, which is also connected to a recently created field called *real-world evidence* (Diebolt et al., 2019). A program's capacity to evaluate data and facilitate tailored care has revolutionized drug discovery and drug-based therapy, reduced recovery times, and boosted treatment precision measures.

AI in healthcare holds promise for uses beyond patient care (Sparrow & Hatherley, 2019). AI systems have been used to identify patterns and trends in both healthy and unhealthy populations, which has helped decision-makers make better choices that could have an impact on their patients and society. By identifying patterns and symptoms that correspond to the severity of the illness in various cohorts, for instance, AI was able to reduce the COVID-19 virus's ability to spread across national borders (Allam & Jones, 2020).

Furthermore, the use of intelligent and portable sensors and devices makes it possible to remotely monitor, diagnose, and treat illnesses as well as abnormal patient behaviors, such as challenging behaviors in individuals with autism spectrum disorders (ASD) and potentially dangerous situations that call for quick preventative measures.

Needless to say, the field of surgery has changed dramatically as a result of the use of AI to increase the efficiency of surgical procedures (McFarlane, 2020). However, the use of AI in medical procedures raises concerns about ethical issues and privacy—all related to patient data. The need to strike a balance between patients' privacy and innovative technology still needs to be carefully considered, as AI is still sensitive to false positive detection issues (Elliott & Soifer, 2020).

8.1.3 AI and education

Of all the changes AI has brought about in a variety of fields, its impact on education has been especially apparent. In recent years, there has been a notable increase in the incorporation of AI into training methods and educational programs (Pedro et al., 2019). In higher education, new learning platforms and intelligent technologies for data science and programming have been implemented. Students have been trained with new tools and capabilities to handle and analyze data.

However, the new AI-based pedagogical tools may cause a number of issues, particularly with content and programming code that automatic tools such as ChatGPT® may use (Denny et al., 2023). As a result, students may be prevented from strengthening their critical thinking and problem-solving abilities. To optimize the advantages of the new AI-based technology in the education sector, all of this should be taken into account.

8.1.4 Social and ethical issues

Concerns regarding AI's ethical implications are growing as the technology advances across numerous fields (Khogali & Mekid, 2023). Given the often "black box" approach of AI programs, it is reasonable to argue that algorithmic bias could result. This raises potential risks related to decision-making, job displacement, and other areas. Furthermore, the notion that a small number of individuals might be exposed to massive volumes of data necessitates regulatory frameworks and careful thought. Machine learning algorithms often use a technique called *supervised learning,* as AI is typically trained on historical data (Krishnan et al., 2022).

The way the training is conducted may encourage the bias of the algorithms, which can take many different forms. For example, it could lead to biased hiring practices for employees and biased criminal and legal decisions made by "justice" algorithms, which would violate the fairness compartment (Gitiaux & Rangwala, 2019). Furthermore, because AI programs aren't always transparent, it can be challenging to determine whether developing and implementing them will advance positive social norms and values in our society.

Virtual chatbots have become a common tool for interpersonal communication as a result of AI's influence on personal communication tools (Ahn et al., 2022). In our society, automatic programs are used to create interpersonal communication and skill norms as well as to provide answers to questions ranging from basic to sophisticated. The ability to engage with AI tools and work remotely has also altered the work-life balance.

8.1.5 Agriculture and environmental change

AI holds significant promise for mitigating climate change and enhancing agricultural productivity through the application of *precision agriculture* (Mishra & Mishra, 2023). Smart cities allow for better control over urban life, which is characterized by reduced energy use, reduced electronic waste, and increased agricultural yields for the benefit of society.

These smart cities are managed by sensor-based AI programs. In many countries, the need to control energy through AI-based IT management systems has resulted in improvements to mobility and urban transportation, including better traffic flow and lower vehicle CO_2 emissions. It is now feasible to plan and focus on environmental conservation efforts and enhance decision-making regarding vulnerable areas that may be affected by natural hazards such as floods and storms, thanks to climate change and earthquake forecasting. To guarantee that these technologies will be used appropriately and to reduce adjusted risks, collaboration between government, business, and academic institutions is essential.

8.1.6 The positive and negative impact of AI

Without a doubt, AI has enormously beneficial effects that redefine industries. In manufacturing lines, intelligent automation that minimizes errors through AI algorithms is well adopted (Floridi et al., 2023). Companies use machine learning algorithms to mine databases for insightful information that helps them better target their strategic goals and provide better customer service in response to dynamic, competitive markets.

Furthermore, it was discovered that AI was a vital tool for scientific research, allowing for the acceleration of advancement in numerous scientific domains that necessitate image processing, grouping, and detecting patterns, as well as finding correlations between variables. Furthermore, the relationship between genetics and artificial intelligence is one of the most well-known fields affecting societal resilience (Xu et al., 2019).

Among the most significant results in precision medicine and the application of genomics in future medicine are the identification of disease markers and drug discovery. These endeavors add to our understanding of genes and diseases and enhance therapeutic treatment, improve patient outcomes, reduce adverse events, and pave the way for the emergence of a new field in medicine known as *personalized medicine.*

AI is also utilized in computer vision and speech recognition to assist people with disabilities. Models of natural language processing (NLP) are used to comprehend speech impairments and help people interact more effectively with their environment. In terms of the economy, using AI tools makes it possible to create new goods and services as well as business models that support long-term growth and entrepreneurship.

However, AI is known to be vulnerable to algorithmic bias and frequently requires a wide variety of datasets (Roselli et al., 2019). Frequent audits of AI systems and an understanding of their decision-making processes are imperative owing to the lack of transparency in algorithmic decision-making. Furthermore, laws and rules requiring data encryption, anonymization, and stringent database access must be taken into account when addressing privacy concerns. In order to prevent malicious software and tools from altering data, security concerns should also be addressed.

8.2 Case studies

In light of the aforementioned, this chapter suggests investigating the following research questions:

- **Research Question I:** How does AI affect people's behavior, and what are the drawbacks for individuals using it?
- **Research Question II:** How much do people trust chatbot-based AI programs such as ChatGPT?

Two complementary studies were conducted in order to address the above questions. Study I was carried out to address Research Question I, and Study 2 was utilized to address Research Question II.

Using text mining techniques recommended by Isoaho et al. (2021) and Grimmer and Stewart (2013), a quantitative content analysis was carried out on the abstracts of scientific publications in the first study. In both studies, Orange data mining version 3.61 was used to analyze data combining quantitative and qualitative content analysis.

8.2.1 Study I

This study set out to survey the scientific literature and explore the role of AI and its impact across a range of scientific fields.

Method: Data collection and analysis

A corpus of scientific articles covering the years 2020–2023 was gathered from the Web of Science (WoS) database, per the recommendations of Gheyas and Abdallah (2016) and Sardi et al. (2017). The graphical search combo box controlled the search and included the following editions:

- Science Citation Index Expanded (SCI-EXPANDED): 1993–present
- Social Sciences Citation Index (SSCI): 1993–present
- Arts & Humanities Citation Index (AHCI): 1993–present
- Conference Proceedings Citation Index–Science (CPCI-S): 1990–present
- Conference Proceedings Citation Index–Social Science & Humanities (CPCI-SSH): 1990–present
- Emerging Sources Citations Index (ESCI): 2015–present

Prior to starting the literature search, "AI challenges and domains" was selected as the search's scope. The search was narrowed down to a corpus that contained only scientific research articles that had been published in peer-reviewed journals. Every paper was assessed in line with the requirements of Sardi et al. (2017) and Isoaho et al. (2021). The abstracts of a few randomly chosen papers (1% of the corpus) were automatically scanned using the Orange data mining model version 3.61 analysis tool (topic modeling and word cloud) (see Figure 8.1).

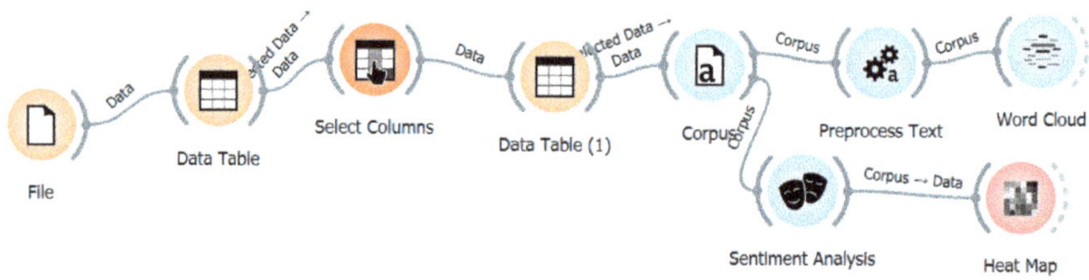

Figure 8.1 Word cloud and sentiment analysis data mining analysis purposed by the model format's creation in Orange version 3.61

8.1.2 Results

The topic query was addressed in 1,114 scientific papers that came up in the first search. However, fewer papers were received overall after the search queue was expanded to include the word "trust." In this phase, 45 papers were received. Following the addition of the word "technology," the corpus consisted of only 22 publications.

The topic of AI technology and its impact on society is still in its infancy, but the number of publications and citations related to it appears to have some bearing, particularly when it comes to technology trust (see Figure 8.2). Furthermore, the fields of computer science and information systems (ranked

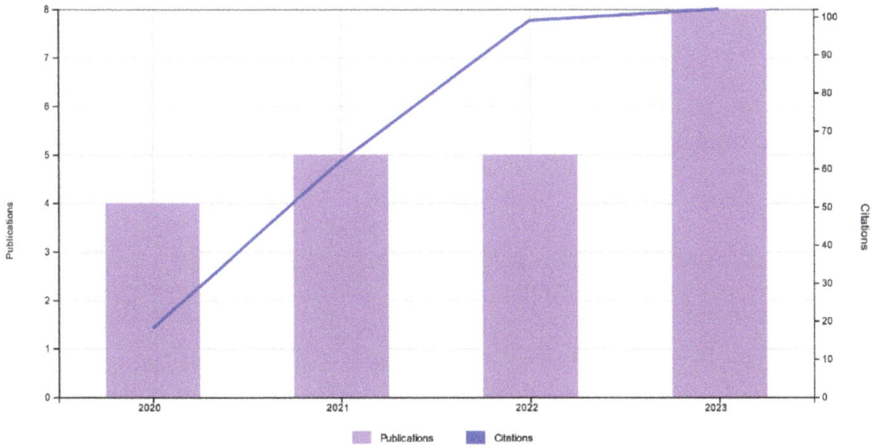

Figure 8.2 WoS citations and publications on AI and technology between 2020 and 2023

first), telecommunication (ranked second), and engineering (ranked third) are the primary areas in which AI technology and trust are discussed in the scholarly literature (see Figure 8.3).

A word cloud analysis of the top papers in this field highlights the fact that chatbots used for consultation are employed mostly in the health sector. People are also looking for guidance and solutions related to their medical issues as well

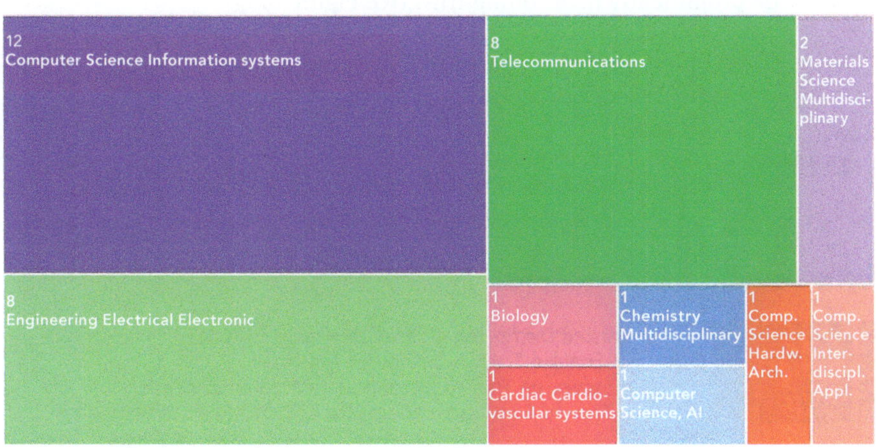

Figure 8.3 Technology and AI-related WoS publication domains

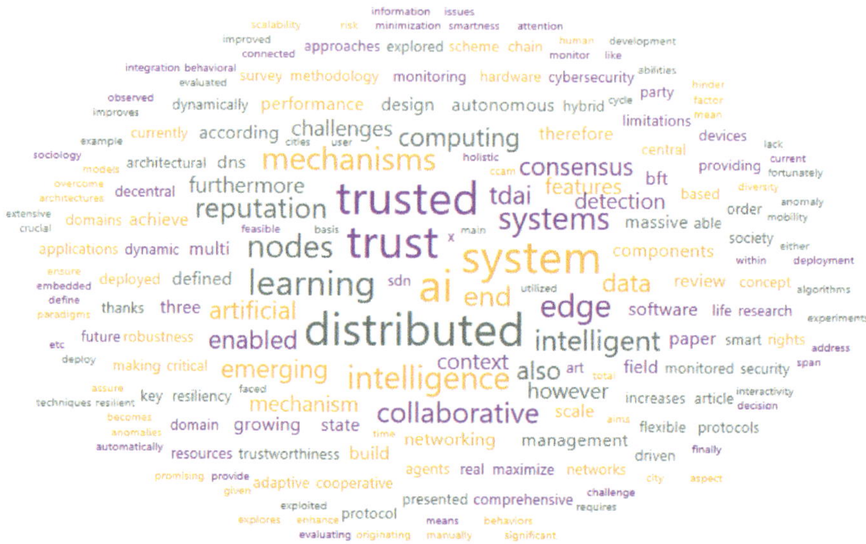

Figure 8.4 A word cloud containing important scientific papers about technology and artificial intelligence

as for diagnostic purposes. Although they are significant, accuracy and expertise are not the primary drivers of chatbot use (see Figure 8.4). In addition, sentiment analysis of the top papers revealed a favorable view of AI technology, with the paper's title prominently mentioning trust (see Figure 8.5).

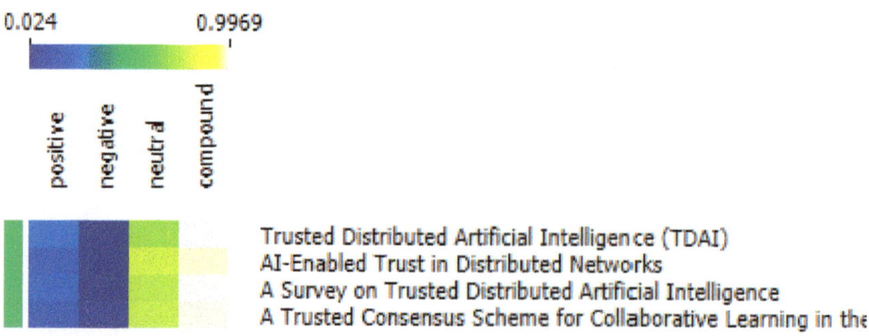

Figure 8.5 Sentiment analysis of leading articles about technology and artificial intelligence

8.2.2 Study II

The purpose of this study was to determine the degree of public trust in chatbot-based AI programs such as ChatGPT versus the belief of the machine themselves, based on a qualitative content analysis of a secondary survey provided by the Mendeley™ repository.

Study II sample and measures

The sample contained two files. There were 80 respondents in the first study sample. A secondary sample based on Moilanen's (2023) questionnaire was used to evaluate the differences in users' trust perceptions when using chatbots as a support tool for mental health self-care. In addition, a second sample from Huh (2023) was used. We analyzed ChatGPT when asked how much respondents believe we can trust AI chatbots when asking them about disease diagnosis and patient care. The formal question presented to the chatbot was: *"Are answers to disease diagnosis and patient care from ChatGPT trustable?"*

Measures, tools, and analysis

To assess ChatGPT's effectiveness, 10 published case reports from Korea (the first sample) were examined. We asked ChatGPT for a precise diagnosis and treatment plan. The secondary sample data was examined with SPSS® version 29.0, and respondents' data was subjected to regression and frequency analysis.

Results

First sample: Out of the ten cases, three were successfully resolved after ChatGPT was provided with the patient's symptoms, examination results, and medical history. With the addition of laboratory, pathological, and radiological results, the accuracy rate rose to seven out of 10. Four times, ChatGPT's response contained inappropriate content; in one instance, it contained no information about appropriate treatment.

Furthermore, word cloud analysis using the Orange 3.61 version is still required for the chatbot learning phase, so long as accurate and professional responses to medical case inquiries are still absent (see Figure 8.6). In other words, the word cloud analysis of chatbot responses indicates that individuals primarily use chatbots as supportive systems to enhance their health and medical consultations, primarily to get information about their diagnostic results and medical condition. They do not, however, view it as a professional recommendation because the chatbot is unable to reliably assess medical cases and offer accurate responses.

Figure 8.6 Sample I: Word cloud prominent words found from a corpus provided by ChatGPT as a response to medical cases

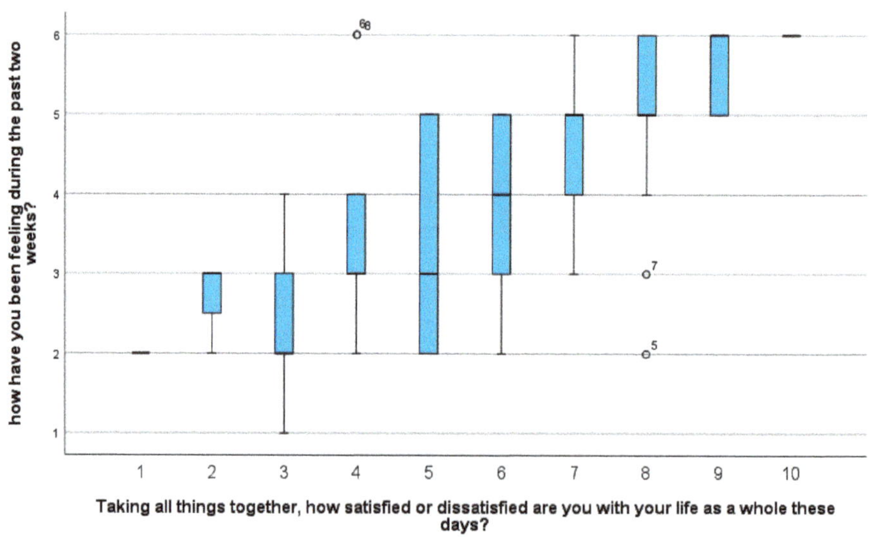

Figure 8.7 Sample II: Box–Plot diagram showing the level of satisfaction of respondents with their life in general versus the past two weeks

Table 8.1 Sample II: Regression Analysis, Second Sample[a]

Model	R	R Square	Adjusted R Square	Std. Error of the Estimate
1	.808[a]	.652	.642	.751
2	.851[b]	.723	.707	.680
3	.874[c]	.765	.743	.636

a. Predictors: (Constant), I am confident in the system.
b. Predictors: (Constant), I am confident in the system, The system is reliable.
c. Predictors: (Constant), I am confident in the system, The system is reliable, Taking all things together, how satisfied or dissatisfied are you with your life as a whole these days?
[a]Trust in AI based technology (chatbot) was used as a dependent variable vs. several predictors that were used as independent variables.

Second Sample: The majority of the 80 respondents (5.77–9.13) are satisfied with their lives, on a Likert scale from 1 (not at all satisfied) to 10 (very satisfied; see Figure 8.7). According to Table 8.1's regression results, just two predictors ($R^2 = .723$) were able to account for 76.5% of the variance. A sufficient degree of trust in chatbots to respond to inquiries about medical or health conditions was found to be predicted by confidence in AI-based systems (chatbots) ($\beta = .525, p < .01$) and dependable responses ($\beta = .389, p < .01$) (see Table 8.2).

8.3 Discussion

The current study's findings demonstrate that AI is still regarded as a significant area of information technology (IT) and that it has a significant impact on a wide range of industries and domains, including education, computer science and cyber security, finance, business, environmental sciences, and health. The academic community has been researching the effects of AI on human behavior in recent years, and an increasing number of studies in this field have been published in an effort to comprehend how technology-based AI affects our evolving global environment. According to the current study, information systems, computer science, and related fields are better connected to AI technology.

People primarily use ChatGPT and related chatbots to answer basic queries, such as getting first medical advice on their health and basic queries that could corroborate the advice of a licensed medical professional. Still, there's a long way to go before these machines can react appropriately and provide their customers with statistically accurate responses. However, it was discovered that people's trust in AI is crucial, and they are more likely to use AI-based technology if it can both

Table 8.2 Sample II: Regression analysis, predictors: Trust in AI-based technology[a]

Model		Unstandardized Coefficients		Standardized Coefficients	t	Sig.
	B	Std. Error	Beta			
1	(Constant)	.329	.580		.567	.574
	I am confident in the system	.894	.110	.808	8.099	**<.001**
2	(Constant)	.288	.525		.549	.587
	I am confident in the system	.581	.145	.525	3.991	**<.001**
	The system is reliable	.345	.116	.389	2.961	**.006**
3	(Constant)	–.236	.538		–.438	.664
	I am confident in the system	.526	.138	.476	3.813	**<.001**
	The system is reliable	.374	.110	.422	3.411	**.002**
	Taking all things together, how satisfied or dissatisfied are you with your life as a whole these days?	.114	.048	.206	2.403	**.022**

[a] Dependent variable: I can trust the system

accurately answer their queries and respect their privacy. This is still a controversial topic from an ethical standpoint, and it should be considered when developing new AI-based technology in the future.

References

Allam, Z., & Jones, D. S. (2020, February). On the Coronavirus (COVID-19) outbreak and the smart city network: Universal data sharing standards coupled with artificial intelligence (AI) to benefit urban health monitoring and management. *Healthcare, 8*(1), 46). MDPI.

Ahn, J., Kim, J., & Sung, Y. (2022). The effect of gender stereotypes on artificial intelligence recommendations. *Journal of Business Research, 141,* 50–59.

Bughin, J., Hazan, E., Ramaswamy, S., Chui, M., Allas, T., Dahlström, P., Henke, N., & Trench, M. (2017). Artificial intelligence: The next digital frontier.

Denny, P., Prather, J., Becker, B. A., Finnie-Ansley, J., Hellas, A., Leinonen, J., Luxton-Reilly, A., Reeves, B. N., Santos, A., & Sarsa, S. (2023). Computing education in the era of generative AI. *arXiv preprint arXiv:2306.02608*

Diebolt, V., Azancot, I., & Boissel, F-H., Adenot, I., Balague, C., Barthélémy, P., Boubenna, N., Coulonjou, H., Fernandez, X., Habran, E., Lethiec, F., Longin, J., Metzinger, A., Merlière, Y., Pham, E., Philip, P., Roche, T., Saurin, W., Tirel, A., Voisin, E., & Marchal, T. (2019). Artificial intelligence: Which services, which applications, which results and which development today in clinical research? Which impact on the quality of care? Which recommendations? *Therapie, 74*(1), 155–164.

Duan, Y., Edwards, J. S., & Dwivedi, Y. K. (2019). Artificial intelligence for decision making in the era of big data—Evolution, challenges and research agenda. *International Journal of Information Management, 48,* 63–71.

Elliott, D., & Soifer, E. (2022). AI technologies, privacy, and security. *Frontiers in Artificial Intelligence, 5,* 826737.

Engel, U., & Dahlhaus, L. (2023). Artificial intelligence and the labor market: Expected development and ethical concerns in the German and European context. In: Engel, U. (Ed.), *Robots in care and everyday life.* SpringerBriefs in Sociology. Springer, Cham. https://doi.org/10.1007/978-3-031-11447-2_2

Floridi, L. (2023). The ethics of artificial intelligence: Principles, challenges, and opportunities. Oxford University Press. https://doi.org/10.1093/oso/9780198883098.001.0001

Gheyas, I. A., & Abdallah, A. E. (2016). Detection and prediction of insider threats to cyber security: A systematic literature review and meta-analysis. *Big Data Analytics, 1*(1), 1–29.

Gitiaux, X., & Rangwala, H. (2019). Multi-differential fairness auditor for black box classifiers. *arXiv preprint arXiv:1903.07609*

Grimmer, J., & Stewart, B. M. (2013). Text as data: The promise and pitfalls of automatic content analysis methods for political texts. *Political Analysis, 21*(3), 267–297.

Isoaho, K., Gritsenko, D., & Mäkelä, E. (2021). Topic modeling and text analysis for qualitative policy research. *Policy Studies Journal, 49*(1), 300–324.

Huh, S. (2023). Can we trust AI chatbots' answers about disease diagnosis and patient care? *J Korean Med Assoc, 66*(4), 218–222. doi: 10.5124/jkma.2023.66.4.218

Khogali, H. O., & Mekid, S. (2023). The blended future of automation and AI: Examining some long-term societal and ethical impact features. *Technology in Society, 73,* 102232.

Krishnan, R., Rajpurkar, P., & Topol, E. J. (2022). Self-supervised learning in medicine and healthcare. *Nature Biomedical Engineering, 6*(12), 1346–1352.

McFarlane, M. (2020). Artificial intelligence: The new frontier in surgery. *European Journal of Medical and Health Sciences, 2*(4).

Mishra, H., & Mishra, D. (2023). Artificial intelligence and machine learning in agriculture: Transforming farming systems. *Research Trends in Agriculture Science, 1,* 1–16.

Moilanen, J. (2023). Supporting mental health self-care discovery through a chatbot: Dataset. figshare. Dataset. https://doi.org/10.6084/m9.figshare.22193803.v1

Parker, S. K., & Grote, G. (2022). Automation, algorithms, and beyond: Why work design matters more than ever in a digital world. *Applied Psychology, 71*(4), 1171–1204.

Pedro, F., Subosa, M., Rivas, A., & Valverde, P. (2019). Artificial intelligence in education: Challenges and opportunities for sustainable development.

Roselli, D., Matthews, J., & Talagala, N. (2019, May). Managing bias in AI. *Companion Proceedings of The 2019 World Wide Web Conference* (pp. 539–544). https://doi.org/10.1145/3308560.3317590

Sardi, L., Idri, A., & Fernández-Alemán, J. L. (2017). A systematic review of gamification in e-Health. *Journal of Biomedical Informatics, 71,* 31–48.

Sparrow, R., & Hatherley, J. J. (2019). The promise and perils of AI in medicine. Monash University.

Xu, J., Yang, P., Xue, S., Sharma, B., Sanchez-Martin, M., Wang, F., Beaty, K. A., Dehan, E., & Parikh, B. (2019). Translating cancer genomics into precision medicine with artificial intelligence: Applications, challenges and future perspectives. *Human Genetics, 138*(2), 109–124. https://doi.org/10.1007/s00439-019-01970-5

Chapter 9

Stochastic Parroting: Leaders Versus the Artificial Intelligence Echo Chamber

Joseph Crawford[1*] and Michael Cowling[2]

[1]University of Tasmania

[2]Central Queensland University

*Corresponding author

9.1 Introduction

Ipsa scientia potestas est, a Latin phrase from Sir Francis Bacon's 1597 text *Meditationes Sacrae,* highlights that knowledge itself is power. This comment was made in a time about 150 years after the emergence of Gutenberg's printing press and many more beyond the woodblock printing model adopted in 9th-century China. It offered a representation that knowledge workers came to know and trust as their call to productive and meaningful work. The pursuit of knowledge, and its management and regulation, was valuable.

Bacon's comment continues to have new meaning some 400 years later. In 1983, the advent of the communication protocol (transfer control protocol/ internetwork protocol [TCP/IP]) enabled what we commonly refer to as the

Internet. The Internet's popularity did not take shape until the late 1990s, as it began being used by companies in building commercial ideas. It did not last, as underlying quality led to a bust in the early 2000s. Yet, the effects were large, and new approaches to knowledge dissemination were key in exciting new investors and users alike.

The dot-com boom and bust saw the NASDAQ index move from less than 1,000 to 5,048.62 in five years and return to 1,139.90 by 2002. The NASDAQ did not again reach the 5,000–6,000 range again until 2015. Technical investment knowledge aside, the rapid emergence of new approaches to engaging with knowledge had significant effects on conversations of equity. According to McCullough (2018), dot-com insiders cashed out ~43 billion between September 1999 and July 2000. Around 100 million individual investors collectively lost 5 trillion, with 45% of 401(k)s losing more than one-fifth of their value during the period. So, those with deep knowledge and expertise profited well, and those without did not. Despite greater access to knowledge, it was individual investors (e.g., families) who typically lost the most.

The popularization of the third generation of the natural language processing (NLP) tool generative pre-trained transformer (GPT®-3) in 2021 and bidirectional encoder representations from transformers (BERT) in 2018 have radically reshaped the processes of knowledge generation and dissemination. These tools, and their counterparts, have the capacity to efficiently organize a vast corpus of knowledge and return a summary of its investigation in moments, and they do so in a way that feels reasonably human. the tools, however, aim for unbiased presentation of the existing corpus of knowledge. As is generally accepted, the representation of human knowledge to date is not unbiased, and nor is it free from prejudice (McCullagh, 2000). This chapter has two primary objectives:

- To explore how the popularization of ChatGPT® and other LLMs are affecting fair and balanced processing of knowledge
- To explore how leaders engage with knowledge in the AI era

9.1.1 The hegemonic problem, race, and stochastic parroting

ChatGPT and similar tools have the potential to perpetuate views that contemporary humanity has sought to respond to. In Newstead et al. (2023, p. 1), ". . . AI generated content can contain and perpetuate harmful leadership-related gender biases." In their study, they asked artificial intelligence to generate examples of top leaders and characteristics of good and bad leaders, and the results were primarily males and male-oriented characteristics. This phenomenon is commonly termed *stochastic parroting*, or the ability to repeat back (parrot) patterns and structures of knowledge found (Boussen et al., 2023) but not analyzed meaningfully. Herein lies the challenge that this chapter seeks to discuss. The nature of stochastic parroting can be increasingly complex to deal with for those expected to consume large volumes of evidence to make good decisions.

In NLP, a common trend has been rapidly growing language models in terms of number of parameters and size of training data (Bender et al., 2021). Bender and colleagues comment that there might be risks with increasingly large databases and that there is a greater need for curation and careful documentation prior to attempting to ingest the entire web. BERT was 16 gigabytes in 2019, GPT-3 was 570 gigabytes in 2020, and Switch-C was 745 gigabytes in 2021. In their comments, Bender et al. articulate that humans tend to infer meaning in conversations where there may not be any, and this can create misleading interpretations of synthetic text. In their words, language models pick up on subtle biases and have the capacity to perpetuate racial bias, among other types. While there are rapidly growing manuscripts on racism linked to generative AI, there are few that have passed preprint. Hagendorff et al. (2023, p. 717), however, write of the "speciesist bias" in AI, and draw heavily on the belief that this bias exists "because the models are trained on datasets in which speciesist patterns prevail."

The same argument can apply to narratives of race. Buolamwini (2016) identifies that her facial recognition AI could not detect black faces, or that the Twitter® tool preferenced white faces and often cropped black faces (Guardian, 2020). NLP does this because of the large volumes of historically "acceptable" but racist practices and texts that exist. In an analysis of children's books, Pescosolido et al. (1997) found that black representations in literature have been underrepresented, and pointed to the relationship that may exist between "black-white relations in the larger society" (p. 443). AI relies on the corpus of knowledge humans have created and likely has difficulty ascertaining concepts of right and wrong in writing. Instead, it relies on volume and interaction of concepts to generate meaning. This is a significant challenge for those who consistently need to draw on a large corpus of knowledge to make good decisions.

9.1.2 The problem for leaders and leadership

If we go back a little, the original model of French et al.'s (1959) "bases of social power" theory suggested five key types of power: *legitimate* (power based on formal role or position), *reward* (power based on the ability to reward or compensate for effort), *expert* (power based on high knowledge and skills), *referent* (power based on perceived attraction, respect, or likeability), and *coercive* (power based on the ability to punish). A later model included one additional power, *information power,* or the ability to control the flow of information others need. Information and export power remains an increasingly important base of power in society, particularly among senior and knowledge workers.

As leaders enter consistent periods of mess, crisis, and complexity, their need to better leverage emergent knowledge continues to be essential. For a leader to make good decisions, they are required to process significant volumes of knowledge to make the best decision possible. In management theory, bounded rationality suggests that most individuals place reasonable limits on the amount of knowledge they need to make a decision (Simon, 1990). To make good decisions, access to high-quality and balanced information is essential. The theory of authentic leadership places the need to process information (particularly self-referent information) in a balanced way at the core of being an effective leader (Crawford et al., 2020; Walumbwa et al., 2008). Yet, with increasing pressures of timeliness, leaders are either using artificial intelligence to generate knowledge reports, or receiving reports informed by artificial intelligence. And, with the underlying bias in the data, this could be catastrophic.

We use a recent case study as an illustrative example. In Australia, there has been a national inquiry into large management consultants' breach and misuse of confidential tax policy to support tax avoidance of multiple clients outside the intent of the law, with the government terming their report "A Calculated Breach of Trust" (Commonwealth of Australia, 2023). In response, a group of respected academics used Google®'s Bard® to generate content based on its live corpus, only to find that it generated false evidence (Guardian, 2023). This included generating false examples of companies audited and even naming a scandal that seems not to have existed. Governmental practice for accusations is to allow the accused to respond prior to publishing, of which these were identified. In the absence of this process, the senators leading the inquiry would likely have trusted this information as factual. For leaders with reduced resources for "checks and balances," and those accused with less legal capacity to respond, this scenario could have ended a different way.

To take a smaller view, and one more aligned to the nature of this edited text, we asked ChatGPT to generate a similar example:

> *In a multinational corporation's diversity training program, employees were encouraged to share personal experiences to foster understanding. One staff member, using AI-generated false stories, recounted discriminatory encounters portraying individuals of a certain ethnicity in a negative light. These fabricated anecdotes aimed to highlight challenges faced by minorities but instead perpetuated harmful stereotypes. As a consequence, the false narratives circulated, influencing decision-makers' perceptions and contributing to unconscious biases within the company. Subsequently, a promotion opportunity arose where a deserving candidate, coincidentally of the misrepresented ethnicity, was overlooked. Investigations revealed the influence of these fictitious stories on the decision-making process, highlighting the insidious impact of AI-generated misinformation.*

While quite specific, using AI for personal advantage will sometimes work but may also have unintended consequences. In this chapter, we focus on how access to good information is needed to make fair and balanced decisions. We adopt a theoretical framework of the behavior of an authentic leader (Crawford et al., 2019, p. 126), or an individual who "influences and motivates followers to achieve goals through their sincerity and positive moral perspective, enabled through heightened awareness and balanced processing." More critically, we focus on the concept of balanced processing that authentic leaders deploy (see Table 9.1). We do this with the intention not to violate Larsson et al.'s (2021) critique that authentic leader dimensions are not isolated but rather interactive.

Table 9.1 Authentic Leader Behavior Dimensions[a]

Awareness is having insight into the behaviors of oneself, other individuals, and groups (p. 121).
Sincerity is presenting one's true self to others, honestly and openly in all relationships and with consideration for the context (p. 122).
Balanced processing is the tendency to consider all relevant information available, and using this to make decisions that benefit the collective (e.g., followers; p. 123).
Positive moral perspective is the commitment to one's intrinsic ethical framework, and a willingness to subdue personal interests and ego to facilitate collective interests (p. 124).
Informal influence is the ability to inspire and motivate individuals to accomplish goals of their own volition, regardless of rank or position (p. 125).

[a] *Source:* Crawford et al., 2019

9.2 Remember before AI? The beginning of the echo chamber

Humans respond well to short lists of information and are biased towards specific rank orders in lists (Isaac & Schindler, 2014)—for instance, the *Billboard* Hot 100, the top 10 locations to holiday this year, top 10 karaoke songs, or the top 10 richest people. Generation of digestible content has been a key performance indicator of digital marketers and content writers alike. These are developed by institutions to "productize" content offerings into "sellable packages for brands" (BuzzFeed Inc, 2023). Generally, humans are not good at detecting the difference between accurate and misleading content (Chen et al., 2015).

In parallel to clickbait like top 10 lists, social media platforms generate spaces that organize people into homophilic clusters—places where likeminded people come together (Aiello et al., 2012). Alignment of values is important for creating a sense of community, yet it can also foster bias in information diffusion (Cinelli et al., 2021) or the likelihood that individuals over-rely on information presented by those with whom they align. As a result, algorithms designed to curate content are primed to maximize content that enables users to engage with likeminded people and have increasingly lower exposure to divergent ideologies (i.e., a filter bubble; Spohr, 2017). In contrast, exposure to diverse views is likely to support more critical thinking and tolerance.

Each of these forces—whether logic towards simplified information or for information from inner circles—have sat against humans who have only a limited capacity for processing. Information overload occurs when too much information is received (Edmunds & Morris, 2000), and this might explain why information simplification occurs. Yet there are inherent risks to leaders' decision-making. Leaders need effective sources of quality knowledge to make good decisions. Digital leaders (e.g., in remote or asynchronous work) will regularly rely on digital sources of information to generate context, and those leaders who are influenced by content algorithms that limit their diversity of views may support the emergence of echo chambers of bad decisions.

9.3 Enter center stage, large language models

Thus far, the discussion has focused primarily on the practices of knowledge consumption and processing for leaders or, in the context of authentic leadership, the attempt to process information in ways that minimize prospective bias. Each of the examples has had limited direct reference to AI, but they did provide important context. In 2018, when GPT-1 was released, it did have a significant effect on public discourse, but it was GPT-3 in November of 2022 that generated greater interest, as it offered a quick and efficient replacement for many human tasks, from computer coding to graphic design, legal research, and more. However, it relies on content generated before its knowledge cutoff point. Since then, live versions including Microsoft® Bing® and Google®'s Bard® have the capacity to process current information.

These tools offer efficient information processing but remain limited by their prospective incoming data. Although AI can be incredibly useful, it also suffers from the limitations of the current dataset. There are three common methods that create bias in the AI system, among others: First, in the live or older datasets used for training contain bias, racial minorities tend to have less information presented about them, and stereotypes occur prominently in historical literature. Second, the AI tools may also use pre-existing characteristic interpretations that are loaded with racial bias or prejudice to continue to perpetuate such logic. Third, datasets that underrepresent certain ethnic or racial groups will naturally continue to do the same. That is, information in *is* information out.

Table 9.2 AFL Player Rankings Generated by ChatGPT*

Who were the top 10 players from the AFL 2019 season born outside Australia	Who were the top 10 players from the AFL 2019 season born in Australia
Mason Cox (USA, Collingwood): Known for his athleticism and impactful performances in key games.	Patrick Dangerfield (Geelong Cats): Dominant midfield presence, impactful performances, and exceptional skill set.
Pearce Hanley (Ireland, Gold Coast Suns): Displayed versatility and skill across multiple positions on the field.	Nat Fyfe (Fremantle Dockers): Strong leadership, versatility, and consistently high-level performances throughout the season.
Callum Twomey (Ireland, Essendon): Rising talent showing exceptional adaptability and quick learning in AFL.	Marcus Bontempelli (Western Bulldogs): Outstanding versatility, leadership, and ability to impact games in various positions.
Stefan Giro (Italy, Fremantle): Demonstrated rapid development and a strong work ethic in his games.	Patrick Cripps (Carlton Blues): Exceptional contested ball-winning ability and influential leadership within the team.
Mason Redman (England, Essendon): Notable for his resilience and steady improvement throughout the season.	Brodie Grundy (Collingwood Magpies): Dominant ruckman, providing a strong presence and impact in crucial games.
Zac Smith (New Zealand, Geelong Cats): Contributed significantly as a reliable ruckman in crucial matches.	Lachie Neale (Brisbane Lions): Exceptional ball-winning ability, consistency, and leadership within the midfield.
Colin O'Riordan (Ireland, Sydney Swans): Showcased adaptability and a quick grasp of the AFL style of play.	Dustin Martin (Richmond Tigers): High impact with his athleticism, game sense, and ability to perform under pressure.
Zach Tuohy (Ireland, Geelong Cats): Known for his consistent performance and experience in AFL.	Jeremy Cameron (GWS Giants): Top-notch goal-scoring ability and consistent performance as a key forward.
Luke Jackson (South Africa, Melbourne Demons): Emerging talent displaying promising skills and potential growth.	Ben Cunnington (North Melbourne Kangaroos): Renowned for his toughness, contested ball-winning skills, and consistency on-field.
Mark O'Connor (Ireland, Geelong Cats): Notable for his defensive prowess and adaptability in different roles.	Tim Kelly (Geelong Cats): Rapid emergence as a star player due to his speed, skill, and consistent performances.

*This table is described on the next page

There are significant historical examples of racial bias in literature (e.g., Forbes, 1963; MacLeod & Newall, 2022; Santoro & Santoro, 2018). In an interesting analysis of Australian rules football (Australian Football League: AFL), a supplement of AFL commentator analyses shows that non-white players were more likely to be praised for their physicality, whereas white players were more likely to receive praise based on perceived intellect and character (MacLeod & Newall, 2022). When asking ChatGPT to generate a list of the top 10 players from that season, it produced a list of 10 Australian players (two were indigenous). The same pattern was true for questions of character and intelligence and for physicality.

In the following generations (text is a verbatim answer from ChatGPT, 4 December 2023), we asked ChatGPT to describe the top 10 players born in and outside Australia. The results showed zero references to leadership and presence in the outside Australian context, but the inside Australian did (see Table 9.2).

These tools have the potential to continue to produce the stereotypes and challenges that we experience in everyday life. Leaders have a responsibility and a moral imperative to respond effectively to this knowledge gap, but is this an increasingly difficult challenge when artificial intelligence is added to the mix?

9.4 A spiral to the bottom? Echo chamber foam!

As AI becomes increasingly used to support everyday work, content producers may be expected to develop and publish more content to support meeting key performance indicators. For other workers, generation of internal resources—such as hiring strategies—may not have a direct effect on future generative AI outputs, although its effect may still be indirect. Employees who produce human resource strategies inevitably inform advertised position descriptions, and appointment of people will be based on AI-generated recommendations (e.g., prototypical selection criteria). Given that AI relies on the incoming corpus of data, the quality of inputs is of essential importance.

Conversely, OpenAI® launched an AI classifier to support detection of AI versus human content, yet it discontinued the product due to low reliability (Hendrik Kirchner et al., 2023). Under these circumstances, AI tools are producing content for employees—or followers, subordinates, and direct reports—and those employees are publishing content that future AI captures will use—or, in the case of live data capture, immediately.

So, the publication of AI-developed blogs, position descriptions, and the like used by other leaders as market insights in a model of balanced processing might dilute the quality of diverse and inclusive knowledge. This could be a perpetual loop subject to content-gaming and content-manufacturing for personal gain—a practical equivalent to painting-the-tape in investment (Porter & Weaver, 1994). In this reality, leaders who are attempting to engage in a balanced assessment of information will be flooded with knowledge well beyond their possible scope of reference. Leaders pursuing self-preservation may seek to rely increasingly on sources of truth—such as their inner circle—and reinforce echo chambers out of a sense of necessity.

When reflecting on this self-reinforcing loop, where content creators rely increasingly on AI to meet competitive demand expectations, leaders respond to this with the equivalent of "echo chamber foam"—that is, a form of insulation used in recording studios to reduce echoing, but which also limits what can be heard from the outside. And this context could lead to perceptions of connection with community and an increasingly less representative dataset entering in.

9.5 Leaders of machines

In an environment where *knowledge itself is power,* effective leadership requires grappling with such power. To influence effectively, leaders need to be conscious of their capacity to process information and engage with an increasingly complex knowledge environment. This is particularly true when engaging with AI that aspires to generate unbiased content yet can only work within the dataset it has available. To this end, scholars and practitioners alike need leadership development strategies that focus on engaging with complexity (e.g., Uhl-Bien et al., 2007) and with information and digital literacy (e.g., McAskill, 2008; Santoso et al., 2019).

This proposition is complex and much more complicated than Bender and colleagues' (2021) recommendation that more data curation prior to uploading or integrating new information into a corpus is needed. Data curation is an important step that responds to symptoms, and effective leadership driven by a focus on enabling balanced processing of information will support responding to the cause. This ought to sit alongside a human focus on more balanced alternative narratives—and greater tolerance of competing views.

Leaders may also take heed of the emergent separation of professions between those who continue to create new knowledge (e.g., an investigative journalist) as compared to those who replicate knowledge in new contexts (e.g., a digital copywriter). The separation may support clearer and more cohesive filtering of information without filter bubbles and echo chambers emerging. Finally, we must keep a critical eye on the challenges likely faced by underrepresented populations in AI datasets.

9.6 Conclusion

This chapter began with an exploration of the challenge leaders face in supporting environments for diverse people in the era of AI. The concept of stochastic parroting poses a significant challenge to leaders who need effective access to data to make good and fair decisions. In reflecting on the balanced processing component of authentic leadership, we explore how leaders might engage with echo chambers, filter bubbles, and AI generators. We offer some propositions for leadership development scholars and for leadership practitioners on how they may respond effectively to an increasingly complex knowledge economy.

References

Aiello, L. M., Barrat, A., Schifanella, R., Cattuto, C., Markines, B., & Menczer, F. (2012). Friendship prediction and homophily in social media. *ACM Transactions on the Web*, *6*(2), 1–33.

Bender, E. M., Gebru, T., McMillan-Major, A., & Shmitchell, S. (2021, March). On the dangers of stochastic parrots: Can language models be too big? *Proceedings of the 2021 ACM Conference on Fairness, Accountability, and Transparency* (pp. 610–623).

Boussen, S., Denis, J. B., Simeone, P., Lagier, D., Bruder, N., & Velly, L. (2023). ChatGPT and the stochastic parrot: Artificial intelligence in medical research. *British Journal of Anaesthesia, 131*(4), e120–e121.

Buolamwini, J. (2016). How I'm fighting bias in algorithms. *TEDxBeaconStreet.* https://www.ted.com/talks/joy_buolamwini_how_i_m_fighting_bias_in_algorithms

BuzzFeed Inc. (2023). [Advert for] Sr manager brand marketing and monetization strategy, FWF. BuzzFeed Inc. https://boards.greenhouse.io/buzzfeed/jobs/5478654?gh_jid=5478654

Chen, Y., Conroy, N. J., & Rubin, V. L. (2015, November). Misleading online content: Recognizing clickbait as "false news". *Proceedings of the 2015 ACM on Workshop on Multimodal Deception Detection* (pp. 15–19).

Cinelli, M., De Francisci Morales, G., Galeazzi, A., Quattrociocchi, W., & Starnini, M. (2021). The echo chamber effect on social media. *Proceedings of the National Academy of Sciences, 118*(9), e2023301118.

Commonwealth of Australia (2023). *PwC: A calculated breach of trust.* https://www.aph.gov.au/Parliamentary_Business/Committees/Senate/Finance_and_Public_Administration/Consultingservices/PwC_Report

Crawford, J. A., Dawkins, S., Martin, A., & Lewis, G. (2020). Putting the leader back into authentic leadership: Reconceptualising and rethinking leaders. *Australian Journal of Management, 45*(1), 114–133.

Edmunds, A., & Morris, A. (2000). The problem of information overload in business organisations: A review of the literature. *International Journal of Information Management, 20*(1), 17–28.

French, J. R., Raven, B., & Cartwright, D. (1959). The bases of social power. *Classics of Organization Theory, 7*(311–320), 1.

Forbes, J. D. (1963). The historian and the Indian: Racial bias in American history. *The Americas, 19*(4), 349–362.

Guardian (2020). Twitter apologises for 'racist' image-cropping algorithm. *The Guardian.* https://www.theguardian.com/technology/2020/sep/21/twitter-apologises-for-racist-image-cropping-algorithm

Guardian (2023). Australian academics apologise for false AI-generated allegations against big four consultancy firms. *The Guardian.* https://www.theguardian.com/business/2023/nov/02/australian-academics-apologise-for-false-ai-generated-allegations-against-big-four-consultancy-firms

Hagendorff, T., Bossert, L.N., Fai, T.Y., & Singer, P. (2023). Speciesist bias in AI: a reply to Arandjelović. *AI and Ethics, 3,* 1043–1047.

Hendrik Kirchner, J., Ahmad, L., Aaronson, S., & Leike, J. (2023). New AI classifier for indicating AI-written text. OpenAI. https://openai.com/blog/new-ai-classifier-for-indicating-ai-written-text.

Isaac, M. S., & Schindler, R. M. (2014). The top-ten effect: Consumers' subjective categorization of ranked lists. *Journal of Consumer Research, 40*(6), 1181–1202.

Larsson, M., Clifton, J., & Schnurr, S. (2021). The fallacy of discrete authentic leader behaviours: Locating authentic leadership in interaction. *Leadership, 17*(4), 421–440.

MacLeod, S. A., & Newall, P. W. (2022). Investigating racial bias within Australian rules football commentary. *PLoS One, 17*(7), e0272005.

McAskill, W. (2008). Information literacy: The leadership role of the academic librarian. *College Quarterly, 11*(1), 1–15.

McCullagh, C. B. (2000). Bias in historical description, interpretation, and explanation. *History and Theory, 39*(1), 39–66.

McCullough, B. (2018). A revealing look at the dot-com bubble of 2000—And how it shapes our lives today. TED. https://ideas.ted.com/an-eye-opening-look-at-the-dot-com-bubble-of-2000-and-how-it-shapes-our-lives-today/

Newstead, T., Eager, B., & Wilson, S. (2023). How AI can perpetuate—or help mitigate—gender bias in leadership. *Organizational Dynamics,* 100998.

Pescosolido, B. A., Grauerholz, E., & Milkie, M. A. (1997). Culture and conflict: The portrayal of Blacks in US children's picture books through the mid- and late-twentieth century. *American Sociological Review,* 443–464

Porter, D. C., & Weaver, D. G. (1994). Do NASDAQ market makers paint the tape? Available at SSRN 5847.

Santoso, H., Elidjen, E., Abdinagoro, S., & Arief, M. (2019). The role of creative self-efficacy, transformational leadership, and digital literacy in supporting performance through innovative work behavior: Evidence from telecommunications industry. *Management Science Letters, 9*(13), 2305–2314.

Santoro, T. N., & Santoro, J. D. (2018). Racial bias in the US opioid epidemic: A review of the history of systemic bias and implications for care. *Cureus, 10*(12).

Simon, H. A. (1990). Bounded rationality. *Utility and Probability,* 15–18.

Spohr, D. (2017). Fake news and ideological polarization: Filter bubbles and selective exposure on social media. *Business Information Review, 34*(3), 150–160.

Uhl-Bien, M., Marion, R., & McKelvey, B. (2007). Complexity leadership theory: Shifting leadership from the industrial age to the knowledge era. *The Leadership Quarterly, 18*(4), 298–318.

Walumbwa, F. O., Avolio, B. J., Gardner, W. L., Wernsing, T. S., & Peterson, S. J. (2008). Authentic leadership: Development and validation of a theory-based measure. *Journal of Management, 34*(1), 89–126.

Chapter 10

Minimizing Hate Speech in Academic Environments with Artificial Intelligence Techniques

Ricardo Pereira,[1*] Florinda Matos,[2*] Neri dos Santos,[1] and Roberto Carlos dos Santos Pacheco[1]

[1]UFSC-Federal University of Santa Catarina

[2]Iscte–University Institute of Lisbon–DINÂMIA'CET-IU–Centre for Socioeconomic Change and Territorial Studies, Lisbon, Portugal

*Corresponding authors

10.1 Introduction

Universities are widely recognized as pluralistic environments in which the debate of ideas finds a haven for its broader externalization to society. Since their origin in the Middle Ages, they have been, by nature, the settings for producing new knowledge for humanity. However, in recent decades, hate speech has been gaining ground in universities, generating a dangerous form of anti-knowledge, as shown in Figure 10.1. This shift has led the once-pluralistic university environment to become one in which the ideology of hate prevails over the diversity of ideas and

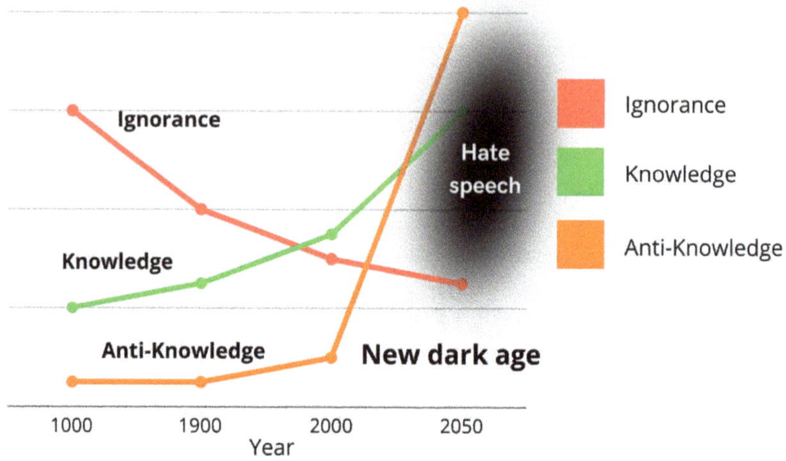

Figure 10.1 Exponential growth of hate speech as a form of anti-knowledge (*Source:* Adapted from Ian Pearson; https://dw2blog.com/2013/02/22/controversies-over-singularitarian-utopianism/)

freedom of expression. This change risks regressing humanity's social development, potentially leading to a new Dark Age reminiscent of the Medieval period.

Figure 10.1 illustrates that from the Middle Ages until the early 20th century, two exponential curves approached each other in divergent directions. On the one hand, humanity's scientific knowledge grew exponentially, and on the other, human ignorance also fell exponentially. However, at the end of the 20th century and the beginning of the 21st century, with the development of the Internet and social media, a third curve has risen sharply: the "curve of anti-knowledge"—of hate speech—which could lead humanity into a new dark age.

Indeed, the entire world is in the midst of a heated debate about how universities should respond to hate speech on campuses. It is emphasized that *hate speech* is the generic term that has come to encompass the use of speech for attacks based on race, ethnicity, religion, and sexual orientation or preference.

This phenomenon can be characterized as public expression in the form of a deliberate attack or incitement to violence, humiliation, insult, or contempt against a person or group based on protected characteristics such as race, religion, ethnic origin, nationality, sex, sexual orientation, gender identity, disability, or serious illness. Hate speech can occur in different ways and linguistic styles, including subtly or when humor is used (Fortuna & Nunes, 2018; Toliyat et al., 2022).

Exposure to hate speech in an academic environment has been associated with various harmful effects, such as the normalization of intolerance, reduction of the sense of belonging of minority groups, impairment of mental health and well-being of students and staff, and the reduction of diversity of ideas and academic freedom, culminating in university dropout (Soral et al., 2018; Ceci & Williams, 2018; Davids, 2019; Welshon, 2020; Kharytonenko et al., 2022).

Nevertheless, the university is not a public square where everyone has the right to say anything. Universities must guarantee the rights essential for fulfilling its purpose of seeking and generating knowledge. The politicization of environments alien to the strictly public sphere, such as universities, has also raised new questions about the meaning and extent of the idea of academic freedom. For many, academic freedom is nothing but a particular case of freedom of expression in general and would be regulated by the same principles.

We understand that this observation is problematic and potentially misleading. Universities need to undertake actions to mitigate such situations and provide the means for identifying and monitoring hate speech, among which is artificial intelligence (AI), as proposed in this chapter. The use of AI, such as machine learning models and natural language processing (NLP), has the potential to analyze patterns in large volumes of text to automatically identify cases of hate speech, assisting in the moderation processes of content posted on academic channels in general.

Mansur et al. (2023) highlight the existence of previous studies (including those by Langham & Gosha, 2018; Fortuna & Nunes, 2018; Modi, 2018; Alrehili, 2019; Dorris et al., 2020) that addressed different aspects of hate speech detection on social media, mainly on Twitter®. However, research on AI monitoring of hate speech in an academic context is sparse.

To properly contextualize this issue, it is essential to understand some of the main justifications usually invoked to protect freedom of expression in general, conducted within the public sphere, such as political, religious, and artistic freedom of expression. According to Macedo Jr. (2023), there are basically three justifications for freedom of expression, sometimes defended on exclusive grounds, other times by their combination and sum:

1. **In knowledge production:** Its importance for the development of knowledge, as it would ensure that the marketplace of ideas could foster and refine the knowledge process.
2. **In human development:** The ethical function to allow the development and self-realization of the human being through the guarantee of their aspiration for self-expression.
3. **In democracy:** Its political role in facilitating the political process necessary for democratic self-government. At this point, freedom of expression would have a legitimizing function of power by ensuring that everyone, indiscriminately, could participate in the process of forming public opinion.

However, as principles, they do not imply that someone can say anything to anyone at any time, especially when it violates academic rules. First, it is important to emphasize that the university environment, guided by its fundamental objectives of promoting teaching, research, and outreach, has as its main focus the pursuit of knowledge built on recognized scientific methodologies. In academia, not all ideas have space. A professor who produces an academic work that is in flagrant disagreement with the criteria of academic excellence will not be able to publish their work in a scientific journal and may even be removed from their functions or not be made permanent in their position. If they present ideas not validated by the academic community, they will have difficulty in even entering the university.

For example, it is inconceivable that a conference on oncology medicine could benefit from the freedom of expression of a conspiracy theory expert to discuss the best therapies for cancer. Society deeply values the knowledge of specialists. We seek doctors when sick because we expect the professional attending us to apply medical knowledge. We consider that an oncologist who does not offer adequate medical treatment, according to accepted medical practices, to a patient, replacing this with religious or mystical lectures, does not act within the limits of their freedom of expression. They can even be held accountable for their professional misconduct. In the office, as a doctor, they do not have the freedom of expression to put forth arbitrary opinions. The same principle that applies to the doctor applies to the professor and researcher and does not give the freedom to disseminate and teach any idea.

Considering this context, this chapter aims to synthesize current knowledge about AI applications, specifically aimed at identifying and mitigating hate speech in an academic context. This chapter is limited to presenting the applications of AI available for monitoring/mitigating hate speech in an academic environment without delving into the technically available solutions to solve the research problem.

10.2 The dichotomy between freedom of expression and hate speech in the academic setting

Hate speech can target individuals or groups based on arbitrary or normatively irrelevant characteristics, portraying them as undesirable and legitimate targets of hostility (Toliyat et al., 2022).

An example of this occurred during the COVID-19 pandemic when hate speech, including derogatory language, racial insults, and xenophobic comments, was directed at Asians, blaming them for the spread of the virus and associating them with negative stereotypes (Toliyat et al., 2022). An example of such hate speech related to these individuals was: "It's the Chinese virus, from China, caused by their disgusting eating habits, their cruelty. Boycott everything Chinese" (He et al., 2021).

Hate speech can take the form of derogatory language, stereotypes, or discriminatory comments, expressing hostility, prejudice, and discrimination, like those directed at Asian individuals or communities in the example above (Ceci & Williams, 2018; Toliyat et al., 2022). These comments, which can take the form of comments, online posts, or tweets, contribute to the perpetuation of hate speech and the marginalization of individuals exposed to it (Toliyat et al., 2022).

Religious conflicts, ideological clashes, and political disputes, combined with migration crises, have potentiated hate speech on issues such as national identity, xenophobia, and religious intolerance, among other issues driving hate speech.

This global panorama is inevitably replicated in academic environments, which should promote the free debate of ideas among a plural and diverse community. Academic freedom is essential for developing new research and creating new knowledge, which only occurs in environments of freedom of expression. However, cases of prejudiced manifestations or personal attacks on members of certain groups (with antagonistic ideological positions) have been generating debates about how far forms of intolerance should be tolerated under the guise of freedom of expression.

There is a tension between the principles of freedom of expression and the need for an inclusive, safe environment conducive to the full participation of all voices (Ceci & Williams, 2018; Davids, 2019). It is argued that universities cannot be considered islands of repression, but they should also not allow speech that compromises fundamental ethical standards (Welshon, 2020).

Therefore, the big question is how to reconcile protection against prejudices that silence and marginalize part of the student body without incurring generalized censorship. Authors such as Welshon (2019) advocate the idea of "armed intolerance" as a demarcation line, distinguishing vigorous debate from content that incites violence.

Other authors highlight the risks of a broad or paternalistic application of public policies in which any dissent already labelled as hate speech will be suppressed. Some advocate for more training and dialogue rather than regulation of speech (Ceci & Williams, 2018).

The key is to enable the development of sufficiently mature academic communities to constructively deal with divergences and build tolerance to monitor and minimize hate speech in the academic sphere, which results from a delirious irrationality of conspiracy theories through artificial intelligence.

10.3 Artificial intelligence as an alternative to monitor/minimize hate speech in the academic environment

Aggressiveness, threats, and other forms of abuse that can harm individuals and disrupt social relationships are part of the language used in online communications. As a response to these challenges, the detection of hate speech and related tasks (for example, recognizing the use of offensive or abusive language, aggressiveness, misogyny, racism, xenophobia, and homophobia) emerge as key research topics in the field of AI, particularly in NLP, arousing interest among researchers (Silva et al., 2020; Mansur, 2023).

Identifying the sentiments expressed in posts and comments written by users on social media represents a challenge. Automating this process increases the level of difficulty. Initially, the task of inspecting hate comments was performed manually. With the growing number of users, manual annotation became extremely difficult and computationally time consuming. Most methodologies employed for the automatic identification of hate texts are based on NLP, which seeks to identify the words used and their corresponding semantics (Barkhashree & Dhaliwal, 2023). NLP is a specialized area that enables computers to understand and process human language, performing tasks such as tokenization, syntactic analysis, semantic analysis, and sentiment analysis (Gallardo et al., 2023).

Initially, the problem of hate speech detection was seen as a binary issue, with hate and non-hate being the only two classes. However, this dual classification evolved over time into a more complex multiclass problem, in which hate speech can be associated with various sentiments.

To cope with the complexities involved, researchers turned to intelligent machine-learning (ML) methodologies for automation. Various social platforms have already implemented ML-based methods to detect and track hate content. However, there is still significant space for improvement, as the categorization of hate speech remains an exceptionally arduous task (Barkhashree & Dhaliwal, 2023).

In recent years, deep learning has significantly advanced NLP with techniques such as word embedding, recurrent neural networks, and transformer models. Researchers have proposed improving deep-learning techniques for hate speech detection on social networks, which can be visualized in terms of combining ideas, such as using the long short-term memory (LSTM) model in the detection of hate speech on social networks using "Bag-of-Words" (BoW), chi-squared and recurrent neural networks (RNNs), which could potentially improve classification performance, as per Gallardo et al. (2023).

The shift began with the use of supervised and unsupervised ML methods, and recently, researchers have started exploring deep learning methods (Barkhashree & Dhaliwal, 2023).

In this research perspective, there is an evolution towards ML techniques, which can be used to analyze facial features in depth and extract behavioural components based on them. The behavioural components obtained through facial reading and hate speech analysis can be combined to offer a more holistic approach. Incorporating deep learning models into this research is also a promising path for future investigations. Deep learning models, such as convolutional neural networks (CNNs) and RNNs, have shown remarkable capabilities in capturing intricate patterns and dependencies in large and diverse datasets. Therefore, if a well-curated and extensive dataset suitable for training deep learning models is available, it has the potential to enhance the results and advance the capabilities of the proposed system (Barkhashree & Dhaliwal, 2023).

Silva et al. (2020), for example, investigated a variety of learning methods and characteristics for three tasks—hate speech detection, aggressiveness classification, and target group—in Spanish and English. Among these methods, a purely data-driven bidirectional encoder representations from transformers (BERT) model, and to some extent, a psycholinguistically informed hybrid CNN model, generally stood out in relation to previous work in the field for specific combinations of task and language.

10.4 Challenges and opportunities for implementing AI in monitoring hate speech in academic environments

Mansur et al. (2023) highlight several challenges and opportunities in detecting hate speech using AI, pointing out significant limitations in characterizing hate speech and operationalizing AI for detection and monitoring activities related to the dissemination of hate speech. The authors emphasize the importance of identifying hate posts generated by users before they are published. Deep learning models, genetic algorithms, and knowledge graphs can be implemented for this hate speech detection function.

The main challenges in identifying hate speech are outlined in Table 10.1 (on next page). Table 10.1 lists a set of challenges involved in detecting hate speech on social media, as well as the various approaches used to address these challenges, which may be related to their application in an academic context. Table 10.2, on the other hand, discusses the challenges related to detecting hate speech based on machine learning issues.

After analyzing how artificial intelligence can be applied in the detection, monitoring, and mitigation of hate speech in an academic environment and pointing out the challenges to be overcome for its effective implementation, it is up to universities and higher education institutions to define a set of guidelines for the construction of a healthy academic environment conducive to the pluralization of ideas.

Table 10.1 Challenges Involved in Detecting Hate Speech on Social Media

Challenges	Description
Understanding online hate speech	It is important to emphasize the need to understand hate speech as a social and social network phenomenon. Due to the lack of individual and universal consensus regarding its definition, categorizing and properly identifying it is an extremely complex task.
Subtle and unreliable annotations	Social networks are valuable sources of information, but they are also less reliable and filled with noise. Hate speech detection is challenging due to subtle instances, sarcasm, and the unreliability of human annotations. Challenges in hate speech detection include false negatives, biases in annotation, and the lack of sufficiently labeled data. The acceptance of a universal concept of what constitutes hate speech is also a limiting factor.
Ambiguity and noise	Most existing methods for categorizing hate speech focus on online content, but users often use evasive typing language to avoid detection, making the collection and annotation of hate speech difficult owing to its incomplete and subjective nature.
Separation of hate speech from an offensive instance	It is imperative to distinguish hate speech from other offensive language so that it is possible to identify hate speech automatically on social networks. Dimensionality reduction and semantic representations are methods mentioned as approaches to solve this problem.
Distinguishing hate speech from profanity	The task of distinguishing between hate speech and swearing is a major challenge in identifying hate speech. Although hate speech may include profane language, the mere presence of such words does not necessarily imply that the text is hateful. This highlights the complexity of the issue and the need for advanced techniques and a nuanced understanding of language semantics to increase the accuracy of hate speech detection systems. Machine learning algorithms are applied to make this distinction.
Misogyny as an instance of hate speech	Misogyny is a form of hate speech targeted towards women. Its detection is an additional challenge in the complex task of detecting hate speech, especially on online social networks. Researchers have been using NLP resources with ML models to address this problem. Additional efforts are being made to reduce unintentional biases in ML models for detecting misogyny, as the occurrence of certain identity words can lead to unrealistic misogyny scores. This highlights the challenge of classifying misogynistic abuse on social networks.

Source: Adapted from Mansur et al., 2023

Table 10.2 Challenges Involved in Detecting Hate Speech in Relation to Machine Learning

Challenges	Description
Overfitting and sampling	It is extremely important to carefully manage data sampling and overfitting issues in hate speech detection to ensure the robustness and generalization of the models.
Imbalance issue	Class imbalance is a challenge in hate speech detection, as it constitutes only a small fraction of what can be found online. To manage datasets with imbalanced classes, a variety of approaches can be used, including resampling, data augmentation, and other distinct mechanisms. This highlights the importance of addressing class imbalance in hate speech detection to ensure the accuracy and effectiveness of the models.
Adversarial examples	The challenge of adversarial examples is discussed, where attempts are made to deceive text detection systems through subtle changes in the text, causing it to be incorrectly identified by detection models. To address this problem, researchers have introduced solutions that preserve importance and readability, performing equally or better than the results of adversarial retraining. This highlights the importance of developing more robust and resilient models that can detect adversarial examples and prevent them from circumventing hate speech detection mechanisms.
Generalization issue	The problem of generalization in hate speech detection arises from the variability of user-generated text across different platforms, which can reduce the model's ability to generalize effectively. Comments collected in the form of user-generated texts can vary among services, and the use of such data can hinder the model's generalization. Therefore, it is essential to develop detection approaches that do not rely on information from any specific platform. This highlights the importance of developing hate speech detection models that can be generalized across different platforms and data distributions, as well as the need to consider various factors that may affect the generalization of the models.
Lack of comparative evaluation	The lack of comparative evaluation makes it difficult to assess the impact of existing efforts. To address this issue, various techniques and resource algorithms are being compared, and performance tests are being conducted in different categories using publicly accessible datasets. Furthermore, researchers have introduced semantic features to understand the nuances of user messages with the possible intention of hate.

(Continues on next page)

Table 10.2 Challenges Involved in Detecting Hate Speech in Relation to Machine Learning (*cont.*)

Challenges	Description
Feature engineering	Hate speech detection is a challenge as a result of the scarcity of typical and special characteristics, making its identification difficult. Feature engineering plays a crucial role in hate speech detection, and researchers have explored various techniques to extract features and improve the performance of the models. Approaches involving resource extraction, resource selection, and dimensionality reduction are discussed
Other challenges	Other challenges mentioned include the detection of COVID-19-related hate speech, detecting hate speech targeting specific groups, and the overlap between hate speech and other forms of offensive language.

Source: Adapted from Mansur et al., 2023

10.5 Building a healthy academic environment for the pluralization of ideas: Guidelines to consider

The importance of a healthy academic environment for the pluralization of ideas is emphasized, especially when discussions involve challenging deeply rooted beliefs (George & West, 2017). This environment is crucial for fostering critical thinking through open debate. However, it is argued that such debate can be conducted without tolerating speech that incites violence or reinforces the marginalization of groups (Davids, 2019; Parini et al., 2017).

One of the significant challenges for academic institutions is to balance the guarantee of freedom of expression with the need to combat expressions that harm the dignity of community members (Ceci & Williams, 2018; Welshon, 2020). Universities must provide an appropriate environment for promoting the free debate of ideas, considering expressions that exceed a productive discourse and infringe upon principles of respect and inclusion.

There are arguments for both a more tolerant and skeptical stance and for a more vigorous "zero tolerance" approach to intolerant speech. Each has its reasons and associated risks, such as censorship versus complacency.

The concept of "armed intolerance" (Welshon, 2020), which at times is interchangeable with hate speech, seeks to delineate that not all controversy qualifies as hate speech requiring intervention. There should be room for respectfully expressed divergent views.

Ceci & Williams (2018) argue that exposing and openly debating controversial ideas, when well-mediated, can reduce polarization and educate about diversity. Limiting or rejecting these discussions could be counterproductive. Universities need to educate professors and students on media literacy and critical thinking to engage productively amid differences.

Davids (2019) maintains that tolerance should be an educational imperative in higher education and democracy. He argues for the importance of higher education in promoting democracy and expanding its definition beyond educating students for a multicultural world. He emphasizes the students' role in society and their responsibility towards human suffering, promoting compassion and empathy.

Davids (2019) also discusses individual autonomy and its relation to tolerance. He highlights that tolerance implies autonomous exercise of conscience but also recognizing the need to restrict this freedom in relation to others in certain contexts. He advocates for exercising autonomy based on rationality and respect for others and encourages students to bring their perspectives, worldviews, and biases into the classroom for debate and confrontation with divergent views.

Althibyani & Al-Zahrani (2023) highlight that digital citizenship education can play a significant role in reducing problems such as hate speech, cyberbullying, and the spread of fake news, especially among higher education students. By promoting a culture of respect and responsibility in the use of digital technology, digital citizenship can empower students to identify and critically evaluate online information.

Welshon (2020) argues that while freedom of expression is a fundamental individual right, there is a limit outside of which this expression turns into armed intolerance or hate speech that threatens community members and academic and professional standards. It involves publicly opposing and protesting against expressions of armed intolerance, highlighting their incompatibility with academic values and norms. Educational institutions should provide spaces in which community members feel safe and protected from intolerance and reaffirm and defend the fundamental principles of the university and the professional standards structuring academic freedom.

Finally, Ceci & Williams (2018) clarify that no group of professors or students has the right to determine for the entire community that a matter is closed for discussion. A goal of academia is to challenge students to think more broadly and rigorously and to encourage thoughtful discussion.

These suggestions reflect a balanced approach that seeks to protect freedom of expression while maintaining a respectful and safe academic environment, emphasizing that academic freedom and freedom of expression are not governed by the same principles.

10.6 Final remarks

Hate speech has advanced alarmingly in academic spaces, once seen as pluralistic environments for the free debate of ideas.

In light of this worrying scenario, the purpose of this chapter is to present the potential of artificial intelligence, through machine learning models and natural language processing, to assist in identifying and mitigating hate speech in an academic context. AI tools enable rapid analysis of large volumes of data in the form of posts and comments on university channels, signalling linguistic and semantic patterns associated with different degrees of intolerance.

However, as discussed throughout the chapter, the application of AI in this context is not without challenges. Well-defined guidelines and what constitutes hate speech are needed to avoid false positives or controversies surrounding these tools. There should also be clarity about the ethical and legal limits of academic freedom of expression so as not to engage in widespread censorship practices.

Thus, combating intolerant discourse in universities cannot be limited solely to identifying and removing hate speech in the form of offensive posts in academic channels. It is necessary to get to the root of the problem, promoting a culture of open dialogue, plurality of views, and critical thinking.

This does not mean that manifestations that violate basic ethical principles should be accepted. On the contrary, the way forward is to educate and raise awareness, not simply "silence". The university needs to train individuals mature enough to deal with disagreements constructively without resorting to aggression or reinforcing stigmas against those who think differently.

In this sense, artificial intelligence can be a relevant aid, proactively identifying cases that go beyond vigorous yet respectful and tolerant debate. However, this technology alone will not bring about the necessary cultural transformation. It is up to academic managers and leaders to cultivate a healthy ecosystem for the pluralization of ideas.

Intolerant discourse is a symptom of deeper problems that require solutions beyond technical issues. Universities need to reclaim their civilizing role, forming conscious, responsible, and supportive citizens. AI can support this mission, but the solution will come from the revival of humanist values that drive the search for knowledge. As long as arrogance, hate, and disqualification of the different prevail, no machine learning model will bring the transformation so necessary for society.

AI can be used for both good and evil. In the case of universities, which often support key technological developments, it is important to promote the ethical use of AI for good, mainly to prevent and combat cases of academic exclusion and hatred. It is up to universities, as knowledge construction centers, to promote the good use of AI, alerting their stakeholders to the challenges of incorrect use. Therefore, universities should be key places for equality and inclusion, and AI tools should be the guardians of their work "for good" in these and other areas.

It is up to those in charge to identify the appropriate tools, but each tool reflects the intentions of its creators and, above all, how they are nourished. Therefore, as in other areas, ethics should guide this use.

References

Alrehili, A. (2019). Automatic hate speech detection on social media: A brief Survey. *ACS/IEEE International Conference on Computer Systems and Applications* (AICCSA), 1–6. doi: 10.1109/AICCSA47632.2019

Althibyani, H. A., & Al-Zahrani, A. M. (2023). Investigating the effect of students' knowledge, beliefs, and digital citizenship skills on the prevention of cybercrime. *Sustainability, 15*(15), 11512.

Barkhashree, & Dhaliwal, P. (2023). Impounding behavioural connotations for hate speech analysis—A view towards criminal investigation using machine learning. *International Journal of Information Technology,* 1–14. https://doi.org/10.1007/s41870-023-01500-7

Ceci, S. J., & Williams, W. M. (2018). Who decides what is acceptable speech on campus? Why restricting free speech is not the answer. *Perspectives on Psychological Science, 13*(3), 299–323.

Davids, N. (2019). Tolerance as an imperative for higher education and democracy. *South African Journal of Higher Education, 33*(4), 62–75.

Dorris, W., Hu, R., Vishwamitra, N., Luo, F., & Costello, M. (2020). Towards automatic detection and explanation of hate speech and offensive language. *Proceedings of the Sixth International Workshop on Security and Privacy Analytics.* doi:10.1145/3375708.3380312

Fortuna, P., & Nunes, S. (2018). A survey on automatic detection of hate speech in text. *ACM Computing Surveys, 51*(4), 1–30.

Gallardo, J. N., Gloria, E. D. G., Landicho, N. R. P., & Sueno, H. T. (2023, August). Detection of hate speech using improved deep learning techniques. *10th International Conference on Information Technology, Computer, and Electrical Engineering* (ICITACEE) (pp. 184–189). IEEE.

George, R. P., & West, C. (2017). Sign the statement: Truth seeking, democracy, and freedom of thought and expression—A statement by Robert P. George and Cornel West. Retrieved from the James Madison Program in American Ideals and Institutions in the Department of Politics at Princeton University. https://jmp.princeton.edu/statement

He, B., Ziems, C., Soni, S., Ramakrishnan, N., Yang, D., & Kumar, S. (2021). Racism is a virus: Anti-Asian hate and counterspeech in social media during the COVID-19 crisis. In *Proceedings of the 2021 IEEE/ACM International Conference on Advances in Social Networks Analysis and Mining* (Hague), 90–94.

Kharytonenko, O., Savenkova, L., Poltavets, Y., & Zainchkivska, I. (2022). Hate speech: Challenges and responses (Example of a university environment). Редакційна колегія Editorial board ВП Андрущенко, 49.

Langham, J., & Gosha, K. (2018). The classification of aggressive dialogue in social media platforms. *Proceedings of the 2018 ACM SIGMIS Conference on Computers and People Research.* doi:10.1145/3209626.3209720

Macedo Jr., R. P., *Liberdade acadêmica ou liberdade de expressão?* https://direito.usp.br/noticia/7190c331f891-liberdade-academica-ou-liberdade-de-expressao

Mansur, Z., Omar, N., & Tiun, S. (2023). Twitter hate speech detection: A systematic review of methods, taxonomy analysis, challenges, and opportunities. *IEEE Access.* doi: 10.1109/ACCESS.2023.3239375

Modi, S. (2018). AHTDT- Automatic hate text detection techniques in social media. *2018 International Conference on Circuits and Systems in Digital Enterprise Technology.* (ICCSDET), 1-3. doi:10.1109/ICCSDET.2018.8821128

Parini, J., Callanan, K., Alvarez, J., Anderson, M., Andres, G., Andrews, C., & Zupan, P. (2017, March 6). Free inquiry on campus: A statement of principles by over one hundred Middlebury college professors [Blog post]. https://freeinquiryblog.wordpress.com

Silva, S. C. D., Ferreira, T. C., Ramos, R. M. S., & Paraboni, I. (2020). Data-driven and psycholinguistics-motivated approaches to hate speech detection. *Computación y Sistemas, 24*(3), 1179–1188.

Soral, W., Bilewicz, M., & Winiewski, M. (2018). Exposure to hate speech increases prejudice through desensitization. *Aggressive Behavior, 44*(2), 136–146.

Toliyat, A., Levitan, S. I., Peng, Z., & Etemadpour, R. (2022). Asian hate speech detection on Twitter during COVID-19. *Frontiers in Artificial Intelligence, 5,* 932381.

Welshon, R. (2020). Hate speech on campus: What public universities can and should do to counter weaponized intolerance. *Res Publica, 26*(1), 45–66.

Index

For Product Safety Concerns and Information please contact our EU representative GPSR@taylorandfrancis.com
Taylor & Francis Verlag GmbH, Kaufingerstraße 24, 80331 München, Germany

www.ingramcontent.com/pod-product-compliance
Ingram Content Group UK Ltd.
Pitfield, Milton Keynes, MK11 3LW, UK
UKHW020827130526
470833UK00021B/342
* 9 7 8 1 0 3 2 6 4 4 3 4 9 *